THE BEST OF
COUNTRY COOKING

taste of home
THE WORLD'S #1 COOKING MAGAZINE

For other Taste of Home books and products,
visit www.ShopTasteofHome.com.

Wholesome Food from the Heartland

Your soon-to-be favorite recipes can be found right here in this year's THE BEST OF COUNTRY COOKING. This wonderful, new book has traditional and reliable go-to recipes that are a welcome addition to your current cookbook collection.

This latest edition in our popular series is full of 325+ STICK-TO-YOUR-RIBS RECIPES that come from readers of our rural- and nostalgia-based magazines. That includes hundreds of hearty, home-style dishes that have been featured in recent issues of *Country*, *Country Woman*, *Country EXTRA*, *Reminisce* and *Reminisce EXTRA*.

This cookbook is chock-full of both old-fashioned and modern recipes that were created by hundreds of home cooks just like you, with every dish sampled and approved by the toughest critic around—a hungry family! Our Test Kitchen staff cooked and taste-tested every recipe in this book, so you can be doubly confident each dish is a "keeper" that doesn't require a tryout first.

Page through this beautiful book and you'll find bubbling casseroles, farm-fresh veggie dishes, hearty soups, and enough cakes, pies and goodies to satisfy your sweet tooth for years to come.

Be sure to watch for the blue-ribbon symbol at left as you thumb through THE BEST OF COUNTRY COOKING. It identifies prize-winning recipes that earned highest honors in national cooking contests sponsored by one of our magazines.

So what are you waiting for? Grab a fork and dig in! It won't be long before you realize why these dishes are simply the BEST IN THE COUNTRY!

VICE PRESIDENT, EDITOR IN CHIEF: Catherine Cassidy
VICE PRESIDENT, EXECUTIVE EDITOR/BOOKS: Heidi Reuter Lloyd
CREATIVE DIRECTOR: Howard Greenberg
FOOD DIRECTOR: Diane Werner, RD
SENIOR EDITOR/BOOKS: Mark Hagen
EDITOR: Krista Lanphier
ASSOCIATE CREATIVE DIRECTOR: Edwin Robles, Jr.
ART DIRECTOR: Gretchen Trautman
CONTENT PRODUCTION MANAGER: Julie Wagner
LAYOUT DESIGNER: Kathy Crawford
PROOFREADER: Linne Bruskewitz
RECIPE ASSET SYSTEM MANAGER: Coleen Martin
RECIPE TESTING AND EDITING: Taste of Home Test Kitchen
FOOD PHOTOGRAPHY: Taste of Home Photo Studio
ADMINISTRATIVE ASSISTANT: Barb Czysz
COVER PHOTOGRAPHER: Rob Hagen
COVER FOOD STYLIST: Alynna Malson
COVER SET STYLIST: Jenny Bradley Vent

NORTH AMERICAN CHIEF MARKETING OFFICER: Lisa Karpinski
VICE PRESIDENT/BOOK MARKETING: Dan Fink
CREATIVE DIRECTOR/CREATIVE MARKETING: Jim Palmen

THE READER'S DIGEST ASSOCIATION, INC.
PRESIDENT AND CHIEF EXECUTIVE OFFICER: Mary G. Berner
EXECUTIVE VICE PRESIDENT, RDA,
& PRESIDENT, LIFESTYLE COMMUNITIES: Suzanne M. Grimes

INTERNATIONAL STANDARD BOOK NUMBER (10): 0-89821-894-2
INTERNATIONAL STANDARD BOOK NUMBER (13): 978-0-89821-894-7
LIBRARY OF CONGRESS NUMBER: 2011922589

Printed in U.S.A.
1 3 5 7 9 10 8 6 4 2

PICTURED ON FRONT COVER:
Holiday Glazed Ham (p. 45), Broccoli Mac and Cheese Bake (p. 44) and Poppy Seed Chiffon Cake (p. 112).

PICTURED ON BACK COVER:
Glazed Carrots and Sugar Snap Peas (p. 79), Roasted Citrus & Herb Turkey (p. 60) and Baked Onion Cheese Dip (p. 16).

CONTENTS

SNACKS
& BEVERAGES

*Zesty dips, hot morsels, tasty bites and no-fuss sippers make the
perfect finger food and refreshments for friendly get-togethers.*

GUACAMOLE

ANNE TIPPS ❖ DUNCANVILLE, TEXAS

Lemon juice keeps this dip looking fresh and prevents discoloration until serving. Or, before chilling, place plastic wrap directly on the dip so there isn't any air between the dip and the wrap.

    1 medium ripe avocado, halved, seeded and peeled
4-1/2 teaspoons lemon juice
    1 small tomato, seeded and finely chopped
1/4 cup finely chopped onion
    1 tablespoon finely chopped green chilies
    1 garlic clove, minced
1/4 teaspoon salt, optional
Tortilla chips

In a large bowl, mash avocado with lemon juice. Stir in the tomato, onion, chilies, garlic and salt if desired. Cover; chill. Serve with tortilla chips. YIELD: about 1-1/2 cups.

BARBECUED MEATBALLS

GWEN GOSS ❖ GARDEN CITY, KANSAS

A sweet, thick barbecue sauce clings to these large tasty meatballs. This recipe is one of my favorites to take to potlucks or to serve as a meal after the harvest.

    1 cup quick-cooking oats
    1 egg
1/3 cup evaporated milk
3/4 teaspoon chili powder
3/4 teaspoon salt
1/4 teaspoon pepper
1/8 teaspoon garlic powder

1-1/2 pounds ground pork
    1 cup ketchup
3/4 cup packed brown sugar
2-1/2 teaspoons Liquid Smoke, optional
1/2 teaspoon lemon juice

In a large bowl, combine the first seven ingredients. Crumble pork over mixture and mix well. Shape into 2-in. balls. Place meatballs on a greased rack in a shallow baking pan. Bake, uncovered, at 375° for 20-25 minutes or until a meat thermometer reads 160°. Drain on paper towels. Transfer to an ungreased 2-qt. baking dish.

Meanwhile, in a saucepan, combine ketchup, brown sugar, Liquid Smoke if desired and lemon juice; cook and stir until brown sugar is dissolved. Pour over meatballs. Bake, uncovered, at 375° for 10-15 minutes longer or until heated through. YIELD: 6 servings.

HORSERADISH CHEESE SPREAD

MARGIE WAMPLER ❖ BUTLER, PENNSYLVANIA

Here's a recipe that's simple, but oh-so good! This tangy cheese spread has a wonderful combination of flavors that taste even better when served with crisp rye crackers. It's a fine appetizer or snack!

    1 pound process cheese (Velveeta), cubed
    1 cup mayonnaise
1/2 cup horseradish
Assorted crackers

Melt the cheese in the top of a double boiler. Remove from the heat and stir in the mayonnaise and horseradish. Pour into a small crock or ceramic bowl. Chill. Serve with crackers. YIELD: about 2-1/2 cups.

GREEK CHEESE BALLS

ANNE KASSLY ❖ BELLEVILLE, ILLINOIS

This quick, easy party pleaser is best served with crackers, pita chips or pita bread cut in wedges.

2 packages (8 ounces *each*) cream cheese, softened
2 cups (8 ounces) crumbled feta cheese
1 can (4-1/4 ounces) chopped ripe olives
1/2 cup finely chopped cucumber
1/2 cup chopped roasted sweet red peppers
1 teaspoon pepper
2 cups finely chopped walnuts, toasted
Assorted crackers

In a large bowl, beat cream cheese until fluffy. Stir in the feta cheese, olives, cucumber, red peppers and pepper. Shape into two balls; roll in chopped walnuts. Wrap tightly in plastic wrap. Chill until serving. Serve with crackers. YIELD: 2 cheese balls (2-1/4 cups each).

SMOKED TROUT PATE

JUDY WALLE ❖ TOLEDO, OHIO

This yummy spread is easy to make in a food processor, and it's a guaranteed winner at any party. The recipe is versatile, so feel free to substitute other favorite smoked fish.

1 pound flaked smoked trout
1 package (3 ounces) cream cheese, softened
1/2 cup half-and-half cream
1 tablespoon horseradish sauce
1 tablespoon lemon juice
1/8 teaspoon pepper
2 teaspoons minced fresh parsley
Assorted crackers

Place the first seven ingredients in a food processor; cover and process until blended. Transfer to a small bowl. Chill until serving. Serve with crackers. YIELD: 2-2/3 cups.

SOUR CREAM AND BEEF TURNOVERS

ELVA KELLY ❖ PRINCE GEORGE, BRITISH COLUMBIA

I always serve these turnovers at family gatherings. If you like, add a tossed green salad and serve them for dinner. They freeze well, too.

2 cups all-purpose flour
1 tablespoon sugar
1 teaspoon salt
1/2 cup shortening
1 cup (8 ounces) sour cream
1 egg yolk

FILLING
3/4 pound ground beef
1 large onion, finely chopped
1/4 cup finely chopped fresh mushrooms
1/2 cup sour cream
1/2 teaspoon salt
1/2 teaspoon dried oregano
1/4 teaspoon pepper
1 egg
2 teaspoons water

In a large bowl, combine the flour, sugar and salt. Cut in shortening until crumbly. Stir in sour cream and egg yolk just until moistened. Shape into a ball. Cover and refrigerate for 2 hours or until easy to handle.

In a large skillet over medium heat, cook the beef, onion and mushrooms until meat is no longer pink. Remove from the heat; drain. Stir in the sour cream, salt, oregano and pepper.

On a floured surface, roll out dough to 1/8-in. thickness. Cut with a floured 3-in. round cutter. Place a rounded teaspoon of filling on one side of each circle; fold dough over filling. Press edges with a fork to seal. Prick the tops with a fork. Re-roll the scraps; repeat.

Place on greased baking sheets. Beat egg with water; brush over turnovers. Bake at 450° for 12-15 minutes or until lightly browned. YIELD: about 4-1/2 dozen.

TURKEY CIGARS WITH CRANBERRY-DIJON DIPPING SAUCE

DONNA MARIE RYAN ❖ TOPSFIELD, MASSACHUSETTS

With or without the dipping sauce, this crunchy crowd-pleaser is tasty. The cranberry-Dijon sauce gives the fun snack plenty of tang.

1/2 pound ground turkey
  4 teaspoons grated Parmesan cheese
  2 teaspoons minced fresh parsley
  2 teaspoons jellied cranberry sauce
  2 teaspoons ground walnuts, *divided*
  1 teaspoon honey
  1 teaspoon Dijon mustard

1/2 teaspoon salt
1/2 teaspoon pepper
  12 sheets phyllo dough (14 inches x 9 inches)
  6 tablespoons butter, melted

DIPPING SAUCE
1/2 cup jellied cranberry sauce
1/4 cup Dijon mustard

In a small skillet, cook turkey over medium heat until no longer pink; drain. Remove from the heat. Stir in the cheese, parsley, cranberry sauce, 1 teaspoon walnuts, honey, mustard, salt and pepper.

Place one sheet of phyllo dough on a work surface with a long side facing you; brush with butter. Repeat with three more sheets of phyllo, brushing each layer. (Keep remaining phyllo dough covered with plastic wrap and a damp towel to prevent it from drying out.)

Cut the stack widthwise into four strips. Place 2 tablespoons turkey mixture along one long side of each strip; roll up tightly. Pinch edges to seal. Cut roll in half; place seam side down on an ungreased baking sheet. Repeat. Brush tops with butter; sprinkle with remaining walnuts.

Bake at 425° for 10-12 minutes or until golden brown. For dipping sauce, in a microwave, heat cranberry sauce until softened. Stir in mustard. Serve with appetizers. YIELD: 2 dozen (1 cup sauce).

TURKEY SLIDERS WITH CHILI CHEESE MAYO

LISA HUNDLEY ❖ ABERDEEN, NORTH CAROLINA

Serve these juicy sliders with an assortment of toppings as a scrumptious appetizer. The chili cheese mayo adds a kick!

    4 bacon strips
    1 medium onion, finely chopped
    2 garlic cloves, minced
    2 tablespoons Worcestershire sauce
1/2 teaspoon salt
1/4 teaspoon pepper
    1 pound ground turkey
    2 tablespoons olive oil
  12 heat-and-serve rolls

MAYO
    1 cup mayonnaise
    1 jar (5 ounces) sharp American cheese spread
    1 teaspoon onion powder
    1 teaspoon garlic powder
    1 teaspoon chili powder

TOPPINGS
  12 small lettuce leaves
    2 plum tomatoes, thinly sliced

In a large skillet, cook bacon over medium heat until crisp. Remove to paper towels; drain. Crumble bacon and set aside. In the same skillet, saute onion in the drippings until tender. Add garlic; cook 1 minute longer.

Transfer to a large bowl. Add the bacon, Worcestershire sauce, salt and pepper. Crumble turkey over mixture and mix well. Shape into 12 patties.

Cook in a large skillet in oil over medium heat for 3-4 minutes on each side or until a meat thermometer reads 165° and juices run clear. Meanwhile, bake rolls according to package directions.

For mayo, in a small bowl, combine the mayonnaise, cheese spread, onion powder, garlic powder and chili powder. Split rolls; spread with mayo. Top each burger with lettuce and tomato. YIELD: 1 dozen.

HOT PEPPER PLEASERS

DARIUS KOVACINA ❖ ACME, PENNSYLVANIA

Here's a real crowd-pleaser. The banana peppers pack a subtle punch, and the pepperoni adds spice. Have knives, forks and napkins ready so folks can eat them up neatly.

  10 banana peppers
    1 package (8 ounces) cream cheese, softened
    1 egg
    1 cup (4 ounces) shredded cheddar cheese
1/2 cup shredded part-skim mozzarella cheese
    1 small onion, finely chopped
1/2 cup finely chopped pepperoni
    2 tablespoons olive oil

Cut peppers in half lengthwise; open and lay flat. Remove seeds if desired.

In a small bowl, beat cream cheese and egg until blended. Stir in the cheddar, mozzarella, onion and pepperoni. Spoon into the halved peppers.

Place in two 15-in. x 10-in. x 1-in. baking pans and drizzle with oil. Bake at 350° for 25-30 minutes or until lightly browned. YIELD: 20 appetizers.

EDITOR'S NOTE: When cutting hot peppers, disposable gloves are recommended. Avoid touching your face.

STUFFED MUSHROOMS

BRYAN ANDERSON ✤ GRANITE FALLS, MINNESOTA

These scrumptious mushroom hors d'oeuvres from my grandmother's recipe box are perfect for serving at special-occasion dinners and birthdays.

16 to 18 large fresh whole mushrooms
1 small onion, chopped
1 garlic clove, minced
2 tablespoons butter
8 butter-flavored crackers, crushed
3 ounces pepperoni *or* summer sausage, finely chopped
1/4 cup grated Parmesan cheese
1 tablespoon minced fresh parsley
1/8 teaspoon pepper

Remove stems from mushrooms; set caps aside. Mince stems. In a skillet over medium heat, saute stems, onion and garlic in butter until soft. Remove from heat; stir in the remaining ingredients. Firmly stuff into mushroom caps; place on a greased baking sheet. Bake at 375° for 15-20 minutes or until tender. YIELD: about 1-1/2 dozen.

NUTTY CARAMEL POPCORN

SHARON BUCHINSKI ✤ ENDEAVOUR, SASKATCHEWAN

Folks who've tasted my snack are quick to remind me to make it again for them the following Christmas! The sugary combination of popcorn and crunchy nuts hits the spot.

4 quarts popped popcorn
1-1/3 cups pecan halves, toasted
2/3 cup whole unblanched almonds, toasted
1-1/3 cups sugar
1 cup butter
1/2 cup light corn syrup
2 teaspoons vanilla extract

PRESSURE-COOKED POPCORN

Did you ever pop popcorn in a pressure cooker? It's delicious. Just leave the steam vent open so the steam can escape. Use 2 tablespoons of oil and 1/3 cup popcorn for a 4-quart cooker.

Place popcorn in a large greased bowl. Sprinkle pecans and almonds over top; set aside. In a heavy saucepan, combine the sugar, butter and corn syrup; cook and stir over medium heat until a candy thermometer reads 300°-310° (hard-crack stage).

Remove from the heat; stir in vanilla. Immediately pour over popcorn mixture; toss gently. Spread on greased baking sheets. When cool, break into small pieces. Store in airtight containers. YIELD: about 20 cups.

HOMEMADE CRANBERRY JUICE

CAROL DOMES ✤ WHITEHORSE, YUKON

This refreshing and sweet cranberry juice has a very mild level of tartness. Its jewel red color looks very attractive served in glassware.

2 quarts water
8 cups fresh *or* frozen cranberries
1-1/2 cups sugar
1/2 cup lemon juice
1/2 cup orange juice

In a soup kettle, bring the water and cranberries to a boil. Reduce the heat; cover and simmer for 20 minutes or until the berries begin to pop.

Strain through a fine strainer, pressing mixture with a spoon; discard berries. Return cranberry juice to the pan. Stir in the sugar, lemon juice and orange juice. Bring to a boil; cook and stir until sugar is dissolved.

Remove from the heat. Cool. Transfer to a pitcher; cover and refrigerate until chilled. YIELD: 8 servings (2 quarts).

GORGONZOLA & CRANBERRY CHEESE BALL

KATHY HAHN ✤ POLLOCK PINES, CALIFORNIA

A cheese ball is a classic appetizer to take to any gathering, and it's so easy to make. This version, studded with tangy dried cranberries, is a Yuletide hit.

    1 package (8 ounces) cream cheese, softened
    1 cup (4 ounces) crumbled Gorgonzola cheese
    1 cup dried cranberries
    2 tablespoons *each* finely chopped onion, celery, green pepper and sweet red pepper
    1/4 teaspoon hot pepper sauce
    3/4 cup chopped pecans
Assorted crackers

In a small bowl, combine cheeses. Stir in the cranberries, vegetables and pepper sauce. Shape into a ball; wrap in plastic wrap. Refrigerate for 1 hour or until firm. Roll cheese ball in pecans. Serve with crackers. YIELD: 2 cups.

BRAUNSCHWEIGER VEGETABLE DIP

BARBARA FLEMING ✤ KINGSTON SPRINGS, TENNESSEE

I like to serve this spread around the holidays, but my family likes it so much that they often request it throughout the year.

    1 package (8 ounces) braunschweiger sausage
    1 cup (8 ounces) sour cream
    2 tablespoons onion soup mix
    1 teaspoon Worcestershire sauce

    3 to 6 drops hot pepper sauce
Raw vegetables for dipping

In a bowl, combine the first five ingredients. Cover and chill for at least 1 hour. Serve with vegetables. YIELD: 2 cups.

SNACK PIZZAS

MARGARET ALLEN ✤ ABINGDON, VIRGINIA

These filling bites on snack rye bread resemble sloppy joe sandwiches. They're hard for meat-lovers, and just about everyone else, to resist.

    1 pound ground beef
    1 medium onion, chopped
    1/2 cup chopped green pepper
    1 garlic clove, minced
    1 can (6 ounces) tomato paste
    3/4 cup water
    4-1/2 teaspoons minced fresh oregano *or* 1-1/2 teaspoons dried oregano
    1-1/2 teaspoons minced fresh thyme *or* 1/2 teaspoon dried thyme
    1/2 teaspoon fennel seed
    1/2 to 1 teaspoon garlic salt
    36 slices snack rye bread
Grated Parmesan cheese

In a large skillet, cook the beef, onion, green pepper and garlic over medium heat until meat is no longer pink; drain. Add tomato paste, water and seasonings; cook over low heat until thickened, about 10 minutes.

Spread 1 tablespoonful on each slice of bread. Place on ungreased baking sheets; sprinkle with cheese. Bake at 350° for 8-10 minutes or until heated through. YIELD: 3 dozen.

PINECONE-SHAPED SPREAD

LISA POINTER ✦ LEADORE, IDAHO

Spreading Christmas cheer is simple with this tasty novelty. Originally my mother's recipe, it always gets raves.

   1 package (8 ounces) cream cheese, softened
1/2 cup mayonnaise
   5 bacon strips, cooked and crumbled
   1 tablespoon finely chopped green onion
1/2 teaspoon dill weed
1/8 teaspoon pepper
1-1/4 cups whole unblanched almonds, toasted
Fresh rosemary sprigs, optional
Assorted crackers *or* raw vegetables

In a bowl, combine the cream cheese, mayonnaise, bacon, onion, dill and pepper; chill. Form into two pinecone shapes on a serving platter. Beginning at the narrow end of each shape, arrange almonds in overlapping rows. Garnish with rosemary if desired. Serve with crackers or vegetables. YIELD: 1-1/2 cups.

ARTICHOKE DIP

MRS. WILLIAM GARNER ✦ AUSTIN, TEXAS

To give this golden dip some color after it comes out of the oven, sprinkle the top with chopped fresh tomatoes and minced green onions.

   1 can (14 ounces) water-packed artichoke hearts, rinsed, drained and chopped
   1 cup mayonnaise
1/3 to 1/2 cup grated Parmesan cheese
   1 garlic clove, minced
Dash hot pepper sauce
Paprika, optional
Assorted crackers

In a large bowl, combine the artichokes, mayonnaise, Parmesan, garlic and pepper sauce. Transfer to a greased 1-qt. baking dish. Sprinkle with paprika if desired.

   Bake, uncovered, at 350° for 20-25 minutes or until top is lightly browned. Serve warm with crackers. YIELD: 2 cups.

PESTO SWIRLED CHEESECAKE

ELIZABETH JACKSON ✤ PORTLAND, OREGON

My savory cheesecake was so popular at Thanksgiving, it was gone before my husband got a bite. He joined the appetizer line faster when I made it for Christmas and subsequent football parties.

2/3 cup dry bread crumbs
  5 tablespoons finely chopped pine nuts, toasted
  2 tablespoons butter, melted

FILLING
  1 carton (15 ounces) ricotta cheese
1/2 cup half-and-half cream
  2 tablespoons grated Parmesan cheese
  2 tablespoons all-purpose flour
1/2 teaspoon salt
1/4 teaspoon garlic salt
  2 eggs, lightly beaten

PESTO TOPPING
1/2 cup loosely packed basil leaves

  2 tablespoons grated Parmesan cheese
  1 tablespoon pine nuts, toasted
  2 garlic cloves, peeled
  2 tablespoons olive oil
Assorted crackers

In a small bowl, combine the bread crumbs, pine nuts and butter. Press onto bottom of a greased 9-in. springform pan; set aside.

In a small bowl, beat the ricotta cheese, cream, Parmesan cheese, flour, salt and garlic salt until smooth. Add eggs; beat on low speed just until combined. Pour into crust.

For the topping, combine the basil, Parmesan cheese, pine nuts and garlic in a food processor; cover and process until finely chopped. While processing, gradually add the oil in a steady stream. Drop by teaspoonfuls over filling; cut through with a knife to swirl.

Place pan on a baking sheet. Bake at 350° for 35-40 minutes or until center is almost set. Cool on a wire rack for 10 minutes. Carefully run a knife around edge of pan to loosen; cool 1 hour longer. Refrigerate overnight.

Serve with assorted crackers. Refrigerate any leftovers. YIELD: 24 servings.

CREAMY CRAB DIP

TERI LINDQUIST ❖ GURNEE, ILLINOIS

This irresistible dip, served warm, never fails to gather guests around the bowl with veggies and crackers in hand. It's been a staple on my appetizer table for over 20 years.

2 packages (8 ounces *each*) cream cheese, softened
1/2 cup sour cream
1/4 cup mayonnaise
1 garlic clove, minced
2 tablespoons white wine *or* chicken broth
2 tablespoons grated onion
1 tablespoon Dijon mustard
1/8 teaspoon ground nutmeg
3 drops hot pepper sauce
6 ounces premium crabmeat, drained
4 tablespoons minced fresh parsley, *divided*
1/3 cup slivered almonds, toasted
Paprika
Assorted crackers

In a large heavy saucepan over low heat, combine the first nine ingredients. Cook and stir until cream cheese is melted and mixture is heated through. Stir in crab and 2 tablespoons parsley; heat through.

Transfer to a serving bowl; sprinkle with almonds, paprika and remaining parsley. Serve warm with crackers. Refrigerate leftovers. YIELD: 3-1/4 cups.

CHUNKY SEAFOOD SAUCE

JUANITA MYERS ❖ SAN DIEGO, CALIFORNIA

This recipe has been in our family for so long, it has become a tradition. Served with cold shrimp, the sauce is refreshing and looks elegant on the table.

1/2 cup ketchup
3/4 cup finely chopped celery
1/2 cup finely chopped green pepper
3 tablespoons finely chopped onion
2 tablespoons lemon juice
1/2 teaspoon prepared mustard

1/4 teaspoon salt
1/4 teaspoon paprika
1/4 teaspoon Worcestershire sauce

In a small bowl, combine all the ingredients. Cover and refrigerate for at least 1 hour before serving. YIELD: about 1-1/3 cups.

🎗 GRILLED STUFFED JALAPENOS

MARY J. POTTER ❖ STERLING HEIGHTS, MICHIGAN

These cheese-stuffed jalapenos are always popular when my husband and I host tapas (appetizers) parties. There's a flavor explosion in each crisp and tender pepper.

4 ounces cream cheese, softened
1/2 cup shredded Monterey Jack cheese
1/2 teaspoon garlic powder
1/2 teaspoon ground cumin
1/2 teaspoon chili powder
1/4 teaspoon salt
1/4 teaspoon smoked paprika *or* paprika
10 jalapeno peppers

In a small bowl, combine the first seven ingredients. Cut a lengthwise slit down each pepper, leaving the stem intact; remove membranes and seeds. Fill each pepper with 1 tablespoon cheese mixture.

Prepare grill for indirect heat. Place peppers in a disposable foil pan. Grill, covered, over indirect medium heat for 8-10 minutes or until peppers are tender and cheese is melted. Serve warm. YIELD: 10 appetizers.

EDITOR'S NOTE: When cutting hot peppers, disposable gloves are recommended. Avoid touching your face.

EASY JALAPENO PREPARATION

When handling jalapeno peppers, always wear plastic gloves. To easily remove the seeds and membranes from the inside of the pepper, use the small end of a melon baller to easily scrape them out.

TINY TACO MEATBALLS

JOYCE MARKHAM ✛ BELMOND, IOWA

These meatballs may be tiny, but they're big on flavor. Taco seasoning adds a tasty twist to these appetizers that my grandson gobbles up!

  2 eggs
  1 medium onion, finely chopped
  1 envelope taco seasoning
1/2 teaspoon salt
1/4 teaspoon pepper
  2 pounds ground beef
Taco sauce, optional

In a bowl, combine the first five ingredients. Add beef; mix well. Shape into 1-in. balls. Place meatballs on a greased rack in a shallow baking pan.

Bake at 400° for 14-18 minutes or until meat is no longer pink. Serve with taco sauce if desired. YIELD: 14-16 servings.

CHEESY MUSHROOM MORSELS

MARIAN PLATT ✛ SEQUIM, WASHINGTON

There's plenty of happy munching all around the table when I dish up these luscious morsels. Ideal for a large crowd, they taste like quiche without the crust or the fuss.

  1 pound fresh mushrooms, sliced
  1 large onion, chopped
1/2 cup butter
  1 large green pepper, chopped
  2 garlic cloves, minced
10 eggs, lightly beaten
  4 cups (16 ounces) shredded Monterey Jack cheese
  2 cups (16 ounces) small-curd cottage cheese

1/2 cup all-purpose flour
  1 teaspoon baking powder
3/4 teaspoon salt
3/4 teaspoon dried basil
3/4 teaspoon ground nutmeg

In a large skillet, saute mushrooms and onion in butter until tender. Add green pepper and garlic; saute 1 minute longer. Remove from the heat; drain.

In a large bowl, combine the eggs, cheeses, flour, baking powder, salt, basil and nutmeg. Add mushroom mixture. Pour into a greased 15-in. x 10-in. x 1-in. baking pan.

Bake, uncovered, at 350° for 30-35 minutes or until edges are golden and a knife inserted near the center comes out clean. Let stand for 15 minutes. Cut into squares. YIELD: about 12 dozen.

LEMONY ICED TEA

SHARON EMERY ✛ NEW BURNSIDE, ILLINOIS

This beverage is one of our favorites to serve during the hot, humid summer months. We keep a jug in the refrigerator ready to surprise family and guests.

  8 cups water
3/4 cup sugar
1/2 cup lemon juice
1/2 cup white grape juice
1/4 cup unsweetened lemon-flavored instant tea mix
Ice cubes
Lemon slices

In a large pitcher, combine the water, sugar, lemon juice, grape juice and tea mix. Stir well to dissolve the sugar. Serve in chilled glasses over ice with lemon slices. YIELD: 8 servings.

THREE-CHEESE NACHOS

CARI HINZ ❖ EAU CLAIRE, WISCONSIN

I received the recipe for these fun nachos from a coworker a few years back. They're fun to serve as party appetizers or as the main course at a casual dinner with family.

> 2 packages (one 8 ounces, one 3 ounces) cream cheese, softened
> 1 can (4 ounces) chopped green chilies
> 3 tablespoons chopped onion
> 2 garlic cloves, minced
> 1 tablespoon canned chopped jalapeno pepper
> 1-1/2 teaspoons ground cumin
> 1-1/2 teaspoons chili powder
> 2 cups cubed cooked chicken
> 2 cups (8 ounces) shredded Monterey Jack cheese, *divided*
> 1 package (14 ounces) pita bread (6 inches)
> 1 cup (4 ounces) shredded cheddar cheese
> Salsa, optional

In a large bowl, beat the cream cheese, chilies, onion, garlic, jalapeno, cumin and chili powder until smooth. Stir in chicken and 1 cup Monterey Jack cheese.

Split each pita into two circles. Spread 1/4 cup of chicken mixture on each circle; place on ungreased baking sheets.

Bake at 400° for 5-10 minutes. Combine the cheddar cheese and remaining Monterey Jack; sprinkle over circles. Bake 5 minutes longer or until cheese is melted. Cut into wedges and serve with salsa if desired. YIELD: 10-12 servings.

🏅 CAPPUCCINO MIX

SUSAN PRILLHART ❖ ROCKLEDGE, FLORIDA

One day, my friends and I were swapping recipes for hot chocolate, and someone shared this change-of-pace mix. I put it in jars as gifts for Christmas.

> 1 cup powdered nondairy creamer
> 1 cup instant chocolate drink mix
> 2/3 cup instant coffee crystals
> 1/2 cup sugar
> 1/2 teaspoon ground cinnamon
> 1/4 teaspoon ground nutmeg

Combine all ingredients. Store in an airtight container. To prepare one serving, stir 3 tablespoons mix into 6 oz. hot water. YIELD: 3 cups dry mix.

BAKED ONION CHEESE DIP

BONNIE HAWKINS ✦ ELKHORN, WISCONSIN

This cheddar-Vidalia dip gets a nice kick from an added cup of pepper Jack cheese. It is fun to serve with an assortment of crackers and breadsticks.

2 cups (8 ounces) shredded cheddar cheese
1 cup (4 ounces) shredded pepper Jack cheese
4 ounces cream cheese, cubed
1/2 cup mayonnaise
1/4 teaspoon dried thyme
2 cups chopped sweet onions, *divided*
Assorted crackers

In a food processor, combine the cheeses, mayonnaise, thyme and 1 cup onions; cover and process until blended. Stir in remaining onions.

Transfer to a greased 3-cup baking dish. Bake, uncovered, at 375° for 20-25 minutes or until bubbly. Serve with crackers. YIELD: 3 cups.

FIESTA APPETIZERS

SHARON SKILDUM ✦ MAPLE GROVE, MINNESOTA

The fact that these go from freezer to oven means there is less last-minute kitchen fuss...and more time to spend with your guests!

1 pound ground beef
1 pound bulk pork sausage
1 medium onion, chopped
1 pound Mexican process cheese (Velveeta), cubed
1 tablespoon Worcestershire sauce
1 teaspoon dried oregano

Salt and pepper to taste
   1 loaf (1 pound) snack rye bread
Minced fresh parsley, optional

In a large skillet, cook the beef, sausage and onion over medium heat until meat is no longer pink; drain. Stir in the cheese, Worcestershire sauce and seasonings.

Spread rye bread slices with 1 heaping tablespoon of mixture; place on baking sheets. Broil 4-6 in. from heat for 3 minutes or until bubbly. May be frozen and broiled without thawing. If desired, sprinkle with minced parsley before serving. YIELD: about 4 dozen.

BACON ROUNDS

EDIE DESPAIN ❖ LOGAN, UTAH

On my family's list of favorite nibbles, this appetizer is tops. I have served the satisfying canapes at showers and brunches and received many compliments!

   1 cup mayonnaise
   1 tablespoon grated Parmesan cheese
   2 teaspoons Worcestershire sauce
  1/4 teaspoon paprika
  1/8 teaspoon celery seed
  1/8 teaspoon garlic powder
  1/8 teaspoon pepper
   2 cups (8 ounces) shredded cheddar cheese
   8 bacon strips, cooked and crumbled
  1/3 cup chopped salted peanuts
   4 green onions, thinly sliced
  48 slices French bread baguette (1/4 inch thick)
Additional sliced green onions, optional

In a large bowl, combine the first seven ingredients. Stir in the cheddar cheese, bacon, peanuts and onions. Spread over bread. Sprinkle with additional onions if desired.

Place on ungreased baking sheets. Bake at 400° for 8-10 minutes or until lightly browned. YIELD: 4 dozen.

BRAIDED PIZZA LOAF

DEBBIE MEDUNA ❖ PLAZA, NORTH DAKOTA

Working women can take the frozen bread dough out in the morning and then prepare this hearty loaf when they get home. It's important to let the filling cool completely before spreading it on the dough.

   1 loaf (1 pound) frozen bread dough, thawed
   1 pound ground beef
   1 medium onion, finely chopped
   1 can (8 ounces) tomato sauce
   1 teaspoon salt
   1 teaspoon dried oregano
   1 teaspoon paprika
   1 teaspoon pepper
  1/2 teaspoon garlic salt
   1 cup (4 ounces) shredded cheddar cheese
   1 cup (4 ounces) shredded part-skim mozzarella cheese
Melted butter

Place dough in a greased bowl, turning once to grease top. Cover and let rise in a warm place until doubled, about 1 hour.

Meanwhile, in a large skillet, cook beef and onion over medium heat until meat is no longer pink; drain. Stir in tomato sauce and seasonings. Bring to a boil. Reduce heat; simmer, uncovered, for 30 minutes, stirring occasionally.

Cool completely. Punch dough down. Turn onto a lightly floured surface; roll into a 15-in. x 12-in. rectangle. Place on a greased baking sheet. Spread filling lengthwise down center third of rectangle. Sprinkle cheeses over filling.

On each long side, cut 1-1/2-in.-wide strips about 2-1/2 in. into center. Starting at one end, fold alternating strips at an angle across filling. Brush with butter.

Bake at 350° for 30-35 minutes or until golden brown. Serve warm. Refrigerate leftovers. YIELD: 1 loaf.

SOUPS, SALADS & SANDWICHES

Fixing a simple recipe of hearty soup, salad or favorite sandwich is easy with these classic luncheon combinations.

AVOCADO AND GRAPEFRUIT SALAD

MARION SELL ❖ SANTA MARIA, CALIFORNIA

This simple colorful salad is easy to make. We eat a lot of grapefruit so I was happy to come up with this pleasing combination. The honey in the dressing enhances the taste of both fruits.

    4 Bibb or Boston lettuce leaves
    1 medium grapefruit, peeled
    1 medium ripe avocado, peeled and sliced
    1 tablespoons canola oil
1 1/2 teaspoon white wine vinegar
    1/2 teaspoon honey
    1/8 teaspoon salt

Place lettuce on two salad plates. Section the grapefruit over a bowl to reserve juice. Arrange grapefruit sections and avocado slices on lettuce.

In a small bowl, whisk the oil, vinegar, honey, salt and 1-1/2 teaspoons reserved grapefruit juice. Drizzle over salads; serve immediately. YIELD: 2 servings.

OVERNIGHT CHICKEN FRUIT SALAD

JUDY RUGG ❖ FAIRPORT, NEW YORK

When planning a luncheon, I like to use recipes that can be prepared the night before to make the next day's lunch run smoothly. The tropical taste in this make-ahead salad appeals to the ladies...as well as the men!

    3 cups cubed cooked chicken
    1 pound seedless red grapes, halved

    1 cup sliced celery
    1 can (8 ounces) sliced water chestnuts, drained
    1 cup mayonnaise
    1 tablespoon soy sauce
    1 tablespoon lemon juice
    1 teaspoon curry powder
    1 cup slivered almonds, toasted

In a large bowl, combine chicken, grapes, celery and water chestnuts. Combine mayonnaise, soy sauce, lemon juice and curry powder. Pour over chicken mixture; toss lightly until coated. Cover and chill 8 hours or overnight. Stir in almonds just before serving. YIELD: 8 servings.

PEAR TEA SANDWICHES

LAURIE BALCOM ❖ LYNDEN, WASHINGTON

The gals at your next event will have fun guessing the secret ingredients in these delightfully different sandwiches. They're a sweet mix of creamy and crunchy textures.

    1 cup dried pears
    1/4 cup spreadable cream cheese
    2 tablespoons maple syrup
    2/3 cup chopped walnuts, toasted
    8 slices cinnamon-raisin bread, toasted and crusts removed

Place pears in a small bowl. Cover with boiling water; let stand for 5 minutes. Drain. Cool slightly; chop pears.

In a small bowl, combine cream cheese and syrup. Stir in pears and nuts.

Spread over four slices of toast; top with remaining toast. Cut each sandwich into two triangles. YIELD: 8 tea sandwiches.

In a small saucepan, saute the mushrooms, onions and garlic in oil until tender. Stir in the broth, parsley, thyme and pepper.

Bring to a boil. Stir in the orzo, lemon juice and peel. Cook for 5-6 minutes or until pasta is tender. YIELD: 2 servings.

🎗 ROASTED RED PEPPER SOUP

KATHY RAIRIGH ❖ MILFORD, INDIANA

I love oven-roasted peppers, especially when I transform them into this silky soup seasoned with garlic and thyme. Dip a grilled cheese sandwich into it and enjoy!

- 2 pounds sweet red peppers, cut into 1-inch pieces (about 6 medium)
- 1 large onion, sliced
- 2 medium carrots, sliced
- 1 jalapeno pepper, quartered and seeded
- 2 tablespoons olive oil
- 5 garlic cloves, minced
- 2 tablespoons whole fresh thyme leaves plus 1 teaspoon minced fresh thyme, *divided*
- 4 cups vegetable broth *or* water
- 4 cups chicken broth
- 2 cups cubed peeled potatoes
- 2 cups cubed peeled sweet potato
- 2 cups cubed peeled butternut squash
- 1 teaspoon salt
- 1/8 teaspoon pepper

Place red peppers, onion, carrots and jalapeno in two greased 15-in. x 10-in. x 1-in. baking pans; drizzle with oil and toss to coat. Bake at 425° for 25-30 minutes or until tender, stirring occasionally. Add the minced garlic and whole thyme leaves; bake 5 minutes longer.

LEMONY MUSHROOM-ORZO SOUP

EDRIE O'BRIEN ❖ DENVER, COLORADO

Here's a versatile soup that works as an appetizer or side for a sandwich lunch. It's loaded with mushrooms and orzo pasta—lemon livens up the soup's mild flavor.

- 2-1/2 cups sliced fresh mushrooms
- 2 green onions, chopped
- 1 garlic clove, minced
- 1 tablespoon olive oil
- 1-1/2 cups chicken broth
- 1-1/2 teaspoons minced fresh parsley
- 1/4 teaspoon dried thyme
- 1/8 teaspoon pepper
- 1/4 cup uncooked orzo pasta
- 1-1/2 teaspoons lemon juice
- 1/8 teaspoon grated lemon peel

RICE VS. ORZO

Because of orzo's similar shape and mild flavor, it can be substituted for rice in many recipes. Nutritionally speaking, ounce for ounce, rice and orzo contain similar amounts of fat, sugar, carbohydrates and even sodium.

Meanwhile, in a Dutch oven, combine the vegetable broth, chicken broth, potatoes, sweet potato, squash, salt, pepper and minced thyme. Bring to a boil. Reduce heat; cover and simmer for 15 minutes or until vegetables are tender.

Add roasted pepper mixture; cook 5 minutes longer. Cool slightly. In a blender, process soup in batches until smooth. Return all to pan; heat through. YIELD: 12 servings (3 quarts). EDITOR'S NOTE: When cutting hot peppers, disposable gloves are recommended. Avoid touching your face.

ASPARAGUS PASTA SALAD

TERESA KOKX ❖ HART, MICHIGAN

This salad is one of my favorites to make for potlucks in the springtime when the asparagus is the best. It is so tasty that everyone will ask you for the recipe.

3 cups cut fresh asparagus (1-inch pieces)
3 cups medium pasta shells, cooked and drained
1 small red onion, chopped
1 small cucumber, sliced
1 cup sliced carrots
1/2 cup sliced radishes
1/2 cup Italian salad dressing
1/2 cup shredded Parmesan cheese

Cook asparagus in a small amount of water until crisp-tender, about 4 minutes. Rinse in cold water; drain and cool. Place asparagus in a large bowl; add the pasta, onion, cucumber, carrots and radishes.

Combine salad dressing and Parmesan cheese; pour over pasta mixture and toss to coat. Cover and refrigerate for at least 2 hours. YIELD: 8-10 servings.

BACON 'N' EGG SALAD SANDWICHES

DELORES SUTTON ❖ DOVER, PENNSYLVANIA

One day I decided to make egg salad and just started adding a little of this and a little of that. I came up with this recipe that my family really loves.

12 hard-cooked eggs, chopped
1/2 cup mayonnaise
1 small onion, chopped
1 small sweet pickle, diced
1 tablespoon prepared mustard
2 teaspoons sweet pickle juice
1-1/2 teaspoons salt
1 teaspoon minced fresh parsley
1/4 teaspoon pepper
1/4 teaspoon Italian seasoning
1/4 teaspoon dried oregano
1/8 teaspoon garlic powder
1/8 teaspoon chili powder

1/8 teaspoon paprika
5 bacon strips, cooked and crumbled
Lettuce leaves
6 to 8 sandwich rolls, split

In a large bowl, combine the first 14 ingredients. Cover and refrigerate for at least 1 hour. Just before serving, stir in the bacon. Place a lettuce leaf and about 1/2 cup egg salad on each roll. YIELD: 6-8 servings.

THANKSGIVING CABBAGE SALAD

SUZY HORVATH ❖ GLADSTONE, OREGON

Here's a terrific coleslaw to include with all the fixings for your holiday meal. Just dice up apples and cabbage, whisk the sauce and don't forget the pretty red cranberries.

2 medium apples, chopped
1 tablespoon lemon juice
1 cup heavy whipping cream
2 tablespoons sugar
2 tablespoons cumin seeds
1/2 teaspoon salt
1/4 teaspoon pepper
1 tablespoon red wine vinegar
6 cups shredded green cabbage
2 cups shredded red cabbage
2/3 cup dried cranberries

In a small bowl, combine apples and lemon juice. In another bowl, combine the cream, sugar, cumin seeds, salt and pepper; gradually whisk in vinegar.

In a large bowl, combine the green cabbage, red cabbage, cranberries and apples. Add dressing and gently toss to coat. Cover and refrigerate for at least 1 hour before serving. YIELD: 10 servings.

Add the haddock, dill, salt and pepper. Bring to a boil. Reduce the heat; cook for 5-10 minutes or until the fish flakes easily with a fork.

Combine flour and cold water until smooth; gradually stir into chowder. Bring to a boil; cook and stir for 2 minutes or until thickened. Add cream; heat through (do not boil). Discard spice bag. Stir in bacon. Garnish with parsley. YIELD: 5 servings.

SPLIT PEA AND HAM SOUP

LUCILLE SCHREIBER ✤ GLEASON, WISCONSIN

Not a winter goes by that I don't fix at least one batch of this traditional pea soup. It's a hot and hearty meal that really warms up my family.

- 1 pound dried green split peas (2 cups)
- 7 cups water
- 1 teaspoon canola oil
- 2 cups cubed fully cooked ham
- 2 cups chopped carrots
- 1 cup chopped celery
- 1 cup chopped onion
- 1 cup diced peeled potato
- 1 teaspoon salt, optional
- 1/2 teaspoon garlic powder
- 1/2 teaspoon pepper
- 1/4 cup minced fresh parsley

In a Dutch oven or soup kettle, bring the peas, water and oil to a boil. Reduce heat; cover and simmer for 2 hours, stirring occasionally. Add the next eight ingredients; cover and simmer for 30 minutes or until vegetables are tender. Stir in parsley. YIELD: 10 servings (2-3/4 quarts).

HADDOCK CHOWDER

ELEANOR ATTERIDG ✤ ROLESVILLE, NORTH CAROLINA

Warming bowls of this chilly weather chowder can include most any type of seafood or whitefish. We especially like it with haddock, cod or grouper. Crispy rolls and a green salad complete the meal.

- 1/2 pound sliced bacon, diced
- 1 large onion, chopped
- 2 medium carrots, sliced
- 1 bay leaf
- 2 whole cloves
- 1 medium potato, peeled and cubed
- 2 cups water
- 1/4 cup white wine or chicken broth
- 1 pound haddock fillets, cut into chunks
- 1 teaspoon dill weed
- 1/2 teaspoon salt
- 1/8 teaspoon white pepper
- 1 tablespoon all-purpose flour
- 2 tablespoons cold water
- 1 cup half-and-half cream
- 1 tablespoon minced fresh parsley

In a large saucepan, cook bacon over medium heat until crisp. Using a slotted spoon, remove to paper towels; drain, reserving 1 tablespoon drippings. In the drippings, saute onion and carrots until tender.

Place bay leaf and cloves on a double thickness of cheesecloth; bring up corners of cloth and tie with string to form a bag. Add to saucepan. Stir in the potato, water and wine. Bring to a boil. Reduce heat; cover and simmer for 15-20 minutes or until potatoes are tender.

SINGAPORE SATAY SANDWICHES

DIANE HALFERTY ❖ CORPUS CHRISTI, TEXAS

My grandkids think this shredded chicken is the best thing under a bun. The peanut butter flavor, fresh fruit and vegetable toppings make it a fun, packable sandwich for delicious lunches.

1-1/2 pounds boneless skinless chicken breasts
    1 teaspoon steak seasoning
    1 tablespoon canola oil
    3 tablespoons reduced-fat chunky peanut butter
1/4 cup unsweetened apple juice
    2 tablespoons lime juice
    2 tablespoons reduced-sodium soy sauce
    2 teaspoons hot pepper sauce
    6 kaiser rolls, split

    2 cups torn romaine
    1 cup shredded carrots
1/2 cup julienned peeled cucumber
    6 tablespoons unsweetened crushed pineapple

Sprinkle the chicken breasts on both sides with the steak seasoning. In a large skillet, cook the chicken in oil for 4-7 minutes on each side or until juices run clear. Transfer to a cutting board and shred.

In a large microwave-safe bowl, melt peanut butter. Whisk in the apple juice, lime juice, soy sauce and hot pepper sauce. Add chicken and toss to coat.

Spoon 1/2 cup chicken mixture onto roll bottoms; top with romaine, carrots, cucumber and pineapple. Replace roll tops. YIELD: 6 servings.

EDITOR'S NOTE: This recipe was tested with McCormick's Montreal Steak Seasoning. Look for it in the spice aisle.

CHICKEN PITA SALAD

CATHY SLUSSLER ❖ MAGNOLIA, TEXAS

I make this refreshing dish to take to family get-togethers. Its great Greek flavors and crispy chewiness guarantee it will be gone in a blink.

    3 pita breads (6 inches)
1/4 cup olive oil
1/4 cup balsamic vinegar
    3 tablespoons lemon juice
    1 tablespoon minced fresh oregano *or*
        1 teaspoon dried oregano
    2 garlic cloves, minced
    2 teaspoons grated lemon peel
    1 teaspoon sugar
    1 teaspoon salt
1/4 teaspoon pepper
    2 cups shredded cooked chicken
    1 can (15 ounces) garbanzo beans *or* chickpeas,
        rinsed and drained
    1 English cucumber, halved and sliced
    1 pint cherry tomatoes, halved
    1 small red onion, quartered and sliced
1/2 cup crumbled feta cheese

Cut each pita bread round into eight triangles, then split in half. Place on a baking sheet. Bake at 350° for 10-12 minutes or until lightly toasted.

For dressing, in a small bowl, whisk the oil, vinegar, lemon juice, oregano, garlic, lemon peel, sugar, salt and pepper.

In a large bowl, combine the chicken, garbanzo beans, cucumber, tomatoes and onion. Stir in pita triangles. Drizzle with dressing and toss to coat.

Cover and refrigerate for at least 30 minutes. Just before serving, sprinkle with cheese. YIELD: 16 servings.

CREMINI & BUTTERNUT SQUASH SOUP

GILDA LESTER ❖ MILLSBORO, DELAWARE

When the weather turns chilly, wholesome soup hits the spot. This one tastes like autumn, with vitamin-rich squash and the earthy flavor of mushrooms. Adding cream makes it velvety smooth.

    1 large butternut squash (about 5 pounds)
    1 carton (32 ounces) reduced-sodium chicken broth, *divided*
    1 large onion, chopped
    1 tablespoon olive oil
1/2 pound chopped baby portobello (cremini) mushrooms
    3 garlic cloves, minced
    1 teaspoon minced fresh thyme
1/2 teaspoon rubbed sage
1/8 teaspoon ground nutmeg
1/4 cup heavy whipping cream
1/4 cup grated Romano cheese

Cut squash in half lengthwise; discard seeds. Place squash, cut side down, in a 15-in. x 10-in. x 1-in. baking pan coated with cooking spray. Bake at 400° for 55-65 minutes or until the squash is tender.

Cool slightly; carefully scoop out pulp. Place in a food processor with 1 cup broth; cover and process until smooth.

In a large saucepan over medium heat, cook onion in oil until tender. Add the mushrooms, garlic, thyme and sage; cook 3-4 minutes longer or until mushrooms are tender. Stir in the nutmeg, squash puree and remaining broth. Bring to a boil. Reduce heat; simmer, uncovered, for 20 minutes.

Stir in cream; heat through (do not boil). Ladle soup into bowls; sprinkle with cheese. YIELD: 8 servings (2 quarts).

BUYING & STORING WINTER SQUASH

Common varieties of winter squash include the butternut, acorn, Hubbard, spaghetti and turban. Winter squash should feel heavy for their size, have hard, deep-colored rinds and be free of blemishes. Store in a dry, cool, well-ventilated place for up to 1 month.

BEEF SANDWICHES
WITH BEET SPREAD

DAWN SCHUMILAS ❖ WHITE FOX, SASKATCHEWAN

Stack it up! This old-fashioned beef sandwich has a zesty horseradish spread featuring flavors that really come alive in your mouth. Topped with fresh onion, lettuce and tomato, it is simply unbeatable.

    4 ounces cream cheese, softened
    1 whole fresh beet, cooked, peeled and mashed
      (about 1/2 cup)
1/4 cup prepared horseradish
    2 tablespoons lemon juice
    1 tablespoon white vinegar
1-1/2 teaspoons sugar
Dash cayenne pepper
    8 hard rolls, split and toasted
    8 teaspoons butter, softened
    1 pound thinly sliced deli roast beef
    8 lettuce leaves
    8 slices tomato
    8 slices onion

In a small bowl, beat cream cheese and beet until blended. Beat in the horseradish, lemon juice, vinegar, sugar and cayenne.

Spread rolls with butter and beet spread. Layer with beef, lettuce, tomato and onion. YIELD: 8 servings.

SHRIMP SALAD LEMON BASKETS

RENATA STANKO ❖ LEBANON, OREGON

Sunny lemon baskets brimming with shrimp salad are a feast for the eyes, nose and taste buds. Guests will appreciate the creative presentation and flavors.

    2 envelopes unflavored gelatin
1-1/2 cups cold water
    1 cup mayonnaise
    6 medium lemons
    1 package (5 ounces) frozen cooked salad shrimp,
      thawed, *divided*
1/2 cup chopped seeded peeled cucumber
1/4 cup chopped pimiento-stuffed olives
    2 teaspoons sugar
    2 teaspoons prepared horseradish
1/4 teaspoon salt
1/4 teaspoon paprika
1/2 cup heavy whipping cream, whipped
    12 sprigs fresh parsley

In a small saucepan, sprinkle gelatin over cold water; let stand for 1 minute. Cook and stir over low heat until gelatin is completely dissolved. Remove from the heat; whisk in mayonnaise. Refrigerate for 30 minutes or until partially set.

Cut lemons in half; juice lemons, reserving 3 tablespoons juice (save remaining juice for another use). Scoop out and discard pulp. With a sharp knife, cut a thin slice off the bottom of each lemon basket so it sits flat; set aside.

Set aside 2 dozen shrimp for garnish; chop remaining shrimp. In a small bowl, combine cucumber, olives, sugar, horseradish, salt, paprika and reserved lemon juice; fold into gelatin mixture. Fold in chopped shrimp and whipped cream.

Spoon into lemon baskets. Garnish with parsley and reserved shrimp. Chill until set. YIELD: 1 dozen.

GRILLED CHEESE & PEPPER SANDWICHES

ARLINE HOFLAND ✿ DEER LODGE, MONTANA

This is a tasty and wholesome sandwich to make for one or two. It's a nice twist on traditional grilled cheese. It's especially good with rye bread!

    4 slices rye bread with caraway seeds
    2 tablespoons butter, softened, *divided*
1/2 cup chopped onion
1/2 cup chopped green pepper
1/2 cup chopped sweet red pepper
    2 teaspoons chopped seeded jalapeno pepper
    2 tablespoons olive oil
3/4 cup shredded Monterey Jack cheese

Butter one side of each slice of bread with 1/2 teaspoon butter; set aside. In a small skillet, saute onion and peppers in oil until tender. Spoon onto two bread slices; top with cheese and remaining bread. Spread the outsides of sandwiches with remaining butter.

In a large skillet, toast sandwiches for 3 minutes on each side or until golden brown. YIELD: 2 servings.

EDITOR'S NOTE: When cutting hot peppers, disposable gloves are recommended. Avoid touching your face.

BAKED HAMBURGERS

MARG BISGROVE ✿ WIDEWATER, ALBERTA

Preparing hamburgers this way makes them different than plain old hamburgers. They're hearty and moist, and the onion gives it a special flavor. The sweet sauce further enhances the taste. I serve these as an entree with accompanying vegetables or each on a bun as a sandwich.

    1 small onion, chopped
1/4 cup dry bread crumbs

    2 tablespoons milk
3/4 teaspoon salt, *divided*
1/4 teaspoon pepper
1/2 pound ground beef
1/3 cup water
    2 tablespoons brown sugar
    2 tablespoons ketchup
1/2 teaspoon ground mustard
1/2 teaspoon white vinegar
    2 hamburger buns, optional

In a small bowl, combine the onion, bread crumbs, milk, 1/2 teaspoon salt and pepper. Crumble beef over mixture and mix well. Shape into two patties. Place in a greased 11-in. x 7-in. baking dish.

Combine the water, brown sugar, ketchup, mustard, vinegar and remaining salt; pour over patties.

Bake, uncovered, at 350° for 35-40 minutes or until meat is no longer pink. Serve on buns if desired. YIELD: 2 servings.

CURRIED APPLE SOUP

XAVIER PENNELL ✿ MAULDIN, SOUTH CAROLINA

Harvest-fresh soup is a perfect salute to the riches of Indian summer. Sweet apples, spicy curry and tangy lemon strike a delicious balance.

    1 medium onion, chopped
    2 tablespoons butter
    1 teaspoon curry powder
1/4 teaspoon ground cinnamon
1/8 teaspoon salt
Dash cayenne pepper
Dash ground cloves
    3 medium McIntosh apples, peeled and sliced

3 cups chicken broth
1-1/2 teaspoons lemon juice
Crackers and additional ground cinnamon, optional

In a small saucepan, saute onion in butter until tender. Add the curry, cinnamon, salt, cayenne and cloves; cook and stir for 1 minute. Add apples and broth; bring to a boil. Reduce heat; cover and simmer for 5-7 minutes or until apples are tender.

In a blender, puree soup until smooth. Return to the pan. Stir in lemon juice and heat through. Garnish with crackers and additional cinnamon if desired. YIELD: 4 servings.

SOUTHWEST SALAD

SHARON EVANS ✢ ROCKWELL, IOWA

Friends served us this wonderful salad when we were vacationing in Arizona. My husband particularly liked the fresh-tasting citrus-flavored dressing, and asked me to be sure to get the recipe. It's since become one of our family's favorite salads.

SALAD DRESSING
1/2 teaspoon grated orange peel
1/4 cup orange juice
1/2 cup canola oil
2 tablespoons sugar
3 tablespoons red wine vinegar
1 tablespoon lemon juice
1/4 teaspoon salt

SALAD
3 heads Boston lettuce, washed and cubed
1 small cucumber, thinly sliced
1 medium ripe avocado, peeled and sliced
1 small red onion, sliced and separated into rings
1 can (11 ounces) mandarin oranges, drained or fresh orange sections

In a small bowl, whisk salad dressing ingredients; set aside. Arrange the lettuce, cucumber, avocado, onion and oranges on individual plates. Drizzle with dressing just before serving. YIELD: 6 servings.

CHEESY TORTILLA SOUP

LAVONDA OWEN ❖ MARLOW, OKLAHOMA

My daughter successfully created this dish when trying to duplicate a soup she sampled at a restaurant. I always pass on to her the rave reviews whenever this is served.

  1 envelope chicken fajita seasoning mix
  1 pound boneless skinless chicken breasts, diced
  2 tablespoons canola oil
  1/2 cup chopped onion
  1/4 cup butter, cubed
  1/3 cup all-purpose flour
  2 cans (14-1/2 ounces *each*) chicken broth
  1/3 cup canned diced tomatoes with chilies
  1 cup cubed process cheese (Velveeta)
  1-1/2 cups (6 ounces) shredded Monterey Jack cheese, *divided*
  1-1/2 cups half-and-half cream
Guacamole
  1/2 cup shredded cheddar cheese
Tortilla chips

Prepare fajita mix according to package directions; add chicken and marinate as directed. In a large skillet, cook chicken in oil until no longer pink; set aside.

In a large saucepan, saute onion in butter until tender. Stir in flour until blended. Gradually stir in broth. Bring to a boil. Cook and stir for 2 minutes or until thickened and bubbly. Add the tomatoes, process cheese and 1 cup Monterey Jack; cook and stir until cheese is melted.

Stir in the cream and reserved chicken; heat through (do not boil). Garnish with the guacamole, cheddar cheese and remaining Monterey Jack cheese; add the tortilla chips. YIELD: 8 servings (2 quarts).

CLASSIC FRENCH DRESSING

MARON CRAIG BIELOVITZ ❖ ELMHURST, PENNSYLVANIA

Making salad dressings at home is very easy! This recipe uses pantry staples, so it's simple to whip up any time. It tastes wonderful on any type of greens.

  1/2 cup ketchup
  1/3 cup sugar
  1/4 cup white vinegar
  1 small onion, minced
  1 garlic clove, minced
  1 tablespoon paprika
  1/2 to 1 teaspoon salt
  1/2 cup vegetable oil

In a blender or food processor, combine the first seven ingredients; cover and process until blended. While processing, gradually add the oil in a steady stream. Process until thickened. Store in the refrigerator. YIELD: 1-2/3 cups.

FESTIVE CRANBERRY FRUIT SALAD

ROUSHEEN AREL WOLF ❖ DELTA JUNCTION, ALASKA

This fruit salad is a tradition on my Christmas table. It goes together quickly, which is a plus on such a busy day.

  1 package (12 ounces) fresh *or* frozen cranberries
  3/4 cup water
  1/2 cup sugar
  5 medium apples, diced
  2 medium firm bananas, sliced
  1-1/2 cups fresh *or* frozen blueberries, thawed
  1 can (11 ounces) mandarin oranges, undrained
  1 cup fresh *or* frozen raspberries, thawed
  3/4 cup fresh strawberries, halved

In a large saucepan, combine the cranberries, water and sugar. Cook and stir over medium heat until berries pop, about 15 minutes. Remove from the heat; cool slightly.

In a large bowl, combine the remaining ingredients. Add cranberry mixture; stir gently. Refrigerate until serving. YIELD: 12-14 servings.

BUYING FRESH CRANBERRIES

Fresh cranberries are in season from early fall through December. When buying, look for packages that contain shiny, bright red (light or dark) berries. Avoid berries that are bruised, shriveled or have brown spots.

OPEN-FACED
VEGGIE SANDWICHES

VIRGINA LAWSON ❖ CORTEZ, COLORADO

This sandwich is a great recipe during the summer season when your garden is filled with ripe vegetables. I jazz up this delightful sandwich with a tasty dressing and slices of Muenster cheese.

2 tablespoons olive oil
3 garlic cloves, minced
1/2 teaspoon salt
1/2 teaspoon dried oregano
1/2 teaspoon dried basil
1 medium eggplant, thinly sliced
2 medium zucchini, halved and sliced
1 large onion, sliced
1 medium sweet red pepper, sliced
1 medium green pepper, sliced
1/4 cup mayonnaise
2 tablespoons balsamic vinegar
1 teaspoon Dijon mustard
4 slices Italian bread (1/2 inch thick), toasted
1 medium tomato, thinly sliced
4 slices Muenster cheese

In a large bowl, combine the oil, garlic, salt, oregano and basil. Add vegetables and toss to coat. Transfer to two 15-in. x 10-in. x 1-in. baking pans.

Bake, uncovered, at 425° for 15-20 minutes or until lightly browned, stirring occasionally.

Combine the mayonnaise, vinegar and mustard; spread over toast. Place on a baking sheet. Top with vegetable mixture, tomato and cheese. Broil 6-8 in. from the heat for 2-3 minutes or until cheese is melted. YIELD: 4 servings.

FRESH CORN AND TOMATO SOUP

CLYDA CONRAD ❖ YUMA, ARIZONA

This light and fresh soup is an excellent choice. Sieving the tomatoes, celery, onion and green pepper offers silky smoothness, and it lets the corn flavor stand out nicely.

1 celery rib, chopped
1 small onion, chopped
1/4 cup chopped green pepper
2 tablespoons butter
4 cups chopped seeded peeled tomatoes
2 cups chicken broth
1 teaspoon sugar
1/2 teaspoon salt
1/8 teaspoon white pepper
2 cups fresh sweet corn
1 tablespoon minced fresh basil
2 tablespoons minced fresh parsley
1 green onion, finely chopped

In a large saucepan, saute the celery, onion and green pepper in butter until tender. Stir in tomatoes and broth. Bring to a boil. Reduce heat; cover and simmer for 20 minutes.

Press through a sieve or food mill; return to the pan. Add the sugar, salt and white pepper. Bring to a boil. Stir in the corn and basil. Reduce the heat; simmer, uncovered, for 3-5 minutes or until corn is tender. Garnish with parsley and green onion. YIELD: 6 servings.

Picnic Pasta Salad

Everyone loves a hearty pasta salad, and it makes the perfect dish for any get-together...especially outdoor barbecues and picnics!

HOT BACON MACARONI SALAD

KAY BELL ✤ PALESTINE, TEXAS

Start your picnic right with this delicious macaroni salad. It's loaded with diced veggies and smoky bacon, and coated with a zesty dressing similar to one you'd use for German potato salad.

    1 package (7 ounces) elbow macaroni
    1/4 pound sliced bacon, diced
    1/2 pound sliced fresh mushrooms
    1/3 to 1/2 cup sugar
    2 tablespoons all-purpose flour
    1/2 teaspoon salt
    1/8 teaspoon pepper
    2/3 cup cider vinegar
    1/2 cup chopped onion
    1/2 cup chopped celery
    1/2 cup sliced radishes
    2 tablespoons minced fresh parsley

Cook macaroni according to package directions.

Meanwhile, in a large skillet, cook bacon over medium heat until crisp. Remove to paper towels with a slotted spoon. In the same skillet, saute mushrooms in drippings until tender; remove with a slotted spoon. Add the sugar, flour, salt and pepper to the skillet; gradually stir in vinegar until smooth. Bring to a boil. Cook and stir for 1-2 minutes or until thickened.

Drain macaroni. In a large bowl, combine the macaroni, onion and celery. Drizzle with vinegar mixture. Add mushrooms and bacon; toss to coat. Garnish with radishes and parsley. YIELD: 6 servings.

CHEESY PASTA SALAD

SANDI GREEN ✤ JACKSON, MICHIGAN

This creamy pasta salad came about when I combined ingredients from two different recipes. It's so hearty and delicious, it's like eating an entree. It got rave reviews when I served it at a baby shower.

    4 cups cubed cooked chicken
    1 package (8 ounces) spiral pasta, cooked,
        drained and cooled
1-1/2 cups cubed Gouda *or* Monterey Jack cheese
    1 cup sliced celery
    1 cup seedless green grapes
    1 cup mayonnaise
    1/4 cup sour cream
    3 tablespoons lemon juice
    3 tablespoons honey
    1 teaspoon dried thyme
    1/2 teaspoon ground mustard
    1/4 teaspoon white pepper
    2/3 cup chopped pecans, toasted

In a large bowl, combine chicken, pasta, cheese, celery and grapes. In a small bowl, combine next seven ingredients. Pour over chicken mixture and toss to coat. Cover and chill until ready to serve; toss with pecans. YIELD: 12 servings.

VEGGIE BOW TIE SALAD

ELEKTRA HARRIS ✤ VANCOUVER, BRITISH COLUMBIA

Here's a healthy salad full of fresh vegetables, tender pasta and zippy, homemade vinaigrette dressing. It's a perfect accompaniment for lean meat or fish.

    2 cups uncooked bow tie pasta
    2 cups fresh broccoli florets
    1 cup fresh cauliflowerets
    1 medium sweet red pepper, chopped

1/2 cup cherry tomatoes, halved
1/2 cup chopped pitted green olives
1 jar (4-1/2 ounces) marinated artichoke hearts, drained
1/4 cup unsalted sunflower kernels
1/4 cup minced fresh basil
1/4 cup oil-packed sun-dried tomatoes, chopped, optional

VINAIGRETTE
1/2 cup olive oil
1/4 cup balsamic vinegar
2 tablespoons lemon juice
1 teaspoon sugar
1/2 teaspoon salt
1/4 teaspoon pepper

Cook pasta according to package directions. Meanwhile, in a small saucepan, bring 1 in. of water to a boil. Add broccoli and cauliflower; cook for 2-3 minutes. Drain and immediately place vegetables in ice water; drain and pat dry. Drain pasta and rinse in cold water.

In a large salad bowl, combine the pasta, broccoli mixture, red pepper, cherry tomatoes, olives, artichokes, sunflower kernels, basil and sun-dried tomatoes if desired.

In a small bowl, whisk the vinaigrette ingredients. Pour over the salad; toss to coat. Cover and refrigerate until serving. YIELD: 9 servings.

❧ LAYERED TORTELLINI SALAD

NITA RAUSCH ✤ DALLAS, TEXAS

My tempting tortellini salad combines layers upon layers of flavors and textures, and its colors are amazing. It's ideal for a salad luncheon. Other cheese options are Havarti, fontina or Monterey Jack.

1/2 cup buttermilk
1/2 cup plain yogurt
1/4 cup mayonnaise
1 teaspoon sugar
1/4 teaspoon salt
1/4 teaspoon dill weed
1/4 teaspoon dried basil
1/8 teaspoon white pepper
SALAD
1 package (9 ounces) refrigerated cheese tortellini
2 cups shredded red cabbage
6 cups fresh baby spinach
1 block (8 ounces) part-skim mozzarella cheese, cubed
1 cup cherry tomatoes, halved
1 small red onion, thinly sliced
8 bacon strips, cooked and crumbled
1/2 cup crumbled feta cheese

For the dressing, place the first eight ingredients in a blender. Cover and process until blended; process 1-2 minutes longer or until smooth.

Cook tortellini according to package directions. Drain and rinse in cold water.

In a large glass bowl, layer the cabbage, spinach and tortellini. Top with mozzarella cheese, tomatoes, onion, bacon and feta cheese. Cover and refrigerate for at least 3 hours. Drizzle with dressing; toss to coat. YIELD: 12 servings (1-1/2 cups dressing).

GRILLED EGGPLANT PEPPER SANDWICHES

PAULA MARCHESI ❖ LENHARTSVILLE, PENNSYLVANIA

I love eggplant! These savory, filling sandwiches give the vegetable new meaning. One bite, and you're hooked. Even my grandchildren love them.

1/2 cup pitted ripe olives
2 to 3 tablespoons balsamic vinegar
1 garlic clove, minced
1/8 teaspoon salt
Dash pepper
1/4 cup olive oil

SANDWICHES
1/4 cup olive oil
3 garlic cloves, minced
1 teaspoon pepper
1/2 teaspoon salt
1 large eggplant, cut lengthwise into 1/2-inch slices
2 large sweet red peppers, quartered
8 slices firm white bread (1/2 inch thick)
1/4 cup fresh basil leaves, thinly sliced

Place the first five ingredients in a food processor; cover and process until pureed. While processing, gradually add oil in a steady stream; process until blended. Set aside.

For sandwiches, in a small bowl, combine the oil, garlic, pepper and salt; brush over eggplant and red peppers. Prepare grill for indirect heat, using a drip pan. Arrange vegetables on a grilling grid; place on a grill rack over drip pan.

Grill, covered, over indirect medium heat for 10-12 minutes or until tender. Remove and keep warm. Grill bread over medium heat grill for 1-2 minutes on each side or until toasted.

Spread olive mixture over toast. Top four slices with vegetables and basil; top with remaining toast. YIELD: 4 servings.

EDITOR'S NOTE: If you do not have a grilling grid, use a disposable foil pan. Poke holes in the bottom of the pan with a meat fork to allow liquid to drain.

🎗 GORGONZOLA PEAR SALAD

CANDACE MCMENAMIN ❖ LEXINGTON, SOUTH CAROLINA

This quick, easy recipe really showcases pears. When I have leftover cooked chicken, I often add it to the recipe to make a main-dish salad.

1/3 cup white wine vinegar
1 can (15 ounces) pear halves, drained
1/2 teaspoon salt
1/3 cup olive oil
6 cups torn mixed salad greens
2 medium pears, chopped
1 medium tomato, seeded and finely chopped
3/4 cup chopped walnuts
1/4 cup crumbled Gorgonzola cheese
Coarsely ground pepper, optional

For dressing, in a blender, combine the vinegar, pear halves and salt; cover and process until smooth. While processing, gradually add oil in a steady stream.

In a salad bowl, combine the greens, chopped pears, tomato, walnuts and cheese. Drizzle with desired amount of dressing; toss to coat. Serve with pepper if desired. Refrigerate any leftover dressing. YIELD: 6 servings (1-1/4 cups dressing).

WILD RICE AND CHEDDAR DUMPLING SOUP

TERESA CHRISTENSEN ❖ OSCEOLA, WISCONSIN

I enjoy preparing hearty soups and stews for my husband and two daughters. This is one of their favorites.

    10 cups water
     1 pound sliced fresh mushrooms
     2 cups diced potatoes
     2 cups chopped carrots
 1-1/2 cups chopped celery
     1 medium onion, chopped
     3 chicken bouillon cubes
     3 to 4 cups cubed cooked roast beef
     2 cups cooked wild rice
   3/4 cup all-purpose flour
     3 cups milk
   1/4 cup butter
     1 tablespoon minced fresh parsley
     2 to 3 teaspoons salt
   3/4 teaspoon dried basil
   3/4 teaspoon pepper

DUMPLINGS
     2 cups biscuit/baking mix
     1 cup (4 ounces) shredded cheddar cheese
   2/3 cup milk

Place the first seven ingredients in a stockpot. Bring to a boil. Reduce heat; cover and simmer for 10-15 minutes or until vegetables are tender. Add beef and rice.

In a small bowl, combine flour and milk until smooth. Stir into the soup. Bring to a boil; cook and stir for 2 minutes or until thickened. Stir in the butter and seasonings.

Combine the baking mix, cheese and milk. Drop by tablespoonfuls onto simmering soup. Cover and simmer for 12 minutes or until a toothpick inserted in a dumpling comes out clean (do not lift the cover while simmering). YIELD: 14 servings (about 5 quarts).

ABOUT WILD RICE

A dark-hulled, aquatic grass native to North America, it has a chewy texture, nutty flavor, and the grains expand 3 to 4 times their original size and some of the kernels may pop.

 # MOROCCAN CHICKPEA STEW

CINDY BEBERMAN ❖ ORLAND PARK, ILLINOIS

When I served this spicy stew to guests, including three vegetarians, they were thrilled with the abundance of squash, potatoes, tomatoes and onion.

     1 large onion, finely chopped
     2 tablespoons olive oil
     1 tablespoon butter
     2 garlic cloves, minced
     2 teaspoons ground cumin
     1 cinnamon stick (3 inches)
   1/2 teaspoon chili powder
     4 cups vegetable broth
     2 cups cubed peeled butternut squash
     1 can (15 ounces) chickpeas or garbanzo beans,
       rinsed and drained
     1 can (14-1/2 ounces) diced tomatoes, undrained
     1 medium red potato, cut into 1-inch cubes
     1 medium sweet potato, peeled and cut into 1-inch cubes
     1 medium lemon, thinly sliced
   1/4 teaspoon salt
     2 small zucchini, cubed
     3 tablespoons minced fresh cilantro

In a Dutch oven, saute onion in oil and butter until tender. Add the garlic, cumin, cinnamon stick and chili powder; saute 1 minute longer.

Stir in the broth, squash, chickpeas, tomatoes, potatoes, lemon and salt. Bring to a boil. Reduce the heat; cover and simmer for 15-20 minutes or until potatoes and squash are almost tender.

Add the zucchini; return to a boil. Reduce heat; cover and simmer for 5-8 minutes or until the vegetables are tender. Discard cinnamon stick and lemon slices. Stir in cilantro. YIELD: 9 servings (about 2 quarts).

CUCUMBERS IN CREAM

PHYLLIS KIRSLING ❖ JUNCTION CITY, WISCONSIN

When I was a child, my family had an enormous vegetable garden, so we enjoyed freshly picked cucumbers during the summer. My mother would slice the cucumbers, soak them for a bit in some salt water and add thick cream, which she carefully scooped from the top of fresh milk.

    3 medium cucumbers, peeled and thinly sliced
    1 medium onion, sliced
    2 cups water
    1/2 teaspoon salt
    3/4 cup heavy whipping cream
    1/4 cup sugar
    1/4 cup cider vinegar
Minced fresh parsley, optional

In a bowl, combine cucumbers, onion, water and salt. Let stand for 1 hour; drain and rinse. In a serving bowl, beat cream, sugar and vinegar. Add cucumbers and onion; toss gently. Sprinkle with parsley if desired. YIELD: 6-8 servings.

SAUSAGE SLOPPY JOES

DIXIE TERRY ❖ GOREVILLE, ILLINOIS

I came up with this barbecued burger recipe using pork sausage when I ran out of ground beef one night. It's one of our grandkids' favorites, and my husband likes it, too.

    1/2 pound bulk pork sausage
    1/3 cup chopped onion
    1/2 cup tomato sauce

    1/4 cup water
    2 tablespoons ketchup
  1-1/2 teaspoons Worcestershire sauce
Dash to 1/8 teaspoon hot pepper sauce
    2 hamburger buns, split

In a skillet, cook sausage and onion over medium heat until meat is no longer pink; drain. Stir in the tomato sauce, water, ketchup, Worcestershire sauce and pepper sauce. Bring to a boil. Reduce heat; cover and simmer for 30 minutes. Serve on buns. YIELD: 2 servings.

TRULY TEXAN CHILI

BETTY BROWN ❖ SAN ANTONIO, TEXAS

I am a native Texan, and this is the best chili recipe I've ever tasted. It's meaty and spicy. I'd make this whenever I was homesick during the years we spent away from Texas due to my hubby's military career.

    3 pounds ground beef
    2 to 3 garlic cloves, minced
    3 tablespoons chili powder (or to taste)
    1 tablespoon ground cumin
  1/4 cup all-purpose flour
    1 tablespoon dried oregano
    2 cans (14-1/2 ounces *each*) beef broth
    1 teaspoon salt
  1/4 teaspoon pepper
    1 can (15 ounces) pinto beans, rinsed and drained, optional
Optional garnishes: shredded cheddar cheese, tortilla chips, sour cream *and/or* lime wedges

In a Dutch oven, cook beef over medium heat until no longer pink; drain. Reduce heat; stir in garlic. Combine the chili powder, cumin, flour and oregano; sprinkle over meat, stirring until evenly coated. Add the broth, salt and pepper; bring to a boil, stirring occasionally. Reduce heat; cover and simmer for 1-1/2 to 2 hours, stirring occasionally. (Chili can be transferred to a slow cooker for simmering if desired.)

Cool. Cover and refrigerate overnight. Reheat in a Dutch oven or 3-qt. slow cooker over low heat. If desired, add beans and heat through. Garnish individual bowls if desired with cheddar cheese, tortilla chips, sour cream and/or lime wedges. YIELD: 4-6 servings (5 cups).

CREAM OF CHICKEN NOODLE SOUP

DONNIE KINGMAN ❖ SAN JACINTO, CALIFORNIA

When we were at a restaurant, my husband remarked that I could make a better soup than they could. A challenge! We began discussing what we'd add and take out, and soon came up with this comforting soup.

2 medium onions
2 celery ribs
4 cups water
3 boneless skinless chicken breast halves (6 ounces *each*)
1-1/2 teaspoons salt
1/4 teaspoon pepper
2 tablespoons butter
1 can (14-1/2 ounces) chicken broth
1 large carrot, chopped
1 medium potato, peeled and chopped
2 teaspoons chicken bouillon granules
1-1/2 teaspoons dried basil
2 cups uncooked wide egg noodles
1-3/4 cups milk, *divided*
1/3 cup all-purpose flour

Chop one onion and one celery rib; set aside. Cut remaining onion and celery into chunks; place in a Dutch oven. Add the water, chicken, salt and pepper. Bring to a boil. Reduce heat; cover and simmer for 25-30 minutes or until a meat thermometer reads 170°. Remove chicken and strain broth; set both aside.

In the same pan, saute chopped onion and celery in butter until tender. Add the canned broth, carrot, potato, bouillon, basil and reserved broth. Bring to a boil. Reduce heat; cover and simmer for 20-30 minutes or until vegetables are tender.

Add noodles. Return to a boil; cook for 6-8 minutes or until noodles are tender. Cut chicken into chunks; add to soup. Stir in 1-1/4 cups milk; heat through.

Combine flour and remaining milk until smooth; add to soup, stirring constantly. Bring to a boil; cook and stir for 2 minutes or until thickened. YIELD: 8 servings.

Bring to a boil. Reduce heat; cover and simmer for 2 hours or until beans are tender.

Remove ham hocks; when cool enough to handle, remove meat from bones. Discard bones and cut meat into cubes; return to the soup. Add the additional ham, tomatoes and vinegar; heat through. Discard bay leaves and orange peel before serving. YIELD: 27 servings (6-3/4 quarts).

EDITOR'S NOTE: This recipe was tested with Lea & Perrins Marinade for Chicken.

FAVORITE FISH CHOWDER

FRAN GUSTAFSON ❖ BETHESDA, MARYLAND

Economics had a lot to do with what we ate when I was growing up in New Hampshire during the Depression. Money may have been scarce, but fish was plentiful and affordable, so that's how we began eating this dish. When meat rationing came along in World War II, fish chowder again became a staple in our household. Fortunately, my family loved it...it still is one of my favorites!

    1 large onion, chopped
1/2 cup butter, cubed
    4 cups water
    6 cups cubed peeled potatoes
    2 pounds cod fillets, cut into large chunks
    3 tablespoons lemon juice
    2 cups milk
    2 cans (12 ounces *each*) evaporated milk
2-1/2 teaspoons salt
    2 teaspoons pepper
Minced fresh parsley

In a Dutch oven, saute onion in butter. Add water and bring to a boil. Add potatoes; cook for 10 minutes. Add fish and lemon juice; reduce heat and simmer for 10 minutes. Add milk, evaporated milk, salt and pepper. Sprinkle with parsley. YIELD: 4 quarts.

HERBED CHICKEN SOUP

MYRNA HUEBERT ❖ TOFIELD, ALBERTA

I love cooking and turning a simple recipe into my own personal creation. This soup is one I developed gradually over the years.

    1 broiler/fryer chicken (3 to 3-1/2 pounds), cut up
2-1/2 quarts water
    4 medium carrots, cut into 1/2-inch pieces
    1 medium onion, chopped
1/2 cup chopped celery
    5 chicken bouillon cubes
    2 tablespoons dried parsley flakes
    1 tablespoon dried thyme
    1 teaspoon *each* rubbed sage and poultry seasoning
    1 teaspoon salt, optional

SPORTSMAN'S BEAN SOUP

HOWELL VINCENT ❖ GEORGETOWN, KENTUCKY

I've been cooking and freezing soups and stews for 45 years. This hearty, wholesome soup is one of my wife's favorites. The way to a woman's heart is through her stomach, too.

    2 pounds dried navy beans
    3 large onions, chopped
    2 tablespoons butter
    4 medium carrots, chopped
    2 smoked ham hocks
    1 tablespoon marinade for chicken
    12 orange peel strips (1 to 3 inches)
    1 teaspoon salt
1/2 teaspoon dried thyme
    2 bay leaves
    3 cups cubed fully cooked ham
    1 can (28 ounces) diced tomatoes, undrained
1/4 cup cider vinegar

Sort beans and rinse with cold water. Place in a stockpot; add water to cover by 2 in. Bring to a boil; boil for 2 minutes. Remove from the heat; cover and let stand for 1-4 hours or until beans are softened.

Drain and rinse beans; discard liquid and set beans aside. In the same pan, saute onions in butter until tender. Add carrots; saute 4-5 minutes longer.

Add the ham hocks, marinade for chicken, orange peel, salt, thyme, bay leaves, beans and enough water to cover by 2 in.

1/2 teaspoon pepper

1 large bay leaf

1 package (12 ounces) frozen noodles *or* 2 cups cooked noodles

In a Dutch oven or soup kettle, place the first 13 ingredients. Cover and bring to a boil; skim fat. Reduce heat; cover and simmer for 1-1/2 hours or until chicken is tender.

Remove chicken; allow to cool. Debone and cut into chunks. Skim fat from broth; bring to a boil. Return chicken to kettle. Add frozen noodles and cook for 20 minutes or until tender, or add cooked noodles and heat through. Remove bay leaf. YIELD: 16 servings (4 quarts).

WALDORF SALAD

CHUCK HINZ ❖ PARMA, OHIO

The lemon juice gives this easy salad quite a zip, and the apples and nuts offer a nice crunch. It's light, refreshing and effortless to assemble.

2 medium Red Delicious apples, chopped

2 medium Golden Delicious apples, chopped

2 tablespoons lemon juice

2 celery ribs, chopped

3/4 cup chopped walnuts

1/2 cup raisins

1 cup mayonnaise

Ground cinnamon and ground nutmeg, optional

In a large bowl, toss the apples with lemon juice. Gently stir in the celery, walnuts, raisins and mayonnaise. Sprinkle with cinnamon and nutmeg if desired. Refrigerate until serving. YIELD: 9 servings.

HORSERADISH SPINACH SALAD

PATTY BRODERICK ❖ MOORESVILLE, NORTH CAROLINA

Every time I serve this fresh spinach salad, I'm asked for the recipe. Everyone enjoys the zesty dressing, bacon pieces and toasted pecans. It's so simple and impressive.

3/4 cup cream-style cottage cheese

1/2 cup sour cream

2 to 3 tablespoons sugar

4-1/2 teaspoons cider vinegar

2 teaspoons prepared horseradish

3/4 teaspoon ground mustard

1/4 teaspoon salt

10 cups chopped fresh spinach

1 cup chopped pecans, toasted

6 bacon strips, cooked and crumbled

In a food processor, combine cottage cheese and sour cream; cover and process until smooth. Add the sugar, vinegar, horseradish, mustard and salt; cover and process until smooth.

In a salad bowl, toss spinach with pecans and bacon. Serve with dressing. YIELD: 10 servings (1-1/4 cups dressing).

ITALIAN SAUSAGE WITH PEPPERS

BECKI CLEMETSON ❖ SHARPSVILLE, PENNSYLVANIA

Local fairs in these parts are famous for sausage and pepper sandwiches. I came up with my own recipe so our friends and family can savor the tasty treats year-round.

5 Hungarian wax peppers
1 large sweet yellow pepper
1 large sweet red pepper
2 medium sweet onions, chopped
2 tablespoons olive oil
1 can (14-1/2 ounces) Italian diced tomatoes, undrained
1 can (6 ounces) tomato paste
1/2 cup water
4 garlic cloves, minced
2 bay leaves
1 tablespoon dried parsley flakes
1/2 teaspoon dried basil
1/2 teaspoon dried oregano
1/2 teaspoon salt
1/8 teaspoon white pepper
8 Italian sausage links (4 ounces *each*)
8 hoagie buns, split

Seed wax peppers if desired; cut wax and bell peppers into 2-in. pieces. In a large skillet, saute peppers and onions in oil until tender. Stir in the tomatoes, tomato paste, water, garlic, bay leaves and seasonings; heat through.

Meanwhile, in a large skillet, brown sausages. Transfer to an ungreased 13-in. x 9-in. baking dish. Top with pepper mixture.

Cover and bake at 350° for 35-40 minutes or until a meat thermometer reads 160°. Discard bay leaves. Serve on buns. YIELD: 8 servings.

EDITOR'S NOTE: When cutting hot peppers, disposable gloves are recommended. Avoid touching your face.

ROASTED GARLIC POTATO SOUP

MISTY BROWN ❖ GLENDALE HEIGHTS, ILLINOIS

Roasting mellows and sweetens the blend of veggies in this hearty and heartwarming soup. It's ideal for a cozy night.

1 whole garlic bulb
1-1/2 teaspoons plus 2 tablespoons butter, *divided*

2 pounds potatoes (about 6 medium), peeled and cubed
2 medium onions, quartered
2 tablespoons olive oil
1/2 teaspoon salt
1/4 teaspoon pepper
6 cups vegetable broth, *divided*
4-1/2 teaspoons all-purpose flour
1/2 cup milk

Remove papery outer skin from garlic (do not peel or separate cloves); cut top off bulb. Melt 1-1/2 teaspoons butter; drizzle over garlic. Wrap in heavy-duty foil. Place in a 9-in. round baking pan; set aside.

Place potatoes and onions in a single layer in an ungreased 15-in. x 10-in. x 1-in. baking pan. Drizzle with oil; sprinkle with salt and pepper. Toss to coat.

Bake garlic and potato mixture at 400° for 35-40 minutes or until tender, stirring vegetables once. Cool slightly.

In a blender, combine 2 cups broth and half of the vegetable mixture; cover and process until blended. Repeat with 2 cups broth and remaining vegetable mixture; set aside.

In a large saucepan, melt remaining butter. Stir in flour until smooth; gradually add remaining broth. Bring to a boil; cook and stir for 2 minutes or until thickened. Squeeze softened garlic into pan. Stir in milk and pureed vegetables; heat through. YIELD: 8 servings.

THREE CHEESE-STUFFED BURGERS

CAROLYN SCHMELING ✤ BROOKFIELD, WISCONSIN

There's a great flavor to these cheese-packed burgers, with a subtle hint of spices. We like to cook them on the grill but they can be broiled to perfection, too.

1 tablespoon shredded Swiss cheese
1 tablespoon shredded cheddar cheese
1 tablespoon shredded process cheese (Velveeta)
1/8 teaspoon dried oregano

1/8 teaspoon paprika
1/8 teaspoon chili powder
Dash pepper
1/2 pound lean ground beef
2 hamburger buns, split
Optional toppings: tomato, onion, dill pickle slices and ketchup

In a small bowl, combine the first seven ingredients. Shape beef into four thin patties. Sprinkle cheese mixture over two patties; top with remaining patties and press edges firmly to seal.

Grill burgers, covered, over medium heat or broil 4 in. from heat for 4-6 minutes on each side or until a meat thermometer reads 160° and juices run clear. Serve on buns with toppings of your choice. YIELD: 2 servings.

SAUSAGE TORTELLINI SOUP

JOYCE LULEWICZ ✤ BRUNSWICK, OHIO

My husband's grandmother used to make this soup with her own homemade sausage and homemade tortellini. Since it has been passed down, we now use store-bought ingredients but it's almost as good as hers. It's a great way to get the kids to eat spinach!

1/2 pound bulk Italian sausage
1 small onion, thinly sliced
1 garlic clove, minced
1 can (14-1/2 ounces) reduced-sodium chicken broth
1/2 cup water
1-1/2 cups torn fresh spinach
3/4 cup refrigerated cheese tortellini
2 tablespoons shredded Parmesan cheese

In a small saucepan, cook sausage over medium heat until no longer pink; drain. Add onion; cook and stir until tender. Add garlic; cook 1 minute longer. Stir in broth and water; bring to a boil. Reduce heat; simmer, uncovered, for 10 minutes.

Return to a boil. Reduce heat, add spinach and tortellini; cook for 7-9 minutes or until tortellini is tender. Sprinkle with cheese. YIELD: 2 servings.

🏅 TUSCAN STEAK FLATBREADS

MICHAEL COHEN ❖ LOS ANGELES, CALIFORNIA

Take grilled flatbreads jazzed up with pesto, wrap them around steak and top with cheese and you have an instant party! Guests will love the fun presentation and the taste.

SUN-DRIED TOMATO PESTO
- 1/3 cup packed fresh parsley sprigs
- 2 tablespoons fresh basil leaves
- 1 garlic clove, quartered
- 2 tablespoons grated Parmesan cheese
- 2 tablespoons oil-packed sun-dried tomatoes, patted dry
- 2 tablespoons sherry
- 1/4 teaspoon salt
- Dash pepper
- 1/4 cup olive oil

STEAK FLATBREADS
- 1 beef top sirloin steak (3/4 inch thick and 1-1/4 pounds)
- 1/4 teaspoon salt
- 1/4 teaspoon pepper
- 4 flatbreads *or* whole pita breads
- 2 tablespoons olive oil
- 1 cup (4 ounces) shredded fontina cheese
- 1/4 cup fresh basil leaves, thinly sliced

For pesto, place the parsley, basil and garlic in a food processor; cover and pulse until chopped. Add the Parmesan cheese, tomatoes, sherry, salt and pepper; cover and process until blended. While processing, gradually add oil in a steady stream. Set aside.

Sprinkle the steak with salt and pepper. Grill, covered, over medium heat for 6-10 minutes on each side or until the meat reaches desired doneness (for medium-rare, a meat thermometer should read 145°; medium, 160°; well-done, 170°). Remove and keep warm.

Brush one side of each flatbread with oil; place oiled side down on grill rack. Grill, covered, over medium heat for 1-2 minutes or until heated through.

Spread pesto over grilled side of flatbreads. Cut steak into thin strips; place over pesto. Top with fontina cheese and basil. YIELD: 4 servings.

HEARTY CORN CHOWDER

MARK TWIEST ❖ ALLENDALE, MICHIGAN

Everyone in my wife's family is a corn lover, so her mom came up with this wonderful recipe to satisfy their appetites. With the bacon, sausage and potatoes, it's hearty enough to be a one-pot meal, but it's also really good with chicken.

- 1/2 pound sliced bacon
- 1 cup chopped celery
- 1/2 cup chopped onion
- 2 cups cubed peeled potatoes
- 1 cup water
- 2 cups frozen corn
- 1 can (14-3/4 ounces) cream-style corn
- 1 can (12 ounces) evaporated milk
- 6 ounces smoked sausage links, cut into 1/4-inch slices
- 1 teaspoon dill weed

In a large saucepan, cook bacon over medium heat until crisp. Remove to paper towels with a slotted spoon; drain, reserving 2 tablespoons drippings. Crumble bacon and set aside.

Saute celery and onion in drippings until onion is lightly browned. Add potatoes and water. Cover and cook over medium heat for 10 minutes. Stir in corn, milk, sausage, dill and bacon. Cook until the potatoes are tender, about 30 minutes. YIELD: 4-6 servings (1-1/2 quarts).

COUNTRY POTATO SALAD

RAMONA HOOK WYSONG ❖ BARLOW, KENTUCKY

I felt as though my unique potato salad recipe was missing something. So I decided to experiment with a few different ingredients, and the result was this tangy delight!

 5 pounds potatoes, cooked, peeled and diced
 2 hard-cooked eggs, chopped
1/4 cup thinly sliced green onions
1/4 cup finely chopped green *or* sweet red pepper
1/4 cup minced fresh parsley
 1 small garlic clove, minced
 6 slices bacon, cooked and crumbled
 1 teaspoon celery seed
 1 teaspoon dill weed
 1 teaspoon salt
1/2 teaspoon ground pepper
DRESSING
3/4 cup mayonnaise
 2 tablespoons sour cream
 1 teaspoon horseradish
 1 teaspoon Dijon mustard
Pinch oregano
Pinch chives

In a large salad bowl, combine the first 11 ingredients. Set aside. Combine the dressing ingredients; pour over the potato mixture and toss to coat. Cover and refrigerate for up to 24 hours. YIELD: 20 servings.

GREEN-SKINNED POTATOES

The green tint on some potatoes comes from high levels of solanine, which can be toxic if eaten in quantity. It's unlikely that enough solanine would be consumed to cause harm, but it's best to peel it away before eating.

MAIN DISHES

Get ready for the comforting goodness of dozens of hot and hearty dinners that are sure to satisfy the whole family.

SPINACH BEEF STIR-FRY

NANCEE MEYER ✤ STAFFORD, KANSAS

My aunt lived in the town where I went to college, and for my birthday, I could request any meal, and she would prepare it for my friends and me. This recipe of hers remains one of my favorites.

- 4 teaspoons cornstarch
- 1 can (10-1/2 ounces) condensed beef consomme, undiluted
- 1/4 cup reduced-sodium soy sauce
- 2 tablespoons sugar
- 1-1/2 pounds beef top sirloin steak, cut into thin strips
- 1 tablespoon canola oil
- 1 large onion, halved and thinly sliced
- 3 celery ribs, chopped
- 10 large fresh mushrooms, sliced
- 4 green onions, sliced
- 1 package (6 ounces) fresh baby spinach

Hot cooked rice, optional

In a small bowl, combine the cornstarch, consomme, soy sauce and sugar until smooth; set aside. In a large skillet or wok, stir-fry beef in batches in hot oil for 2-3 minutes or until no longer pink. Remove and keep warm.

In the same pan, stir-fry onion and celery for 5 minutes. Add mushrooms and green onions; stir-fry 3-4 minutes longer or until vegetables are tender.

Return beef to the pan. Add spinach. Stir cornstarch mixture and add to the pan. Bring to a boil; cook and stir until thickened. Serve with rice if desired. YIELD: 6 servings.

🏵 JUST-LIKE-THANKSGIVING TURKEY MEAT LOAF

MOLLIE BROWN ✤ LOS ANGELES, CALIFORNIA

For a holiday meal any time of year, this tender turkey meat loaf is perfect. Complemented with a cranberry glaze, it's a mouthwatering dish.

- 1 cup seasoned stuffing cubes
- 1/2 cup milk
- 1 egg, beaten
- 1 celery rib, finely chopped
- 1 small onion, grated
- 1 small carrot, grated
- 1/4 cup dried cranberries
- 1/2 teaspoon salt
- 1/4 teaspoon pepper
- 3 to 4-1/2 teaspoons minced fresh sage, *divided*
- 3 teaspoons minced fresh rosemary, *divided*
- 1-1/2 pounds lean ground turkey
- 1/2 cup whole-berry cranberry sauce
- 1/2 cup ketchup
- 1/8 teaspoon hot pepper sauce

In a large bowl, combine the stuffing cubes and milk. Let stand for 10 minutes; break up stuffing cubes with a fork. Stir in the egg, celery, onion, carrot, cranberries, salt and pepper. Combine the fresh sage and rosemary; add half to the mixture. Crumble the turkey over the mixture and mix well. Pat into an ungreased 9-in. x 5-in. loaf pan.

Bake, uncovered, at 375° for 25 minutes; drain if necessary. Combine the cranberry sauce, ketchup, pepper sauce and remaining herbs; spread over meat loaf. Bake 20-25 minutes longer or until no pink remains and a meat thermometer reads 165°. YIELD: 6 servings.

HEREFORD CASSEROLE

SHAYLA MCCULLERS ❖ FROSTPROOF, FLORIDA

I often serve this easy beef casserole, along with vegetables from my garden, to our hungry family after a full day of ranch work. It uses ingredients I already have on hand and is always satisfying.

4-1/2 cups uncooked fusilli pasta
1-1/2 pounds ground beef
  1 jar (14 ounces) spaghetti sauce
  4 ounces cream cheese, softened
  1 can (10-3/4 ounces) condensed cream of mushroom soup, undiluted
  1 cup (8 ounces) sour cream
  1 cup (4 ounces) shredded cheddar cheese

Cook pasta according to package directions. Meanwhile, in a large skillet, cook beef over medium heat until no longer pink; drain. Stir in spaghetti sauce; set aside.

In a small bowl, beat cream cheese until smooth. Add soup and sour cream; beat until blended. Drain pasta.

Spoon half of the beef mixture into a greased 13-in. x 9-in. baking dish. Top with pasta, soup mixture and remaining beef mixture. Sprinkle with cheddar cheese.

Bake, uncovered, at 350° for 35-40 minutes or until heated through and cheese is melted. YIELD: 7 servings.

CHICKEN IN WHITE WINE SAUCE

LUCIA JOHNSON ❖ MASSENA, NEW YORK

Want to welcome dinner guests with a good meal? This saucy chicken will wow them with its moist and succulent texture and golden-brown coating. The white wine and Parmesan cheese add wonderful flavor.

  2 tablespoons all-purpose flour
1/4 teaspoon salt
1/4 teaspoon paprika
1/4 teaspoon pepper
  4 boneless skinless chicken breast halves (4 ounces each)
  1 teaspoon olive oil
1/2 cup reduced-sodium chicken broth
1/2 cup white wine or additional reduced-sodium chicken broth
  4 teaspoons grated Parmesan cheese

In a large resealable plastic bag, combine the flour, salt, paprika and pepper. Add the chicken, a few pieces at a time, and shake to coat.

In a large ovenproof skillet coated with cooking spray, brown chicken in oil for 1-2 minutes on each side. Add broth and wine; bring to a boil. Remove from the heat.

Cover and bake at 350° for 20-25 minutes or until a meat thermometer reads 170°. Sprinkle with Parmesan cheese. YIELD: 4 servings.

BROCCOLI MAC & CHEESE BAKE

LISA DEMARSH ❖ MT. SOLON, VIRGINIA

My husband made a version of this casserole for me on our first date. Over the years we've been married, we've made several changes to the ingredients and now, it's even better than the original.

  3 cups uncooked elbow macaroni
  4 cups fresh broccoli florets
1/2 cup butter, cubed
  3 tablespoons all-purpose flour
1/2 teaspoon garlic powder
1/2 teaspoon onion powder
1/4 teaspoon pepper
1/8 teaspoon salt
  2 cans (12 ounces each) evaporated milk
2-1/2 cups (10 ounces) shredded cheddar cheese, divided
1/2 cup crushed corn bread-flavored crackers (about 6 crackers)

Cook macaroni according to package directions, adding broccoli during the last 3-4 minutes; drain.

In a large saucepan, melt butter. Stir in the flour, garlic powder, onion powder, pepper and salt until smooth; gradually stir in evaporated milk. Bring to a boil; cook and stir for 2 minutes or until thickened. Remove from the heat; stir in 2 cups cheese.

Place half of the macaroni and broccoli in a greased 13-in. x 9-in. baking dish. Top with half of the cheese sauce. Repeat layers. Sprinkle with cracker crumbs and remaining cheese.

Bake, uncovered, at 375° for 20-25 minutes or until bubbly. YIELD: 12 servings.

CURRY-APPLE TURKEY LOAF

MARY GUDENKAUF ❖ HARRISONVILLE, MISSOURI

I came up with this tender turkey loaf to help my husband and me stick to our healthy-eating habits. Leftover slices make satisfying lunches to take to work the next day.

- 2 cups soft bread crumbs
- 1 medium apple, finely chopped
- 1 cup finely chopped fresh mushrooms
- 1 small red onion, finely chopped
- 2 egg whites, lightly beaten
- 1 egg, lightly beaten
- 1 to 2 teaspoons curry powder
- 1 teaspoon salt
- 1 pound lean ground turkey

TOPPING
- 2 tablespoons butter
- 2 medium apples, finely chopped
- 1 small red onion, finely chopped
- 1/2 cup unsweetened apple juice
- 1 teaspoon curry powder
- 1/4 teaspoon salt

In a large bowl, combine the first eight ingredients. Crumble turkey over mixture and mix well. Pat into a greased 9-in. x 5-in. loaf pan.

Bake, uncovered, at 350° for 50-60 minutes or until no pink remains and a meat thermometer reads 165°.

In a small saucepan, melt butter. Add the remaining topping ingredients; bring to a boil. Reduce heat; simmer, uncovered, for 12-15 minutes or until apples and onion are tender.

Let meat loaf stand for 5-10 minutes before slicing. Serve with warm topping. YIELD: 6 servings.

🎖 HOLIDAY GLAZED HAM

DIANE FREEMAN ❖ FALKLAND, BRITISH COLUMBIA

I like to serve this juicy, mouthwatering ham with mashed potatoes and colorful vegetables. The apricot glaze is delicious, and the pineapple and cloves always assure a truly lovely presentation.

- 1 boneless fully cooked ham (about 6 pounds)
- 1 tablespoon whole cloves
- 1 can (20 ounces) sliced pineapple
- 1 cup apricot preserves
- 1 teaspoon ground mustard
- 1/2 teaspoon ground allspice
- Maraschino cherries

Place ham on a rack in a shallow roasting pan. Score the surface of the ham, making diamond shapes 1/2 in. deep; insert a clove in each diamond. Bake, uncovered, at 325° for 1-1/2 hours.

Drain pineapple, reserving juice. In a small saucepan, combine the pineapple juice, preserves, mustard and allspice. Bring to a boil; cook and stir for 10 minutes or until slightly thickened.

Spoon half of the glaze over ham. Secure pineapple slices and cherries on top and sides of ham with toothpicks.

Bake 30-45 minutes longer or until a meat thermometer reads 140°, basting twice with remaining glaze. Let stand for 10 minutes before slicing. YIELD: 16 servings.

CREOLE STEAKS

NICOLE FILIZETTI ❖ GRAND MARAIS, MICHIGAN

Here's a way to fancy up an economical cut of beef. I created the recipe as a variation on Swiss steak. Serve this entree with rice to catch the flavorful sauce.

    1 large onion, chopped
1/4 cup chopped green pepper
1/4 cup chopped celery
    4 tablespoons canola oil, *divided*
    3 garlic cloves, minced
    1 tablespoon all-purpose flour
1/2 teaspoon salt
1/2 teaspoon dried thyme
1/2 teaspoon cayenne pepper
1/2 teaspoon pepper
    2 cans (14-1/2 ounces *each*) fire-roasted diced tomatoes, undrained
1/4 teaspoon hot pepper sauce
    1 tablespoon lemon juice
    4 beef cubed steaks (4 ounces *each*)
Additional salt and pepper

In a large skillet, saute the onion, green pepper, celery in 2 tablespoons oil or until crisp-tender. Add garlic; cook 1 minute longer. Stir in the flour, salt, thyme, cayenne and pepper.

Add the tomatoes and pepper sauce; bring to a boil. Reduce heat; simmer, uncovered, for 20-25 minutes or until thickened, stirring occasionally. Remove from the heat; stir in the lemon juice and keep warm.

Sprinkle steaks with salt and pepper to taste. In another large skillet, cook steaks in remaining oil over medium heat for 3-4 minutes on each side or until no longer pink. Serve with sauce. YIELD: 4 servings.

POBLANOS STUFFED WITH CHIPOTLE TURKEY CHILI

SONALI RUDER ❖ NEW YORK, NEW YORK

As an emergency room doctor, I like to make dishes that are healthy without sacrificing great taste. These yummy stuffed peppers are family-friendly and nutritious, too.

    8 poblano peppers
    1 package (20 ounces) lean ground turkey
    1 medium onion, chopped
    3 garlic cloves, minced
    2 teaspoons olive oil
    1 can (14-1/2 ounces) fire-roasted diced tomatoes, undrained
    1 can (8-3/4 ounces) whole kernel corn, drained
    1 tablespoon minced chipotle pepper in adobo sauce
    2 teaspoons adobo sauce
1/2 teaspoon salt
1/2 teaspoon ground cumin
1/2 teaspoon chili powder
1/4 teaspoon pepper
    3 tablespoons minced fresh cilantro, *divided*
    1 cup (4 ounces) shredded Mexican cheese blend
1/2 cup reduced-fat sour cream

Broil peppers 4 in. from the heat until skins blister, about 5 minutes. With tongs, rotate peppers a quarter turn. Broil and rotate until all sides are blistered and blackened. Immediately place peppers in a large bowl; cover and let stand for 20 minutes.

Meanwhile, in a large nonstick skillet over medium heat, cook the turkey, onion and garlic in oil until meat is no longer pink; drain. Add the tomatoes, corn, chipotle pepper, adobo sauce, salt, cumin, chili powder and pepper; heat through. Remove from the heat; stir in 2 tablespoons cilantro. Set aside.

Peel off and discard charred skins from poblanos. Cut a lengthwise slit down each pepper, leaving the stem intact; remove membranes and seeds. Fill each pepper with 1/2 cup turkey mixture.

Place peppers in a greased 13-in. x 9-in. baking dish. Sprinkle with cheese. Bake, uncovered, at 375° for 10-15 minutes or until cheese is melted. Sprinkle with remaining cilantro. Serve with sour cream. YIELD: 4 servings.

🎗 CHORIZO-STUFFED TURKEY BREAST WITH MEXICAN GRITS

VERONICA GANTLEY ❖ NORFOLK, VIRGINIA

This recipe features a wonderful combination of well-seasoned ingredients. It's also a simple dinner option for a busy evening.

   1 boneless skinless turkey breast half (2 pounds)
1/2 pound uncooked chorizo, crumbled
   2 tablespoons olive oil
   1 teaspoon salt, *divided*
   1 teaspoon pepper, *divided*
   2 cups water
   1 cup milk
   1 cup quick-cooking grits
   1 can (4 ounces) chopped green chilies
1/2 cup shredded Mexican cheese blend
Minced fresh parsley, optional

Cover turkey with plastic wrap; flatten to 1/2-in. thickness. Remove plastic. Spread chorizo over turkey to within 1 in. of edges. Roll up jelly-roll style, starting with a short side; tie with kitchen string.

Rub turkey with olive oil. Sprinkle with 1/2 teaspoon salt and 1/2 teaspoon pepper. In a large ovenproof skillet, brown turkey on all sides. Bake at 350° for 1-1/4 to 1-1/2 hours or until a meat thermometer reads 170°. Cover and let stand for 10 minutes before slicing.

In a large saucepan, bring the water, milk and remaining salt to a boil. Slowly stir in grits. Reduce heat; cook and stir for 5-7 minutes or until thickened. Stir in the chilies, cheese and remaining pepper. Serve grits with turkey. Sprinkle with parsley if desired. YIELD: 6 servings.

VEGGIE-TUNA NOODLE CASSEROLE

HEIDI FARNWORTH ❖ RIVERTON, UTAH

After adding two sliced zucchini to a traditional tuna casserole, you have a healthier version. The flavor of the fresh basil and tomatoes adds some pizzazz to the zucchini and offers a twist on a classic.

- 3 cups uncooked egg noodles
- 2 medium zucchini, cut into 1/4-inch slices
- 2 teaspoons olive oil, *divided*
- 1 celery rib, chopped
- 1 garlic clove, minced
- 2 cans (5 ounces *each*) tuna, drained and flaked
- 1/2 cup reduced-fat sour cream
- 1/2 cup reduced-fat mayonnaise
- 4 green onions, thinly sliced
- 2 teaspoons Dijon mustard
- 1/2 teaspoon dried thyme
- 1/4 teaspoon salt
- 1/4 teaspoon pepper
- 1 cup (4 ounces) shredded Monterey Jack cheese
- 1 medium tomato, chopped
- 2 tablespoons minced fresh basil

Cook noodles according to package directions. Meanwhile, in a large skillet, saute zucchini in 1 teaspoon oil until crisp-tender; remove from skillet and set aside.

In the same pan, saute celery in remaining oil until crisp-tender. Add garlic; cook 1 minute longer.

Drain noodles; place in a large bowl. Stir in the tuna, sour cream, mayonnaise, green onions, mustard, thyme, salt, pepper and celery mixture.

Spoon half of the noodle mixture into a greased 11-in. x 7-in. baking dish and top with half of the zucchini slices. Repeat the layers one more time.

Cover and bake at 375° for 30 minutes. Uncover; sprinkle with cheese. Bake 5-10 minutes longer or until cheese is melted. Combine the tomato and basil; sprinkle over casserole. YIELD: 6 servings.

MARIE'S CRAB CAKES

PATTY DZBYNSKI ❖ OWINGS, MARYLAND

These crab cakes, from my Baltimore grandmother, are always part of our holiday meals. Sometimes I make them small, as appetizers, and sometimes large, as an entree.

- 1 egg, beaten
- 1/2 cup fat-free mayonnaise
- 1/3 cup crushed saltines
- 1 tablespoon Worcestershire sauce
- 1 teaspoon seafood seasoning
- 1/4 teaspoon salt
- 1 pound fresh crabmeat
- 1/4 cup canola oil

In a small bowl, combine the first six ingredients. Fold in crab. Shape mixture by 1/4 cupfuls into 10 patties. Cover and chill for 1 hour.

In a large skillet over medium-high heat, cook crab cakes in oil in batches for 3-4 minutes on each side or until golden brown. YIELD: 5 servings.

SWEET ONION & CHERRY PORK CHOPS

STEPHANIE RAY ❖ FOLEY, MINNESOTA

When I want to jump-start supper, I opt for these tender pork chops. The sweet and savory cherry sauce makes this recipe a keeper. Try serving it with wild rice pilaf.

- 1/2 cup fresh *or* frozen pitted tart cherries, thawed
- 2 tablespoons chopped sweet onion
- 1 tablespoon honey
- 1/2 teaspoon seasoned salt
- 1/4 teaspoon pepper
- 2 boneless pork loin chops (5 ounces *each*)
- 1 teaspoon cornstarch
- 1 teaspoon cold water

In a 1-1/2-qt. slow cooker, combine the first five ingredients; top with pork chops. Cover and cook on low for 3-4 hours or until meat is tender.

Remove meat to a serving platter; keep warm. Skim fat from cooking juices; transfer to a small saucepan. Bring liquid to a boil. Combine cornstarch and water until smooth. Gradually stir into the pan. Bring to a boil; cook and stir for 2 minutes or until thickened. Serve with meat. YIELD: 2 servings.

TOMATO-BASIL SALMON STEAKS

NELLA PARKER ✤ HERSEY, MICHIGAN

My family has always been big on seafood, and this pan-fried salmon went over really well! The fresh tomato and basil topping complements the fillets beautifully.

4 salmon steaks (6 ounces *each*)
2 tablespoons olive oil
1 large onion, chopped
2 garlic cloves, minced
6 large plum tomatoes, peeled, seeded and chopped
1/4 cup water
2 tablespoons minced fresh basil
1/4 to 1/2 teaspoon salt
1/4 teaspoon pepper
Hot cooked linguine

In a large skillet over medium heat, cook salmon in oil for 2-3 minutes on each side or until golden brown. Remove and keep warm. In the same skillet, cook and stir onion until crisp-tender. Stir in garlic; cook 1 minute longer. Add the tomatoes, water, basil, salt and pepper.

Bring to a boil. Reduce heat to low; carefully return salmon to the pan. Cover and simmer for 10-12 minutes or until fish flakes easily with a fork. Serve with linguine. YIELD: 4 servings.

REUBEN CASSEROLE

PHYLLIS ACKERMAN ✤ KEARNY, NEBRASKA

For a different main dish from the ordinary, this Reuben-flavored bake is sure to be a hit. It has all the ingredients of a Reuben sandwich, but in the form of a casserole.

1/2 cup chopped onion
1 medium tart apple, peeled and chopped
1/4 cup butter, *divided*
1 cup chopped cooked corned beef
1 cup sauerkraut, drained
1/2 teaspoon caraway seeds
1/4 cup Thousand Island salad dressing
1 cup (4 ounces) shredded Swiss cheese
2 slices rye bread, cubed and toasted
1 jar (2 ounces) diced pimientos, drained
1 medium green pepper, cut into 1/4-inch rings

In a saucepan, saute onion and apple in 2 tablespoons butter until tender. Stir in beef, sauerkraut and caraway seeds.

Spoon into an ungreased 2-qt. casserole. Drizzle with salad dressing; sprinkle with cheese. Toss croutons with remaining butter; sprinkle over cheese. Top with pimientos and pepper.

Bake, uncovered, at 400° for 20 minutes or until heated through. YIELD: 4 servings.

CHICKEN FAJITA PIZZA

IOLA EGLE ❖ BELLA VISTA, ARKANSAS

Add a fiesta of flavor to homemade pizza with this Italian twist on fajitas. Salsa lovers will be wild about it. Toss together a salad to serve on the side.

1/4 cup lime juice
  3 tablespoons olive oil, *divided*
  2 garlic cloves, minced
  1 pound boneless skinless chicken breasts, finely chopped
  1 prebaked 12-inch pizza crust
  1 jar (16 ounces) chunky salsa, drained
  1 small sweet red pepper, chopped
1/4 cup chopped green pepper
  1 green onion, chopped
1-1/2 cups (6 ounces) shredded Mexican cheese blend
Sour cream, optional

In a large resealable plastic bag, combine the lime juice, 2 tablespoons oil and garlic. Add the chicken; seal bag and turn to coat. Refrigerate for 15 minutes.

Drain and discard marinade. In a large skillet, saute chicken in remaining oil until no longer pink.

Place crust on an ungreased 14-in. pizza pan; spread with salsa to within 1/2 in. of edges. Layer with chicken, peppers, onion and cheese.

Bake at 450° for 8-10 minutes or until cheese is melted. Serve with sour cream if desired. YIELD: 6 slices.

LEMONS AND LIMES

Lemon and lime juice and zest can be used interchangeably in equal amounts in most recipes. To have fresh juice readily available, whenever lemons and limes are on sale, throw a bag of each in the freezer. When you need fresh lemon or lime juice, just defrost a single lemon or lime in the microwave.

ASIAN BARBECUED PORK LOIN

MELISSA CARAFA ❖ BROOMALL, PENNSYLVANIA

This tender and juicy roast is topped with a sweet and spicy glaze that can't be beat. I like serving the main course with jasmine rice and green beans almondine.

   1 boneless whole pork loin roast (3 to 4 pounds)
 1/2 teaspoon garlic salt
 1/4 teaspoon pepper
 1/4 cup finely chopped onion
   1 tablespoon butter
 1/2 cup ketchup
 1/3 cup honey
   1 tablespoon hoisin sauce
1-1/2 teaspoons Chinese-style mustard
   1 teaspoon reduced-sodium soy sauce
 1/2 teaspoon garlic powder
 1/4 teaspoon ground ginger
 1/4 teaspoon Chinese five-spice powder

Sprinkle pork roast with garlic salt and pepper. Place in a shallow roasting pan lined with heavy-duty foil. Bake, uncovered, at 350° for 50 minutes.

Meanwhile, in a small saucepan, saute onion in butter until tender. Stir in the remaining ingredients. Bring to a boil. Reduce heat; simmer, uncovered, until sauce is reduced to 3/4 cup, about 20-25 minutes, stirring often.

Brush sauce over pork. Bake 10-20 minutes longer or until a meat thermometer reads 160°. Let stand for 10 minutes before slicing. YIELD: 8-10 servings.

MAPLE CHICKEN 'N' RIBS

PHYLLIS SCHMALZ ❖ KANSAS CITY, KANSAS

With its generous portions, this recipe is great for a potluck or family reunion. I also love this entree because the chicken thighs and country-style ribs are affordable.

1-1/2 cups apple cider or juice
 1/2 cup maple syrup
   9 garlic cloves, unpeeled
   3 tablespoons canola oil
   3 tablespoons soy sauce
   2 cinnamon sticks (3 inches)
   3 whole star anise
 3/4 teaspoon crushed red pepper flakes
   8 pork spareribs (about 5-1/2 pounds)
   8 bone-in chicken thighs (about 3 pounds)

In a large bowl, combine the first eight ingredients. Pour 1-1/2 cups marinade into a large resealable plastic bag; add the spareribs and chicken. Seal the bag and turn to coat; refrigerate for at least 8 hours or overnight. Cover and refrigerate the remaining marinade.

Drain and discard marinade. Place ribs and chicken, skin side up, in a greased shallow roasting pan.

Bake at 350° for 1-1/2 to 2 hours or until tender, basting occasionally with reserved marinade. YIELD: 8 servings.

From the Grill

Here are few recipes to choose from when grilling season approaches, making outdoor gatherings and summer meals easier to throw together.

BEEF KABOBS WITH CHUTNEY SAUCE

JUDY THOMPSON ❖ ANKENY, IOWA

I created this speedy grilled entree for our daughter, a fan of Indian food. The mango chutney and subtle curry give the beef a sweet and zippy flavor.

1/2 cup plain yogurt
3 tablespoons mango chutney
1 teaspoon lemon juice
1/2 teaspoon curry powder
1/4 teaspoon ground cumin
1/8 teaspoon cayenne pepper
MARINATED BEEF
1/4 cup mango chutney
1 tablespoon cider vinegar
1 tablespoon water
1 teaspoon curry powder
1/4 teaspoon cayenne pepper
1 pound beef top sirloin steak, cut into 1/4-inch strips

For sauce, in a small bowl, combine the first six ingredients. Cover and refrigerate until serving.

For marinade, in a large resealable plastic bag, combine the chutney, vinegar, water, curry and cayenne; add beef. Seal bag and turn to coat; refrigerate overnight.

Drain and discard marinade. Thread beef onto eight metal or soaked wooden skewers.

Moisten a paper towel with cooking oil; using long-handled tongs, lightly coat the grill rack. Grill kabobs, covered, over medium heat or broil 4 in. from the heat for 4-6 minutes or until meat reaches desired doneness, turning occasionally. Serve with dipping sauce. YIELD: 8 kabobs (about 1/2 cup sauce).

🏵 CEDAR PLANK SALMON WITH BLACKBERRY SAUCE

STEPHANIE MATTHEWS ❖ TEMPE, ARIZONA

Here's my go-to entree for a warm-weather cookout. The salmon has a rich grilled taste that's enhanced by the savory blackberry sauce. I think that it's a perfect balance of sweet, smoky and spicy.

2 cedar grilling planks
2 cups fresh blackberries
2 tablespoons white wine
1 tablespoon brown sugar
1-1/2 teaspoons honey
1-1/2 teaspoons chipotle hot pepper sauce
1/4 teaspoon salt, *divided*
1/4 teaspoon pepper, *divided*
1/4 cup finely chopped shallots
1 garlic clove, minced
6 salmon fillets (5 ounces *each*)

In a large resealable plastic bag, combine the first seven ingredients; add the swordfish. Seal bag and turn to coat; refrigerate for 1 hour.

Drain and discard marinade. Moisten a paper towel with cooking oil; using long-handled tongs, lightly coat the grill rack. Grill swordfish, covered, over medium-high heat or broil 4 in. from the heat for 4-6 minutes on each side or until fish just turns opaque. YIELD: 2 servings.

SOUTHWEST GRILLED CHICKEN

MOLLY SEIDEL ✤ EDGEWOOD, NEW MEXICO

Lime juice and a splash of pepper sauce lend refreshing zest to this flavorful take on grilled chicken. It's so easy, you'll make it often.

    1/4 cup lime juice
1-1/2 teaspoons olive oil
    1 teaspoon hot pepper sauce
    1 garlic clove, minced
    1/2 teaspoon ground cumin
    1/4 teaspoon salt
    2 boneless skinless chicken breast halves (5 ounces *each*)

In a large resealable plastic bag, combine the first six ingredients; add the chicken. Seal bag and turn to coat; refrigerate for up to 1 hour.

Drain and discard marinade. Grill chicken, covered, over medium heat for 4-7 minutes on each side or until juices run clear. YIELD: 2 servings.

Soak grilling planks in water for at least 1 hour.

In a food processor, combine the blackberries, wine, brown sugar, honey, hot pepper sauce, 1/8 teaspoon salt and 1/8 teaspoon pepper; cover and process until blended. Strain and discard the seeds. Stir in the shallots and garlic into the sauce; set aside.

Place the planks on grill over medium-high heat. Cover and heat until the planks create a light to medium smoke and begin to crackle, about 3 minutes (this indicates planks are ready). Turn the planks over.

Sprinkle salmon with remaining salt and pepper. Place on planks. Grill, covered, over medium heat for 12-15 minutes or until the fish flakes easily with a fork. Serve with sauce. YIELD: 6 servings (3/4 cup sauce).

GRILLED ROSEMARY SWORDFISH

LORIE RICE ✤ LIVERPOOL, NEW YORK

My husband loves swordfish, and this is his favorite way to have it—moist, tender and perked up with herbs. Tuna is a good substitute for swordfish. Its firm texture stands up nicely to grilling.

    1 tablespoon lemon juice
    1 tablespoon olive oil
    2 garlic cloves, minced
    1 teaspoon minced fresh rosemary *or* 1/4 teaspoon dried rosemary, crushed
    1 teaspoon grated lemon peel
1/4 teaspoon salt
1/4 teaspoon pepper
    2 swordfish steaks (5 ounces *each*)

🎖 HONEY-BRINED TURKEY BREAST

DEIRDRE DEE COX ✦ MILWAUKEE, WISCONSIN

Here's a traditional turkey breast with a sweet and spicy zest. This savory recipe also makes great leftovers.

- 2 quarts apple cider *or* juice
- 1/2 cup kosher salt
- 1/3 cup honey
- 2 tablespoons Dijon mustard
- 1-1/2 teaspoons crushed red pepper flakes
- 1 fresh rosemary sprig
- 2 large oven roasting bags
- 1 bone-in turkey breast (4 to 5 pounds)
- 1 tablespoon olive oil

In a Dutch oven, bring first five ingredients to a boil. Cook and stir until salt and honey are dissolved. Stir in rosemary. Remove from heat; cool to room temperature. Refrigerate until chilled.

Place a large oven roasting bag inside a second roasting bag; add turkey breast. Carefully pour brine into bag. Squeeze out as much air as possible; seal bags and turn to coat. Place in a roasting pan. Refrigerate for 8 hours or overnight, turning occasionally.

Line bottom of a large shallow roasting pan with foil. Drain turkey and discard brine; place on a rack in prepared pan. Pat dry.

Bake, uncovered, at 325° for 30 minutes. Brush with oil. Bake 1-1/2 to 2 hours longer or until a meat thermometer reads 170°. (Cover loosely with foil if turkey browns too quickly.) Cover and let stand for 15 minutes before carving. YIELD: 8 servings.

EDITOR'S NOTE: This recipe was tested with Morton brand kosher salt. It is best not to use a prebasted turkey breast for this recipe. However, if you do, omit the salt in the recipe.

VEGETABLE PASTA WITH SUN-DRIED TOMATO SAUCE

TASTE OF HOME TEST KITCHEN

This colorful salad easily enhances any spread. The bow tie pasta and sauteed veggies are covered in a creamy sun-dried tomato sauce. It's delicious!

- 2 cups uncooked bow tie pasta
- 1-1/4 cups half-and-half cream
- 1/3 cup sun-dried tomato spread
- 1 large sweet red pepper, julienned
- 1 large sweet yellow pepper, julienned
- 1 cup sliced fresh mushrooms
- 1 small onion, sliced
- 5 teaspoons olive oil
- 1 package (10 ounces) frozen peas, thawed
- 1/2 teaspoon salt
- 1/4 teaspoon pepper

Minced fresh parsley and grated Parmesan cheese, optional

Cook pasta according to package directions. Meanwhile, in a small bowl, combine cream and sun-dried tomato spread until blended. In a large skillet, saute peppers, mushrooms and onion in oil until crisp-tender. Reduce heat. Add cream mixture; bring to a gentle boil. Cook and stir for 2 minutes. Stir in the peas, salt and pepper. Drain pasta; add to sauce mixture. Cook for 5 minutes or until heated through. Garnish with parsley and cheese if desired. YIELD: 6 servings.

TURKEY AND DRESSING CASSEROLE

CONNIE PRUETT ❖ NORTH BEND, OREGON

This custard-style dressing is filled with turkey cubes, bread crumbs and plenty of seasoning. It makes a rustic, soothing meal on a chilly day and has all the flavor of a traditional Thanksgiving dinner. For more servings sizes, double the recipe and use a 2-quart casserole dish.

    1 celery rib, chopped
1/4 cup chopped onion
    2 tablespoons butter
    1 cup coarsely crumbled corn bread
    1 cup cubed day-old bread
    2 tablespoons chicken *or* turkey broth
1/4 teaspoon poultry seasoning
1/4 teaspoon salt
Dash pepper
GRAVY
1/4 cup butter, cubed
1/4 cup all-purpose flour
1/4 teaspoon salt
    1 cup chicken *or* turkey broth
1/4 cup milk
    1 egg, lightly beaten
1-1/2 cups cubed cooked turkey
Dry bread crumbs, optional

In a small skillet, saute the celery and onion in butter until tender. Transfer to a large bowl. Stir in the corn bread, bread cubes, chicken or turkey broth and seasonings. Transfer to a greased 1-qt. baking dish.

For gravy, in a large saucepan, melt the 1/4 cup of cubed butter. Whisk in the flour and salt until smooth. Gradually add the chicken or turkey broth and milk. Bring to a boil. Reduce the heat; cook and stir for 2 minutes. Remove from the heat. Stir a small amount of the hot mixture into the egg and return all to the pan, stirring constantly. Bring to a gentle boil; cook and stir for 2 minutes longer.

Spoon half of the gravy over dressing mixture. Layer with turkey and remaining gravy. Sprinkle with bread crumbs if desired. Cover and bake at 350° for 25-30 minutes or until heated through. YIELD: 4 servings.

HOMEMADE POULTRY SEASONING

When a recipe calls for poultry seasoning, you can make your own at home with this simple recipe that yields 1 teaspoon of poultry seasoning: combine 3/4 teaspoon rubbed sage and 1/4 teaspoon dried thyme or marjoram.

PORK CHOPS WITH SAUERKRAUT

ROBERTA BYERS ❖ CHAFFEE, MISSOURI

In high school, I received this recipe from a friend's mom, who is German. Forty years later, I still love the entree.

    6 bone-in pork loin chops (1 inch thick and 8 ounces *each*)
    3 tablespoons butter
    1 can (14 ounces) sauerkraut, rinsed and well drained
1-1/2 cups sweetened applesauce
1/3 cup chopped onion
    1 garlic clove, minced
    5 teaspoons brown sugar
    1 teaspoon caraway seeds
    1 teaspoon ground cinnamon

In a large skillet over medium-high heat, brown pork chops in butter on both sides. Transfer to a greased 13-in. x 9-in. baking dish. In a bowl, combine the sauerkraut, applesauce, onion, garlic, brown sugar, caraway seeds and cinnamon. Spoon over chops. Cover and bake at 375° for 45-50 minutes or until meat juices run clear. YIELD: 6 servings.

Drain and discard marinade from lamb. Place the flour in a shallow bowl; coat the lamb shanks with flour. In a stockpot, brown the shanks on all sides in 1/3 cup oil in batches. Remove and set aside.

In the same pan, saute onions in remaining oil. Add reserved marinade. Return shanks to the pan. Bring to a boil. Reduce heat; cover and simmer for 1-3/4 hours. Add carrots and return to a boil. Reduce heat; cover and simmer 15-20 minutes longer or until carrots are tender.

Remove shanks to a cutting board. Skim fat from cooking juices. Stir in cookie crumbs and bouillon. In a small bowl, combine cornstarch and water until smooth; gradually stir into juices. Bring to a boil; cook and stir for 1-2 minutes or until thickened. Return the meat to the gravy; heat through. YIELD: 6 servings (about 6 cups gravy).

SWEET & SPICY CHICKEN DRUMMIES

LYNETTE HANUS ✤ FAYETTEVILLE, GEORGIA

We were on a camping trip, and a young bachelor brought these chicken legs for dinner. They were fabulous! I was so impressed, I asked him for the recipe.

> 2 cups sugar
> 1/4 cup paprika
> 2 tablespoons salt
> 2 teaspoons pepper
> 1 teaspoon garlic powder
> 1 teaspoon chili powder
> 1/2 teaspoon cayenne pepper
> 20 chicken drumsticks (5 ounces *each*)

In a large resealable plastic bag, combine the sugar, paprika, salt, pepper, garlic powder, chili powder and cayenne. Add drumsticks, a few at a time; seal and shake to coat.

🎗 SAUERBRATEN LAMB SHANKS

SANDRA MCKENZIE ✤ BRAHAM, MINNESOTA

Fall is a great time to enjoy slow-cooked meats. Here's a recipe for some very tasty lamb shanks in a rich, tangy sauerbraten gravy.

> 7-1/2 cups water
> 2 cups white vinegar
> 1 large onion, sliced
> 1 medium lemon, sliced
> 1/2 cup sugar
> 3 bay leaves
> 1-1/2 teaspoons whole peppercorns
> 5 whole allspice
> LAMB SHANKS
> 6 lamb shanks (20 ounces *each*)
> 3 garlic cloves, sliced
> 6 tablespoons all-purpose flour
> 1/3 cup plus 2 tablespoons canola oil, *divided*
> 2 large onions, thinly sliced
> 3 medium carrots, sliced
> 9 gingersnap cookies, crushed
> 1 tablespoon beef bouillon granules
> 6 tablespoons cornstarch
> 1/3 cup cold water

In a Dutch oven, combine the first eight ingredients. Bring to a boil. Reduce heat; simmer, uncovered, for 2 minutes. Cool completely. Strain half of the marinade; cover and refrigerate.

Cut slits into each lamb shank; insert garlic slices. Place in a large shallow nonmetallic bowl; add the remaining marinade. Cover and refrigerate overnight.

Place chicken in two greased 15-in. x 10-in. x 1-in. baking pans. Cover and refrigerate for 8 hours or overnight. (A small amount of meat juices will form in the pan.)

Bake, uncovered, at 325° for 50-60 minutes or until no longer pink, the chicken juices run clear and a meat thermometer reads 180°. YIELD: 20 drumsticks.

MOROCCAN BEEF KABOBS

JENNIFER SHAW ❖ DORCHESTER, MASSACHUSETTS

My grandmother's homemade marinade adds zest and tenderness to these beefy kabobs. Her blend of herbs and spices punches up the flavor without adding lots of calories.

1 cup chopped fresh parsley
1 cup chopped fresh cilantro
1/4 cup grated onion
3 tablespoons lemon juice
2 tablespoons olive oil
1 tablespoon ground cumin
1 tablespoon ground coriander
1 tablespoon paprika
1 tablespoon cider vinegar
1 tablespoon ketchup
2 garlic cloves, minced
1 teaspoon minced fresh gingerroot
1 teaspoon Thai red chili paste
Dash salt and pepper
2 pounds beef top sirloin steak, cut into 1-inch pieces

In a large resealable plastic bag, combine the parsley, cilantro, onion, lemon juice, oil, cumin, coriander, paprika, vinegar, ketchup, garlic, ginger, chili paste, salt and pepper; add beef. Seal bag and turn to coat; refrigerate for 8 hours or overnight.

Drain and discard the marinade. Thread the beef cubes onto eight metal or soaked wooden skewers. Moisten a paper towel with cooking oil and using long-handled tongs, lightly coat the grill rack.

Grill beef, covered, over medium-hot heat or broil 4 in. from the heat for 8-12 minutes or until meat reaches desired doneness, turning occasionally. YIELD: 8 servings.

PORTOBELLO BURGERS WITH PEAR-WALNUT MAYONNAISE

LINDSAY SPRUNK ❖ NOBLESVILLE, INDIANA

Looking for a gourmet-style veggie burger? Go with portobellos, the filet mignon of mushrooms. A dollop of nutty pear mayonnaise adds a subtle sweetness.

1/4 cup olive oil
1/4 cup balsamic vinegar
  3 garlic cloves, minced
  1 tablespoon minced fresh thyme *or* 1 teaspoon dried thyme
  4 large portobello mushrooms
  1 medium pear, peeled and chopped
  1 tablespoon olive oil
  1 tablespoon lemon juice
  2 tablespoons mayonnaise
4-1/2 teaspoons chopped walnuts
  4 slices onion
  6 ounces Gorgonzola cheese, thinly sliced
  4 whole wheat hamburger buns, split
  2 cups fresh arugula

In a large resealable plastic bag, combine the oil, vinegar, garlic and thyme. Add mushrooms; seal bag and turn to coat. Refrigerate for up to 2 hours.

In a small skillet over medium heat, cook pear in oil and lemon juice until tender. Transfer to a small food processor; cover and process until blended. Stir in mayonnaise and walnuts. Refrigerate until serving.

Drain mushrooms and discard marinade. Grill mushrooms, covered, over medium heat or broil 4 in. from the heat for 3-4 minutes on each side or until tender. Top with onion and cheese. Grill 2-3 minutes longer or until cheese is melted. Serve on buns with mayonnaise mixture and arugula. YIELD: 4 servings.

TANGY MEATBALLS

JOAN ANTONEN ❖ ARLINGTON, SOUTH DAKOTA

These hearty meatballs, boasting a sweet and savory sauce, can be served as an entree or in a hoagie sandwich. Either way, be prepared for compliments.

1/2 cup milk
  2 slices white bread, torn into small pieces
  2 tablespoons onion soup mix
  2 pounds lean ground beef
  6 tablespoons all-purpose flour
1/4 cup canola oil
SAUCE
  1 cup water
  1 cup ketchup
1/3 cup molasses
  3 tablespoons white vinegar
  3 tablespoons prepared mustard
1/2 teaspoon dried oregano
1/4 teaspoon garlic powder
  6 drops hot pepper sauce

In a large bowl, combine the milk, bread and soup mix. Crumble the beef over milk mixture and mix well. Shape into 1-in. balls and roll in flour. In a large skillet, brown meatballs in oil, in batches and drain.

In a small bowl, combine the sauce ingredients. Add to skillet with meatballs. Bring to a boil. Reduce heat; cover and simmer for 25-30 minutes or until meatballs are no longer pink. YIELD: 8 servings.

CHICKEN CONTINENTAL

NAOMI JUDD ❖ NASHVILLE, TENNESSEE

This is the perfect chicken dish to serve to company because it adds a special touch to the evening. It has such a wonderful flavor and will impress all of your guests.

1-1/2 cups uncooked saffron rice
  6 boneless skinless chicken breast halves (4 ounces *each*)
  2 tablespoons butter
  1 can (10-3/4 ounces) reduced-fat reduced-sodium condensed cream of chicken soup, undiluted
  3 tablespoons dried celery flakes
  2 teaspoons dried thyme

Prepare rice according to package directions, omitting the butter. Meanwhile, in a large skillet, brown chicken in butter on both sides in batches. Remove and keep warm.

Whisk the soup, celery flakes and thyme into the drippings until smooth. Add rice; mix well. Remove from the heat.

Transfer to a greased 13-in. x 9-in. baking pan; top with chicken. Cover and bake at 350° for 30 minutes. Uncover; bake 10-15 minutes longer or until a meat thermometer reads 170°. YIELD: 6 servings.

PORK TENDERLOIN WITH SPICED PLUM SAUCE

RUTH LEE ❖ TROY, ONTARIO

This is one of my most requested dishes. I have prepared it for at least twenty years. It's a great dish for potlucks—I always come home with an empty dish.

    2 pounds medium plums, halved and pitted
2/3 cup cider vinegar
    1 cup packed brown sugar
    1 teaspoon ground cinnamon
1/2 teaspoon salt
1/4 teaspoon cayenne pepper
1/8 teaspoon *each* ground cloves, cardamom and allspice
    2 pork tenderloins (1 pound *each*)
1/2 teaspoon pepper

In a large saucepan, bring plums and vinegar to a boil. Reduce heat; cover and simmer 10-15 minutes or until tender. Cool slightly; transfer to a food processor. Cover and process for 1-2 minutes or until blended; strain.

Return plum mixture to the pan; stir in the brown sugar and seasonings. Bring to a boil. Reduce heat; simmer, uncovered, for 8-10 minutes or until thickened, stirring occasionally.

Place pork on a rack in a roasting pan; sprinkle with pepper. Set aside 1/2 cup plum sauce for serving. Spoon half of the remaining sauce over pork.

Bake at 350° for 40-50 minutes or until a meat thermometer reads 160°, basting occasionally with remaining sauce. Serve with reserved sauce. YIELD: 8 servings.

BOHEMIAN POT ROAST

VERA MELVIN ❖ ST. ANN, MISSOURI

This dish got its name because my husband is of Bohemian descent and because he loves this pot roast! I appreciate that it's so easy to prepare. You can get this one-pot supper cooking, then practically forget about it until dinnertime.

1/4 cup all-purpose flour
1/4 teaspoon pepper
    1 boneless beef chuck pot roast (2 to 3 pounds)
    2 tablespoons canola oil
    1 cup water
    1 can (14-1/2 ounces) diced tomatoes
    1 teaspoon caraway seeds
    1 envelope onion soup mix
    2 bay leaves

GRAVY
1/4 cup cold water
    3 tablespoons all-purpose flour

In a large resealable plastic bag, combine flour and pepper. Add beef; turn to coat. In a Dutch oven, brown roast over medium heat in oil on all sides. Drain.

Stir in the water, tomatoes, caraway seeds, onion soup mix and bay leaves. Bring to boil. Reduce heat; cover tightly and simmer 2-3 hours or until roast is tender.

Remove roast to a serving platter; keep warm. Discard bay leaves. For gravy, combine water and flour until smooth. Add to the cooking liquid; bring to a boil. Cook and stir for 1-2 minutes or until thickened. Slice the roast and serve with gravy. YIELD: 6-8 servings.

 ROASTED CITRUS & HERB TURKEY

NANCY NIEMERG ❖ DIETERICH, ILLINOIS

Thanksgiving has never been the same since I tried this recipe. I have made it for the past 3 years, and it never fails to impress both in presentation and taste. This is a true showstopper whenever you serve it!

1 turkey (14 to 16 pounds)
1/4 cup butter, softened
2 tablespoons Italian seasoning
2 teaspoons salt
2 teaspoons pepper
1 large onion, quartered
1 medium lemon, quartered
1 medium orange, quartered

3 fresh rosemary sprigs
3 sprigs fresh sage
3 cups chicken broth, *divided*
1/4 cup all-purpose flour
Additional citrus fruits and herb sprigs, optional

Pat turkey dry. Combine butter and Italian seasoning. With fingers, carefully loosen skin from the turkey breast; rub half of the butter under skin. Rub remaining mixture over the skin. Rub cavity with salt and pepper and fill with onion, lemon, orange, rosemary and sage. Skewer turkey openings; tie drumsticks together. Place breast side up on a rack in a roasting pan. Pour 2 cups broth into pan.

Bake at 325° for 2-3/4 to 3-1/4 hours or until a meat thermometer reads 180°, basting occasionally with pan drippings. Cover loosely with foil if turkey browns too quickly. Cover and let stand for 20 minutes before carving.

Pour drippings into a small saucepan; skim fat. Combine flour and remaining broth until smooth; whisk into the pan. Bring to a boil; cook and stir for 2 minutes or until thickened.

Discard onion, lemon, orange and herbs from the turkey; transfer turkey to a serving platter. Garnish the platter with additional citrus fruits and herb sprigs if desired. YIELD: 14-16 servings (2 cups gravy).

ITALIAN TOMATO PIE

ARLENE BAUERNFEIND ❖ APPLETON, WISCONSIN

Perfect for a ladies' luncheon or even Sunday brunch, my tomato-topped pie is like quiche but without the eggs. Your guests are sure to enjoy the delicious combination of olives, onions, cheese and herbs.

2 large sweet onions, thinly sliced
2 tablespoons olive oil
1 teaspoon salt
2 cups sliced fresh mushrooms
1 unbaked pastry shell (9 inches)
1-1/2 teaspoons *each* minced fresh basil, oregano and rosemary
2 cups (8 ounces) shredded part-skim mozzarella cheese
1 can (2-1/4 ounces) sliced ripe olives, drained
4 large plum tomatoes, cut into 1/4-inch slices
Dash pepper

In a large skillet, saute onions in oil until lightly browned; sprinkle with salt and set aside.

In the same skillet, saute mushrooms until tender. Using a slotted spoon, transfer onions into pastry shell; sprinkle with herbs and cheese.

Top with mushrooms; sprinkle with olives. Arrange tomato slices over top; sprinkle with pepper.

Bake at 375° for 50-60 minutes or until the crust is golden brown. Let the pie stand for 15 minutes before cutting. YIELD: 8 servings.

BARBECUED BEEF SANDWICHES

TATINA SMITH ❖ SAN ANGELO, TEXAS

Chuck roast makes delectable shredded beef sandwiches after simmering in a rich homemade sauce all day. The meat is tender and juicy and takes minutes to prepare for a weeknight dinner or potluck.

1 boneless beef chuck roast (3 pounds)
1-1/2 cups ketchup
1/4 cup packed brown sugar
1/4 cup barbecue sauce
2 tablespoons Worcestershire sauce
2 tablespoons Dijon mustard
1 teaspoon Liquid Smoke, optional
1/2 teaspoon salt
1/4 teaspoon garlic powder
1/4 teaspoon pepper
12 sandwich buns, split
Sliced onions, dill pickles and pickled jalapenos, optional

Cut roast in half and place in a 3- or 4-qt. slow cooker. In a small bowl, combine the ketchup, brown sugar, barbecue sauce, Worcestershire sauce, mustard, Liquid Smoke if desired and seasonings. Pour over beef.

Cover and cook on low for 8-10 hours or until meat is tender. Remove meat; cool slightly. Skim fat from cooking liquid.

Shred beef with two forks; return to the slow cooker. Cover and cook for 15 minutes or until heated through. Using a slotted spoon, place 1/2 cup on each bun. Serve with onions, pickles and jalapenos if desired. YIELD: 12 servings.

CORDON BLEU LASAGNA

KARLENE BURTON ❖ JACKSON, TENNESSEE

Five cheeses and a jar of prepared Alfredo sauce enhance this terrific lasagna recipe. It's effortless to prepare and kid-friendly, too.

  2 eggs, lightly beaten
  1 carton (15 ounces) ricotta cheese
  1 cup (8 ounces) 4% cottage cheese
1/2 cup grated Parmesan cheese
1/4 cup plus 2 tablespoons minced fresh parsley, *divided*
  1 jar (15 ounces) roasted garlic Alfredo sauce
  2 cups cubed cooked chicken
  2 cups cubed cooked ham
1/4 teaspoon garlic powder
  6 lasagna noodles, cooked and drained
  2 cups (8 ounces) shredded part-skim mozzarella cheese
  1 cup (4 ounces) shredded Swiss cheese

In a large bowl, combine the eggs, ricotta, cottage cheese, Parmesan and 1/4 cup parsley; set aside. In another bowl, combine the Alfredo sauce, chicken, ham and garlic powder.

Spread 1/2 cup of the chicken mixture in the bottom of a greased 13-in. x 9-in. baking dish. Layer with half of the cooked noodles and ricotta mixture. Top with half of the remaining chicken mixture and half of the mozzarella and Swiss cheeses. Repeat the layers.

Cover and bake at 350° for 40 minutes. Uncover; bake 10 minutes longer or a meat thermometer reads 160°. Let stand for 15 minutes before serving. Sprinkle with remaining parsley. YIELD: 12 servings.

HERBED TURKEY TETRAZZINI

BRIGITTE GARRINGER ❖ COPPER CANYON, TEXAS

There are many versions of this old-fashioned casserole. Mine offers a little more zip due to the thyme and lemon peel. It's a nice way to use up those turkey leftovers.

  6 cups uncooked egg noodles
1/3 cup sliced green onions
  2 tablespoons olive oil
  1 pound sliced fresh mushrooms
  3 tablespoons minced fresh parsley
  1 tablespoon minced fresh thyme *or* 1 teaspoon dried thyme
  2 bay leaves
  1 garlic clove, minced
  2 teaspoons grated lemon peel
1/4 cup butter
1/4 cup all-purpose flour
  2 cups chicken broth
  1 egg yolk, lightly beaten
  1 cup milk
  4 cups cubed cooked turkey
Salt and pepper to taste
1/3 cup dry bread crumbs
1/3 cup grated Parmesan cheese
1/2 cup sliced almonds, toasted

Cook noodles according to package directions. Meanwhile, in a Dutch oven, saute onions in oil for 3 minutes. Add mushrooms, parsley, thyme and bay leaves. Cook until mushrooms are lightly browned. Add garlic; cook 1 minute longer. Discard bay leaves.

Transfer mushroom mixture to a small bowl; stir in lemon peel and set aside. Drain noodles; set aside.

In the Dutch oven, melt butter over medium heat. Stir in flour until smooth. Whisk in broth. Bring to a boil; cook and stir for 2 minutes or until thickened. Combine egg yolk and milk; stir into white sauce. Cook and stir 2 minutes longer.

Stir in mushroom mixture and turkey; heat through. Fold in noodles. Season with salt and pepper.

Spoon into a greased 13-in. x 9-in. baking dish. Toss bread crumbs and cheese; sprinkle over the top. Bake, uncovered, at 350° for 25-30 minutes or until lightly browned. Sprinkle with almonds. YIELD: 12 servings.

APPLESAUCE-SAUERKRAUT SPARERIBS

LADONNA LIEBERTH ❖ PORT WASHINGTON, OHIO

All seasons are beautiful here, but I especially like fall so I can serve more hearty fare like these ribs. Served with mashed potatoes and pumpkin pie, this dish truly soothes the soul.

    3 to 3-1/2 pounds country-style pork ribs
    1 teaspoon canola oil
    1 can (32 ounces) sauerkraut
    2 cups applesauce
    2 cups thinly sliced onion
 3/4 cup chicken broth
 3/4 cup apple juice

In a large skillet over medium-high heat, brown ribs in oil. Arrange ribs in an ungreased 13-in. x 9-in. baking dish. Rinse and squeeze sauerkraut; layer the sauerkraut, applesauce and onion over ribs. Combine broth and apple juice; pour over all.

Cover and bake at 350° for 1-3/4 hours; uncover and bake 15 minutes longer or until onion begins to brown and meat is tender. YIELD: 6 servings.

COUNTRY-STYLE PORK RIBS

HEIDI MELLON ❖ WAUKESHA, WISCONSIN

Neither my husband nor myself are big pork eaters, but we absolutely love these ribs. My mom has been making them for as long as I can remember.

 3/4 cup soy sauce
 1/2 cup sugar
 1/2 cup water
    1 garlic clove, minced
    4 pounds country-style pork ribs

Combine the first four ingredients; stir to dissolve sugar. Pour into a 2-gal. resealable plastic bag; add ribs and turn to coat. Seal bag; refrigerate overnight, turning occasionally. Drain and discard marinade.

Grill, covered, over medium heat, turning occasionally, for 30-40 minutes or until juices run clear. YIELD: 6-8 servings.

CRUSTED BAKED CHICKEN

BILL EGAN ❖ BURLINGTON, MASSACHUSETTS

Coating your chicken with flour before dipping it in buttermilk and rolling it in crumbs helps make it crisp. Moist and tender, this mouthwatering chicken is covered with a seasoned bread crumb mixture and then baked until golden brown.

    1 cup dry bread crumbs
    1 tablespoon seafood seasoning
 1/2 teaspoon garlic salt
 1/2 teaspoon Creole seasoning
 1/2 teaspoon dried basil
 1/2 teaspoon dried oregano
 1/2 teaspoon dried thyme
 1/8 teaspoon pepper
 3/4 cup buttermilk
 1/2 cup all-purpose flour
    1 broiler/fryer chicken (4 to 5 pounds), cut up
    1 tablespoon butter, melted

In a shallow bowl, combine the first eight ingredients. Place buttermilk and flour in separate shallow bowls. Coat chicken with flour, then dip in buttermilk and coat with bread crumb mixture. Place on a greased 15-in. x 10-in. x 1-in. baking pan. Let stand for 10 minutes.

Bake, uncovered, at 350° for 45 minutes. Drizzle with butter. Bake 10-15 minutes longer or until the juices run clear. YIELD: 6 servings.

EDITOR'S NOTE: The following spices may be substituted for 1 teaspoon Creole seasoning: 1/4 teaspoon each salt, garlic powder and paprika; and a pinch each of dried thyme, ground cumin and cayenne pepper.

PEPPER & JACK SMOTHERED CHEESEBURGERS

DEBORAH BIGGS ✤ OMAHA, NEBRASKA

To add a little bite to your burgers, just add peppers. The cheesy pepper-onion topping and chipotle glaze lend a Southwestern flair to the chicken patties.

1/2 cup honey mustard salad dressing
1 tablespoon lime juice
1 tablespoon minced chipotle pepper in adobo sauce

BURGERS
1 egg white, beaten
1/4 cup crushed tortilla chips
3 tablespoons minced seeded jalapeno peppers
1/2 teaspoon salt
1 pound ground chicken

TOPPINGS
2 poblano peppers, julienned
2 Anaheim peppers, julienned
1 medium sweet red pepper, julienned
1 small onion, halved and sliced
2 tablespoons canola oil
3 tablespoons minced fresh cilantro
1/4 teaspoon salt
4 slices pepper Jack cheese
4 hamburger buns, split

For glaze, combine the salad dressing, lime juice and chipotle pepper in a blender; cover and process until blended. Set aside.

In a large bowl, combine the egg white, tortilla chips, jalapenos and salt. Crumble chicken over mixture and mix well. Shape into four patties.

Place in a greased 15-in. x 10-in. x 1-in. baking pan. Bake at 375° for 9-11 minutes on each side or until a meat thermometer reads 165° and juices run clear, basting occasionally with glaze.

Meanwhile, in a large skillet, saute peppers and onion in oil until crisp-tender. Remove from heat; stir in cilantro and salt.

Top burgers with pepper mixture and cheese. Broil 4 in. from the heat for 2-3 minutes or until cheese is melted. Serve on buns. YIELD: 4 servings.

EDITOR'S NOTE: When cutting hot peppers, disposable gloves are recommended. Avoid touching your face.

ROSEMARY-GARLIC ROAST BEEF

BRENDA HLIVYAK ✤ LA CENTER, WASHINGTON

This tender and juicy roast looks beautiful when I serve it to guests. It also makes the house smell wonderful as it cooks. I usually serve it with warm French bread and a salad topped with buttermilk dressing.

4 garlic cloves, minced
1 tablespoon dried rosemary, crushed
1 teaspoon salt
1/2 teaspoon pepper
1 beef tri-tip roast (2 to 3 pounds)
4-1/2 teaspoons olive oil
12 small red potatoes, quartered
2 medium sweet yellow peppers, cut into 1-inch pieces
1 large sweet onion, cut into 1-inch slices

Combine the garlic, rosemary, salt and pepper; set aside 4 teaspoons. Rub the remaining mixture over roast; place in a greased shallow roasting pan.

In a small bowl, whisk reserved herb mixture with oil. In a large resealable plastic bag, combine the potatoes, yellow peppers and onion; add oil mixture. Seal bag and toss to coat. Arrange vegetables around roast.

Bake, uncovered, at 425° for 30-60 minutes or until meat reaches desired doneness (for medium-rare, a meat thermometer should read 145°; medium, 160°; well-done, 170°).

Transfer roast and peppers to a warm serving platter. Let stand for 10-15 minutes before slicing. Meanwhile, return potatoes and onion to the oven; bake 10 minutes longer or until potatoes are tender. YIELD: 6 servings.

PEPPERED FILLETS WITH TOMATO-MUSHROOM SALSA

ANN HILLMEYER ❖ SANDIA PARK, NEW MEXICO

These fillets are an all-time favorite at our house, and the secret's in the zesty salsa. It's full of fresh veggies and seasonings that bring the true taste of summer days even in the middle of winter.

6 plum tomatoes, seeded and chopped
1 cup chopped fresh mushrooms
1/4 cup minced fresh Italian parsley
2 tablespoons finely chopped shallot
2 teaspoons minced garlic, *divided*
5 teaspoons olive oil, *divided*
1 tablespoon lime juice
1/2 teaspoon salt
1/4 teaspoon pepper
6 beef tenderloin steaks (4 ounces *each*)
2 teaspoons lemon-pepper seasoning
1/3 cup balsamic vinegar
1/4 cup beef broth
4 teaspoons butter
6 lime slices

For salsa, in a small bowl, combine the tomatoes, mushrooms, parsley, shallot, 1 teaspoon garlic, 3 teaspoons oil, lime juice, salt and pepper; set aside.

Sprinkle steaks with lemon-pepper. In a large skillet, cook steaks in remaining oil for 4-5 minutes on each side or until meat reaches desired doneness (for medium-rare, a meat thermometer should read 145°; medium, 160°; well-done, 170°). Remove and keep warm.

Combine the vinegar, broth and remaining garlic; stir into skillet. Bring to a boil; cook until liquid is reduced by half, about 2-3 minutes. Stir in butter.

Spoon sauce over steaks. Serve with salsa. Garnish with lime slices. YIELD: 6 servings.

SEEDING TOMATOES

To seed a tomato, cut in half horizontally and remove the stem. Hold tomato half over a bowl or sink and scrape out seeds with a small spoon or squeeze the tomato to force out the seeds. Then slice or dice as directed in the recipe.

Sensational Seafood

When you feel like taking a break from traditional meat and potatoes meals,
turn to these delicious recipes that feature fresh fish and seafood.

BAKED HERB CATFISH

KATHY GIANNONE ✦ WEST HENRIETTA, NEW YORK

Spice up dinner with these well-seasoned fillets. A healthy twist on batter-fried catfish, the baked entree cuts the calories and saves the flavor.

    2 tablespoons minced fresh parsley
    1 teaspoon salt
    3/4 teaspoon paprika
    1/2 teaspoon dried thyme
    1/2 teaspoon dried oregano
    1/2 teaspoon dried basil
    1/2 teaspoon pepper
    4 catfish fillets (6 ounces *each*)
    2 tablespoons lemon juice
    1 tablespoon reduced-fat butter, melted
    1 garlic clove, minced

Combine the first seven ingredients; sprinkle over fillets on both sides. Place in a greased 13-in. x 9-in. baking dish. Combine the lemon juice, butter and garlic; drizzle over fillets.

Bake, uncovered, at 350° for 15-20 minutes or until fish flakes easily with a fork. YIELD: 4 servings.

EDITOR'S NOTE: This recipe was tested with Land O'Lakes light stick butter.

CHILLED SALMON WITH CUCUMBER-DILL SAUCE

SHERI SIDWELL ✦ ALTON, ILLINOIS

A friend from Boston shared this traditional New England dish. It's a refreshing hot-weather meal and a nice change of pace from heavy cookout food.

1-1/2 cups water
    1 cup white wine *or* chicken broth
    4 green onions, sliced
    10 whole peppercorns
    4 salmon fillets (5 ounces *each*)
SAUCE
    1/2 cup reduced-fat sour cream
    1/4 cup chopped peeled cucumber
4-1/2 teaspoons snipped fresh dill *or* 1-1/2 teaspoons dill weed
    2 teaspoons prepared horseradish
1-1/2 teaspoons lemon juice
    1/8 teaspoon salt
    1/8 teaspoon pepper

In a large skillet, combine the water, wine, onions and peppercorns. Bring to a boil. Reduce heat; carefully add the salmon. Cover and cook for 5-7 minutes or until the fish flakes easily with a fork.

With a spatula, carefully remove salmon; discard cooking liquid. Cool salmon for 10 minutes; refrigerate until chilled. In a small bowl, combine the sauce ingredients. Serve with salmon. YIELD: 4 servings.

Stir the shrimp, crab legs and garlic mixture into the stockpot; cook for 4-6 minutes or until shrimp and crab turn pink. Drain; transfer seafood mixture to a large serving bowl. Serve with condiments of your choice. YIELD: 4 servings.

SOLE THERMIDOR

NELLA PARKER ❖ HERSEY, MICHIGAN

My twin sister passed down this recipe to me several years ago. It's impressive, delicious and nutritious.

    8 sole fillets (4 ounces *each*)
    2 tablespoons butter, melted
1-1/2 teaspoons seasoned salt
    1/8 teaspoon pepper
1-1/4 cups milk, *divided*
    3 tablespoons butter
    3 tablespoons all-purpose flour
    1 cup (4 ounces) shredded cheddar cheese
    3 tablespoons sherry *or* chicken broth
    1 teaspoon dried tarragon
    1/8 teaspoon paprika

Brush fillets with melted butter; sprinkle with seasoned salt and pepper. Starting with a short side, roll up. Place seam side down in a greased 9-in. square baking pan. Pour 1/2 cup milk over fillets. Bake, uncovered, at 350° for 25-30 minutes or until fish flakes easily with a fork.

Meanwhile, in a small saucepan, melt butter. Stir in flour until smooth; gradually add remaining milk. Bring to a boil; cook and stir for 1 minute or until thickened. Reduce heat; stir in the cheese, sherry and tarragon.

Drain pan juices, reserving 1/4 cup; stir into cheese mixture. Pour over fish; sprinkle with paprika. Broil 4 in. from the heat for 3-4 minutes or until lightly browned. YIELD: 8 servings.

LOW COUNTRY BOIL

MAGESWARI ELAGUPILLAI ❖ VICTORVILLE, CALIFORNIA

Ideal for camping and relaxing trips to the beach, this crowd-pleasing recipe includes a combination of shrimp, crab, sausage, corn and potatoes.

    2 quarts water
    1 bottle (12 ounces) beer
    2 tablespoons seafood seasoning
1-1/2 teaspoons salt
    4 medium red potatoes, cut into wedges
    1 medium sweet onion, cut into wedges
    4 medium ears sweet corn, cut in half
    1/3 pound smoked chorizo *or* kielbasa, cut into 1-inch slices
    3 tablespoons olive oil
    6 large garlic cloves, minced
    1 tablespoon ground cumin
    1 tablespoon minced fresh cilantro
    1/2 teaspoon paprika
    1/2 teaspoon pepper
    1 pound uncooked large shrimp, deveined
    1 pound uncooked snow crab legs
Optional condiments: seafood cocktail sauce, lemon wedges and melted butter

In a stockpot, combine the water, beer, seafood seasoning and salt; add the potatoes and onion. Bring to a boil. Reduce the heat; simmer, uncovered, for 10 minutes. Add the corn and chorizo; simmer 10-12 minutes longer or until the potatoes and corn are tender.

Meanwhile, in a small skillet, heat oil. Add the garlic, cumin, cilantro, paprika and pepper. Cook and stir over medium heat for 2 minutes.

FILET MIGNON WITH RED WINE SAUCE

TARAH PESSEL ❖ CLARKSTON, MICHIGAN

If you need an elegant entree, but have no time to fuss, let them eat steak! The savory wine sauce is scrumptious!

　1 medium onion, thinly sliced
　3 tablespoons butter, *divided*
　2 garlic cloves, minced
3/4 teaspoon salt, *divided*
1/2 teaspoon dried oregano
　2 tablespoons tomato paste
1-1/4 cups dry red wine *or* beef broth
1/2 teaspoon pepper, *divided*
　6 beef tenderloin steaks (4 to 6 ounces *each*)
　3 tablespoons olive oil

In a large saucepan, saute onion in 1 tablespoon butter until tender. Add garlic, 1/4 teaspoon salt and oregano; cook and stir 1 minute. Add tomato paste; cook and stir 2 minutes longer.

Gradually whisk in wine. Bring to a boil. Reduce heat; simmer until reduced by half. Strain sauce and return to pan. Gradually stir in remaining butter until melted. Add 1/4 teaspoon pepper. Remove from the heat; keep warm.

Sprinkle steaks with remaining salt and pepper. Drizzle with oil. Grill, covered, over medium heat or broil 4 in. from the heat for 6-8 minutes on each side or until meat reaches desired doneness (for medium-rare, a meat thermometer should read 145°; medium, 160°; well-done, 170°). Cover and let stand for 3-5 minutes. Serve with wine sauce. YIELD: 6 servings.

SAUSAGE RANCH BREAKFAST CASSEROLE

BONNIE ESSLINGER ❖ CHAPEL HILL, TENNESSEE

This dish is ideal for a crowd-size brunch. Prepare and refrigerate the casserole the night before, and in the morning, bake to perfection.

　2 tubes (8 ounces *each*) refrigerated crescent rolls
　1 pound bulk pork sausage
　1 package (8 ounces) cream cheese, softened
　1 envelope ranch salad dressing mix
　2 cups (8 ounces) shredded sharp cheddar cheese

Unroll one tube of crescent dough into one long rectangle; seal the seams and perforations. Press onto the bottom of a greased 13-in. x 9-in. baking dish. Bake at 375° for 8-10 minutes or until golden brown.

Meanwhile, in a small skillet, brown the sausage; drain and set aside.

Combine the cream cheese and ranch salad dressing mix; spread over the crust. Top with the cooked sausage and shredded cheddar cheese.

On a lightly floured surface, press or roll second tube of crescent dough into a 13-in. x 9-in. rectangle, sealing seams and perforations. Place over cheese.

Bake for 18-22 minutes or until golden brown. Let stand for 5 minutes before cutting. YIELD: 8 servings.

CHERRY-GLAZED PORK TENDERLOIN

SANDRA KENNEDY ❖ ATLANTA, TEXAS

My tangy, glazed tenderloin is so simple to prepare. I serve it with roasted sweet potatoes and apples, a salad and French bread for a festive Sunday dinner.

  1 cup cherry juice blend
  2 tablespoons brown sugar
  1 tablespoon soy sauce
  1 teaspoon cornstarch
1/2 teaspoon ground ginger
  2 pork tenderloins (3/4 pound *each*)
1/2 teaspoon salt
1/2 teaspoon pepper

In a small saucepan, combine the cherry juice, brown sugar, soy sauce, cornstarch and ginger. Bring to a boil. Reduce heat; simmer, uncovered, for 8-10 minutes or until slightly thickened, stirring occasionally.

Meanwhile, place tenderloins on a rack in a foil-lined roasting pan; sprinkle with salt and pepper. Set aside 1/4 cup glaze for serving. Spoon half of the remaining glaze over pork.

Bake, uncovered, at 425° for 35-40 minutes or until a meat thermometer reads 160°, basting occasionally with remaining glaze. Let stand for 5 minutes before slicing. Serve with reserved glaze. YIELD: 6 servings.

GRILLED STUFFED PEPPERS

CAROL GAUS ❖ ELK GROVE VILLAGE, ILLINOIS

After hearing this recipe described at our local Italian restaurant, I decided to try to make these peppers at home. Everyone enjoyed the pretty green shells brimming with a hearty filling.

   3 large green peppers
   1 large tomato, peeled, seeded and chopped
   1 cup (4 ounces) shredded part-skim mozzarella cheese
1/4 cup grated Parmesan cheese
   2 tablespoons minced fresh basil
   2 teaspoons dried oregano
1-1/2 pounds bulk Italian sausage
Additional shredded part-skim mozzarella cheese

Cut peppers in half lengthwise; remove stems and seeds. Set aside. In a large bowl, combine the tomato, cheeses, basil and oregano. Crumble sausage over mixture and mix well. Spoon into pepper halves.

Prepare grill for indirect heat, using a drip pan. Place the peppers over drip pan. Grill, covered, over indirect medium heat for 30-35 minutes or until sausage is no longer pink and peppers are tender. Sprinkle with additional cheese. YIELD: 6 servings.

PREPARING A GRILL FOR INDIRECT HEAT

Bank half of the coals on one side of the grill and the other half on the other side. Place a foil drip pan in the center of the grill, replace the cooking grate and place whatever you are grilling over the drip pan.

HEARTY EGGPLANT PARMESAN

KENDELL CHRISTENSEN ✤ PALATINE, ILLINOIS

Oven-baking instead of frying or sauteing gives this classic eggplant dish a healthy twist. Add a green salad and Italian bread. Meat-free never tasted better!

1/2 cup all-purpose flour
2 eggs, lightly beaten
2 cups dry bread crumbs
1 tablespoon minced fresh basil *or* 1 teaspoon dried basil
2 teaspoons minced fresh oregano *or* 1/2 teaspoon dried oregano
1/2 teaspoon salt
1/2 teaspoon white pepper
1 large eggplant, peeled and cut into 1/2-inch slices
4 tablespoons olive oil
1 jar (25 ounces) marinara sauce
1/2 cup grated Parmesan cheese

Place the flour and eggs in separate shallow bowls. In another bowl, combine the bread crumbs, basil, oregano, salt and pepper. Dip the eggplant slices in flour and then in eggs; coat with the crumb mixture.

In a large skillet, cook eggplant in oil in batches until golden brown on both sides; drain. Arrange in a greased 13-in. x 9-in. baking dish. Top with marinara sauce and cheese.

Cover and bake at 350° for 15 minutes. Uncover; bake 5-10 minutes longer or until golden brown. YIELD: 8 servings.

BISTRO FRENCH ONION CHICKEN

JENNIFER FISHER ✤ AUSTIN, TEXAS

This recipe is sure to please all and will be requested often. The balsamic vinegar and brown sugar add delicious, tangy and sweet flavors at the same time.

1 large sweet onion, thinly sliced
3 teaspoons canola oil, *divided*
2 teaspoons brown sugar
2 teaspoons balsamic vinegar
4 boneless skinless chicken breast halves (4 ounces *each*)
1/2 cup reduced-sodium chicken broth
4 slices French bread baguette
1/4 cup shredded Swiss cheese

In a large nonstick skillet, cook and stir onion in 1 teaspoon oil over medium-low heat for 10 minutes. Stir in brown sugar and vinegar; cook 5-10 minutes longer or until tender and golden brown. Remove and keep warm.

In the same skillet, brown chicken in remaining oil on both sides. Add broth, stirring to loosen browned bits from pan. Transfer to an 11-in. x 7-in. baking dish coated with cooking spray; top with onion mixture. Place a baguette slice over each chicken breast; sprinkle with cheese.

Cover and bake at 350° for 15 minutes. Uncover, bake 3-5 minutes longer or until a meat thermometer reads 170°. YIELD: 4 servings.

SPINACH, MUSHROOM & THREE-CHEESE PIZZA

LILY JULOW ✤ GAINESVILLE, FLORIDA

The magic of mushrooms caps off this yummy pie. A knife-and-fork pizza, it's fully loaded with spinach, onion, garlic and a trio of cheeses.

1 loaf (1 pound) frozen pizza dough, thawed
3 tablespoons olive oil, *divided*
2 thin slices prosciutto *or* deli ham, julienned
1 pound sliced baby portobello mushrooms
1/2 small red onion, sliced
1 tablespoon minced fresh rosemary
2 garlic cloves, minced
1 package (10 ounces) frozen chopped spinach, thawed and squeezed dry
1 log (4 ounces) fresh goat cheese, crumbled
2 cups (8 ounces) shredded fontina cheese
1/2 cup grated Romano cheese

Roll dough into a 12-in. x 9-in. rectangle; transfer to a greased baking sheet and build up edges slightly. Brush with 1 tablespoon oil. In a large skillet, saute prosciutto in remaining oil until crispy. Add mushrooms and onion; saute until tender. Stir in rosemary and garlic; cook 1 minute longer.

Place spinach over dough; top with mushroom mixture and goat cheese. Sprinkle with fontina. Bake at 450° for 15-20 minutes or until edges are golden brown and cheese is bubbly. Sprinkle with Romano cheese. YIELD: 6 pieces.

APRICOT-GLAZED TURKEY BREAST

JANET SPRUTE ✧ LEWISTON, IDAHO

Turkey takes center stage in this tasty dish that is prepared with garlic, ginger and apricot preserves.

1 bone-in turkey breast (5 to 6 pounds)
2 garlic cloves, peeled and thinly sliced
1 tablespoon sliced fresh gingerroot
1/2 cup white wine *or* reduced-sodium chicken broth
1/3 cup reduced-sugar apricot preserves
1 tablespoon spicy brown mustard
2 teaspoons reduced-sodium soy sauce

With fingers, carefully loosen skin from turkey breast. With a sharp knife, cut ten 2-in.-long slits in meat under the skin; insert a garlic and ginger slice into each slit.

Place turkey in a large bowl; pour 1/4 cup wine under the skin. Secure skin to underside of breast with toothpicks. Pour remaining wine over turkey. Cover and refrigerate for 6 hours or overnight.

In a small bowl, combine the preserves, mustard and soy sauce; set aside. Drain and discard marinade; place turkey on a rack in a foil-lined roasting pan.

Bake at 325° for 2 to 2-1/2 hours or until a meat thermometer reads 170°, basting with apricot mixture every 30 minutes (cover loosely with foil if turkey browns too quickly). Cover and let stand for 15 minutes before carving. YIELD: 12 servings.

USING LEFTOVER TURKEY

To use up leftover turkey, make a simple soup. First saute onion and green pepper in oil, add chicken broth, cooked vegetables and chopped turkey, then heat through.

SIDE DISHES & CONDIMENTS

Hearty, wholesome dinner accompaniments, from colorful vegetable medleys to rustic potato casseroles, are here for the taking!

BUTTERY CARROTS AND BRUSSELS SPROUTS

STACY DUFFY ❖ CHICAGO, ILLINOIS

Every cook needs a traditional, standby recipe for brussels sprouts, and I think this is it. The lemon and gingerroot add excellent flavor, and the butter makes them rich.

        1 pound carrots, cut into 1/4-inch slices
    3/4 pound brussels sprouts, halved
    1/4 cup butter, cubed
        1 tablespoon minced fresh gingerroot
        1 tablespoon lemon juice
        2 teaspoons grated lemon peel
        1 teaspoon sugar
Salt and pepper to taste
Minced fresh parsley, optional

In a large saucepan over medium heat, cook carrots and brussels sprouts in boiling water for 8-10 minutes or until tender; drain.

In a small saucepan, melt butter. Add ginger; cook for 2 minutes. Add the lemon juice, peel, sugar, salt and pepper; pour over vegetables. Sprinkle with minced parsley if desired. YIELD: 8 servings.

HERBED PIZZA SAUCE

CATHY BLANKMAN ❖ WARROAD, MINNESOTA

This delicious recipe allows you to create pizza sauce at home instead of buying it in the store. Flavorful and simple, it's so easy to throw together you'll be making this recipe every time you want homemade pizza.

        1 can (8 ounces) tomato sauce
        1 can (6 ounces) tomato paste
        1 teaspoon sugar
        1 teaspoon dried basil
        1 teaspoon dried oregano
    1/2 teaspoon garlic powder
    1/2 teaspoon dried marjoram
    1/2 teaspoon dried thyme

    1/4 teaspoon salt
    1/8 teaspoon pepper

In a small saucepan, combine all ingredients; cook and stir over medium heat for 2 minutes. YIELD: 1-1/2 cups.

RAINBOW VEGETABLE SKILLET

JENNIFER SCHMIDT ❖ DICKENS, TEXAS

Even my kids eat their veggies when I serve this nicely spiced skillet that is as pretty as it is scrumptious. Turn it into a main dish by stirring in cubes of cooked chicken.

        1 medium butternut squash (about 2 pounds)
    1/4 cup reduced-fat butter, melted
        2 tablespoons brown sugar
        1 tablespoon chili powder
        1 tablespoon minced fresh cilantro
        1 teaspoon salt
    1/2 teaspoon pepper
    1/4 teaspoon ground cinnamon
        1 medium green pepper, cut into 1-inch pieces
        1 medium sweet yellow pepper, cut into 1-inch pieces
        1 medium red onion, cut into wedges
        1 tablespoon olive oil
        2 cups grape tomatoes

Cut squash in half; discard seeds. Place cut side down in a microwave-safe dish; add 1/2 in. of water. Microwave, uncovered, on high for 10-12 minutes or until almost tender.

Meanwhile, in a small bowl, combine the butter, brown sugar, chili powder, cilantro, salt, pepper and cinnamon; set aside. When squash is cool enough to handle, peel and discard rind. Cut pulp into 1/2-in. pieces.

In a large skillet, saute peppers and onion in oil until tender. Add tomatoes and squash; heat through. Transfer to a large bowl; add butter mixture and toss to coat. YIELD: 9 servings.

EDITOR'S NOTE: This recipe was tested with Land O'Lakes light stick butter in a 1,100-watt microwave.

FAMILY-FAVORITE BAKED BEANS

LEA ANN ANDERSON ❖ TULSA, OKLAHOMA

Here's a quick, simple and familiar dish that is perfect for reunions and other large gatherings. The sweet-tasting and hearty dish includes three kinds of beans and plenty of ground beef and bacon.

    1/2 pound ground beef
    1/2 pound sliced bacon, diced
      1 small onion, chopped
    1/2 cup ketchup
    1/2 cup barbecue sauce
    1/3 cup packed brown sugar
      2 tablespoons molasses
      1 can (16 ounces) kidney beans, rinsed and drained
      1 can (15-3/4 ounces) pork and beans
      1 can (16 ounces) butter beans, rinsed and drained

In a large skillet, cook beef over medium heat until no longer pink; drain and set aside. In the same skillet, cook bacon over medium heat until crisp. Remove with a slotted spoon to paper towels to drain.

In a large bowl, combine the onion, ketchup, barbecue sauce, brown sugar and molasses. Stir in the beans, beef and bacon.

Transfer to a greased 3-qt. baking dish. Cover and bake at 350° for 1 hour or until the consistency of the beans reach desired thickness. YIELD: 8 servings.

CRISPY BAKED CAULIFLOWER

ELVERA DALLMAN ❖ FRANKLIN, NEBRASKA

This unique recipe for cauliflower is a delicious way to eat your vegetables.

      4 cups cauliflowerets
      6 tablespoons all-purpose flour
    1/4 teaspoon garlic powder
    1/4 teaspoon paprika
    1/4 teaspoon pepper
  2-1/2 cups cornflakes, crushed
      2 egg whites

❦ ASPARAGUS AND SUN-DRIED TOMATOES

PAT STEVENS ❖ GRANBURY, TEXAS

Crisp-tender asparagus is drizzled with lemon butter sauce and sprinkled with flavorful sun-dried tomatoes in this effortless, time-saving recipe.

      3 pounds fresh asparagus, trimmed
    1/3 cup butter, cubed
    1/3 cup chicken broth
      3 tablespoons olive oil
      4 teaspoons grated lemon peel
    1/4 teaspoon salt
    1/4 teaspoon pepper
    1/3 cup oil-packed sun-dried tomatoes, patted dry and chopped
    1/4 cup minced fresh basil

Place asparagus in a steamer basket; place in a large saucepan over 1 in. of water. Bring to a boil; cover and steam for 6-8 minutes or until crisp-tender.

Meanwhile, in a small saucepan, melt butter. Stir in the broth, oil, lemon peel and salt.

Transfer asparagus to a serving platter; drizzle with butter mixture. Sprinkle with pepper; top with tomatoes and basil. YIELD: 12 servings.

BUYING & STORING CAULIFLOWER

When purchasing fresh cauliflower, look for a head with compact florets that are free from yellow or brown spots and with leaves that are crisp and green. Tightly wrap and refrigerate for up to 5 days. Before using, wash and remove the leaves at the base and trim the stem.

Place cauliflower in a saucepan with a small amount of water. Cover and cook for 5-10 minutes or until crisp-tender; drain.

In a small resealable plastic bag, combine flour, garlic powder, paprika and pepper. Place cornflake crumbs in another resealable bag. Lightly beat egg whites in a shallow bowl. Toss the cauliflowerets one at a time in flour mixture, then roll in egg whites and coat with crumbs.

Place on a baking sheet coated with cooking spray. Bake at 425° for 15-20 minutes or until golden brown. Serve immediately. YIELD: 6 servings.

SPAGHETTI SQUASH WITH MOROCCAN SPICES

LILY JULOW ❖ GAINESVILLE, FLORIDA

Here's an easy recipe that's best prepared in the microwave versus a conventional oven. A colorful blend of spices livens up the delicate strands of squash. Be sure to adjust the amount of hot pepper sauce to your taste.

- 1 medium spaghetti squash (4 pounds)
- 2 garlic cloves, minced
- 2 tablespoons butter
- 1 teaspoon ground cumin
- 3/4 teaspoon salt
- 1/2 teaspoon ground cinnamon
- 1/8 teaspoon hot pepper sauce
- 2 tablespoons minced fresh cilantro

Cut squash in half lengthwise; discard seeds. Place squash cut side down on a microwave-safe plate. Microwave, uncovered, on high for 15-18 minutes or until tender.

In a small skillet, saute garlic in butter for 1 minute. Stir in the cumin, salt, cinnamon and pepper sauce. When squash is cool enough to handle, use a fork to separate strands. Toss with butter mixture and cilantro. YIELD: 6 servings.

EDITOR'S NOTE: This recipe was tested in a 1,100-watt microwave.

GRILLED CABBAGE

ELIZABETH WHEELER ❖ THORNVILLE, OHIO

I don't really like cabbage, but I fixed this recipe and couldn't believe how good it was. We threw some burgers on the grill, and our dinner was complete. It's a great way to use up a leftover head of cabbage.

- 1 medium head cabbage (about 1-1/2 pounds)
- 1/3 cup butter, softened
- 1/4 cup chopped onion
- 1/2 teaspoon garlic salt
- 1/4 teaspoon pepper

Cut cabbage into eight wedges; place on a double thickness of heavy-duty foil (about 24 in. x 12 in.). Spread cut sides with butter. Sprinkle with onion, garlic salt and pepper.

Fold foil around cabbage and seal tightly. Grill, covered, over medium heat for 20 minutes or until tender. Open foil carefully to allow steam to escape. YIELD: 8 servings.

Popular Potatoes

When it comes to side dishes, you can't go wrong when using the ever-popular potato. These four recipes make wonderful accompaniments to any meal.

MOIST POTATO PANCAKES

ARLEEN OSVATIC ✦ WAUKESHA, WISCONSIN

Just pass these potato pancakes around your table and compliments will follow. I serve the creamy, golden-brown pleasers with homemade apple sauce.

    2 tablespoons all-purpose flour
    1 egg
    1/4 cup milk
    1 teaspoon salt
    1/8 teaspoon pepper
    2 cups grated peeled potatoes
    1 tablespoon finely chopped onion
    2 to 4 tablespoons canola oil
Applesauce

In a large bowl, whisk the flour, egg, milk, salt and pepper. Pat potatoes dry; stir into egg mixture. Add onion.

Pour the batter by 1/4 cupfuls onto a hot griddle coated with cooking spray; turn when bubbles form on top. Cook until the second side is golden brown. Serve pancakes with applesauce. YIELD: 6 pancakes.

🏵 SWISS-ONION POTATO BAKE

ANNETTA BALLESTEROS ✦ KUTTAWA, KENTUCKY

When I was growing up, my mother told me I would starve my future brood because I didn't like to cook. Thankfully, I enjoy it now! This flavorful side dish goes nicely with any kind of meat loaf.

    1 cup finely chopped sweet onion
    2 tablespoons butter
    1 package (30 ounces) frozen shredded hash brown
      potatoes, thawed
    2 cups (8 ounces) shredded Swiss cheese
    1 teaspoon salt
  1/4 teaspoon pepper
    2 eggs
    1 cup milk
Minced fresh parsley, optional

In a small skillet, saute onion in butter until tender. In a large bowl, combine the hash brown potatoes, cheese, salt, pepper and onion mixture.

Transfer to a greased 13-in. x 9-in. baking dish. In a small bowl, whisk eggs and milk; pour over potato mixture.

Bake, uncovered, at 350° for 35-40 minutes or until a thermometer reads 160°. Let stand for 5 minutes before cutting. Sprinkle with parsley if desired. YIELD: 12 servings.

GOLDEN POTATO SURPRISE

KAREN SHEETS ❖ SHELTON, WASHINGTON

I've had this recipe forever and have tinkered with it over the years to perfect it. The Dijon mustard adds a nice touch. Now it's a family favorite, so I serve it often during special occasions and holidays.

    4 to 5 medium white potatoes, peeled and diced
    2 tablespoons butter
    2 medium red onions, chopped
    2 tablespoons all-purpose flour
    1/2 teaspoon dried thyme
    1/2 teaspoon salt
    1/2 teaspoon pepper
    1 cup half-and-half cream
    1/2 cup mayonnaise
    1 teaspoon Dijon mustard
    4 bacon strips, cooked and crumbled

Place potatoes in a large saucepan and cover with water. Bring to a boil. Reduce heat; cover and cook for 10-15 minutes or until tender. Drain and set aside.

In large saucepan, melt butter. Saute onions until tender; stir in the flour, thyme, salt and pepper until blended. Gradually add cream. Bring to a boil. Cook and stir for 2 minutes or until thickened. Remove from the heat; let cool slightly. Stir in the mayonnaise and mustard. Pour sauce over potatoes; transfer to a 1-1/2-qt. baking dish.

Bake, uncovered, at 350° for 30 minutes. Just before serving, sprinkle with crumbled bacon. YIELD: 4-6 servings.

IRISH HERBED POTATOES

CONNIE LOU BLOMMERS ❖ PELLA, IOWA

Celebrate St. Patrick's Day with this unique potato dish. The wedges are tasty from dill and chive seasoning.

2-1/2 pounds potatoes, peeled and cut into wedges
    1/2 cup butter, melted
    1 tablespoon lemon juice
    1/4 cup minced fresh parsley
    3 tablespoons minced chives
    3 tablespoons snipped fresh dill *or* 3 teaspoons dill weed
    1/8 teaspoon salt
    1/8 teaspoon pepper

Place potatoes in a large saucepan and cover with water. Bring to a boil. Reduce heat; cover and simmer for 15-20 minutes or until tender. Drain. Transfer to a large serving bowl.

In a small bowl, combine the remaining ingredients; pour over potatoes and toss to coat. YIELD: 8-10 servings.

CRUMB-TOPPED BROCCOLI WITH LEMON

PATRICIA NIEH ❖ PORTOLA VALLEY, CALIFORNIA

Dress up broccoli with a lemony bread crumb topping, and you might be surprised with the luscious result, not to mention the positive reaction from guests.

1 garlic clove, minced
1 teaspoon olive oil
1 slice multigrain bread, toasted and crumbled
1/2 teaspoon grated lemon peel
2 tablespoons minced fresh parsley
3 cups fresh broccoli florets
1 tablespoon water
2 tablespoons lemon juice

In a small skillet, saute garlic in oil for 30 seconds. Stir in bread crumbs and lemon peel; cook 1 minute longer. Remove from the heat. Stir in parsley; set aside.

Place broccoli and water in a microwave-safe bowl. Cover and microwave on high for 2-3 minutes or until crisp-tender; drain. Drizzle with lemon juice; toss to coat. Sprinkle with crumb mixture. YIELD: 4 servings.

EDITOR'S NOTE: This recipe was tested in a 1,100-watt microwave.

SEASONED SALT

RENE AMMUNDSEN ❖ VICTORIA, BRITISH COLUMBIA

Our gang likes to make things from scratch. The kids jostle for a turn to make this recipe. It's a tradition, especially sprinkled on our sliced homegrown tomatoes.

2/3 cup fine sea salt
1/2 cup sugar
4-1/2 teaspoons paprika
1 tablespoon onion powder

1 tablespoon garlic powder
1 teaspoon ground turmeric
1/4 teaspoon dried thyme
1/4 teaspoon dried marjoram

In a small bowl, combine all ingredients. Store in an airtight container for up to 1 year. YIELD: 1-1/4 cups.

SWEET-SOUR GREEN BEANS

CLAIRE MOSER ❖ MIDDLETOWN, MARYLAND

This is a side dish my mother made for family and friends. It has a very nice blend of sweet and sour flavors. I often take it to picnics and church dinners as it can be served warm or cold—it's delicious either way.

2 cups fresh green beans, cut into 2-inch pieces
2 bacon strips, diced
1/4 cup chopped onion
4 teaspoons brown sugar
4 teaspoons cider vinegar

Place the green beans in a small saucepan and cover with water. Bring to a boil; cook, uncovered, for 8-10 minutes or until the beans are crisp-tender.

Meanwhile, in a small skillet, cook bacon over medium heat until crisp. Using a slotted spoon, remove to paper towels. Drain, reserving 2 teaspoons drippings; saute onion in the drippings. Stir in brown sugar and vinegar; heat through. Drain beans and place in a bowl; stir in onion mixture. Top with cooked bacon. YIELD: 2 servings.

GLAZED CARROTS AND SUGAR SNAP PEAS

BETTY NEPTUNE ❖ WALKER, MINNESOTA

Busy cooks will appreciate the simplicity of this side dish that pairs the summery taste of baby carrots with fresh snap peas. The veggie medley brightens up any plate.

- 1 pound fresh baby carrots
- 1 pound fresh sugar snap peas, trimmed
- 1 teaspoon cornstarch
- 1/4 teaspoon salt
- 1/8 teaspoon pepper
- 2/3 cup reduced-sodium chicken broth
- 2 teaspoons butter, melted

Place 1 in. of water in a large saucepan; add carrots. Bring to a boil. Reduce heat; cover and simmer for 5 minutes. Stir in peas; cover and cook 2 minutes longer. Drain.

In a small bowl, whisk the cornstarch, salt, pepper and broth until smooth. Add to vegetables with the butter. Bring to a boil over medium heat; cook and stir for 2-3 minutes or until glaze is slightly thickened. YIELD: 6 servings.

CHERRY BAKED BEANS

MARGARET SMITH ❖ SUPERIOR, WISCONSIN

Here's a perfect dish to bring to any get-together. It's fast, easy to prepare, and you don't have to worry about bringing leftovers home...because there won't be any!

- 1 pound lean ground beef (90% lean)
- 2 cans (15 ounces *each*) pork and beans
- 2 cups frozen pitted tart cherries, thawed
- 1 can (16 ounces) kidney beans, rinsed and drained
- 1 cup ketchup
- 1/2 cup water
- 1 envelope onion soup mix
- 2 tablespoons prepared mustard
- 2 teaspoons cider vinegar

In a large skillet, cook beef over medium heat until no longer pink; drain. In a large bowl, combine the remaining ingredients; stir in beef.

Transfer to an ungreased 2-1/2-qt. baking dish. Bake, uncovered, at 400° for 40-45 minutes or until heated through, stirring occasionally. YIELD: 12 servings.

BUTTERNUT ORZO RISOTTO

TASTE OF HOME TEST KITCHEN

This creamy dish resembles traditional rice risotto, only it's quicker and easier to make.

  3 cups cubed peeled butternut squash (about 1/2-inch cubes)
  1 teaspoon olive oil
1/8 teaspoon salt
1/4 teaspoon pepper, *divided*
  3 cups reduced-sodium chicken broth
  1 small onion, chopped
  2 teaspoons butter
  1 cup uncooked orzo pasta
  1 garlic clove, minced
  2 tablespoons minced fresh parsley
1-1/2 teaspoons minced fresh sage
1/2 teaspoon minced fresh thyme
Shaved Parmesan cheese, optional

Place squash in a greased 15-in. x 10-in. x 1-in. baking pan. Drizzle with oil; sprinkle with salt and 1/8 teaspoon pepper. Bake at 400° for 15-20 minutes or until tender, stirring occasionally.

Meanwhile, in a small saucepan, heat broth and keep warm. In a large nonstick skillet, saute onion in butter until tender. Add orzo and garlic; cook and stir for 2-3 minutes. Carefully stir in 1 cup warm broth. Cook; stir until all of the liquid is absorbed.

Add remaining broth, 1/2 cup at a time, stirring constantly. Allow liquid to absorb between additions. Cook until risotto is creamy and orzo is almost tender. (Cooking time is about 20 minutes.) Add herbs, cooked squash and remaining pepper; heat through. Garnish with cheese if desired; serve immediately. YIELD: 5 servings.

SQUASH-APPLE BAKE

JUDITH HAWES ❖ CHELMSFORD, MASSACHUSETTS

This is my mother-in-law's recipe, but I've made it so often I feel as though it's my own! Squash and apples are traditional to a New England fall, and taste even better when baked together. It's a wonderful Thanksgiving dish.

  1 medium buttercup *or* butternut squash (about 1-1/4 pounds), peeled and cut into 3/4-inch slices
  2 medium apples, peeled and cut into wedges
1/2 cup packed brown sugar
  1 tablespoon all-purpose flour
1/4 cup butter, melted
1/2 teaspoon salt
1/2 teaspoon ground mace

Arrange squash in a 2-qt. baking dish. Top with apple wedges. Combine the remaining ingredients; spoon over apples.

Bake, uncovered, at 350° for 50-60 minutes or until tender. YIELD: 4-6 servings.

HERBED PEAS

MARY ANN DELL ❖ PHOENIXVILLE, PENNSYLVANIA

Fresh herbs produce peas that please! Here's a great idea I love to serve with my favorite meat dishes.

3/4 cup thinly sliced green onions
1/3 cup butter
  6 cups fresh *or* frozen peas, thawed
  3 tablespoons minced fresh parsley
  3 tablespoons minced fresh basil
  1 teaspoon sugar
3/4 teaspoon salt
1/2 teaspoon pepper

In a large skillet, saute onions in butter until tender. Stir in the peas, parsley, basil, sugar, salt and pepper; saute for 3 minutes.

Reduce heat; cover and cook 3-5 minutes longer or until peas are tender. Serve with a slotted spoon. YIELD: 8 servings.

BAKED CREAMED ONIONS

MARGARET (PEGGY) BLOMQUIST ❖ NEWFIELD, NEW YORK

I often fix this comforting dish for my grown children when they visit. They love it when I double the recipe so they can take leftovers home! This recipe can be prepared a day ahead and refrigerated before baking.

    5 medium onions, sliced and separated into rings
    3 tablespoons butter
3/4 cup water
1/8 teaspoon ground allspice
    2 tablespoons all-purpose flour
    1 can (5 ounces) evaporated milk
    1 teaspoon sugar
1/2 teaspoon salt
    2 tablespoons grated Parmesan cheese
    2 tablespoons dry bread crumbs

In a large skillet, saute onions in butter for 5 minutes. Add water and allspice; bring to a boil. Reduce heat; cover and simmer for 15-20 minutes or until tender.

Combine flour and evaporated milk until smooth; gradually stir into the onion mixture. Bring to a boil; cook and stir for 2 minutes or until thickened. Stir in sugar and salt.

Transfer to a greased 1-qt. baking dish; sprinkle with cheese and bread crumbs. Bake, uncovered, at 350° for 30-35 minutes or until bubbly. YIELD: 5 servings.

BAKED APPLESAUCE

MARY MOOTZ ❖ CINCINNATI, OHIO

Once you taste this applesauce, you won't want the store-bought variety anymore. Baking the apples locks in their delicious flavor! This recipe can easily be adjusted for any amount of servings.

    2 large tart apples, peeled and sliced
    3 tablespoons sugar
1/4 to 1/2 teaspoon ground cinnamon
1/4 teaspoon vanilla extract

Place apples in a greased 1-qt. baking dish. In a small bowl, combine the sugar, cinnamon and vanilla. Sprinkle over apples.

Cover and bake at 350° for 40-45 minutes or until the apples are tender. Uncover and mash with a fork. Serve warm. YIELD: 2 servings.

PREVENT APPLES FROM BROWNING

To prevent apple slices from turning brown, rub them with lemon or lime juice. This coats the apple slices and prevents air from discoloring them. They store nicely in a resealable plastic bag in the refrigerator.

MICROWAVE CORN PUDDING

CAROL ERDLEY ❖ WATSONTOWN, PENNSYLVANIA

Here's a favorite home-style casserole that is ready to pop in the microwave in about 15 minutes. It is a real time-saver and delicious, too.

    4 eggs
    2 cans (14-3/4 ounces *each*) cream-style corn
    1 cup evaporated milk
1/4 cup all-purpose flour
    2 tablespoons sugar
    2 tablespoons butter, melted
1/2 teaspoon salt
1/4 teaspoon white pepper
Dash paprika

In an ungreased 2-qt. microwave-safe dish, beat the eggs. Stir in the corn, milk, flour, sugar, butter, salt and pepper. Cover and microwave on high for 9 minutes, stirring every 3 minutes.

Uncover; sprinkle with paprika. Microwave 15 minutes longer or until a knife inserted near the center comes out clean. Let stand for 5 minutes before serving. YIELD: 7 servings.

EDITOR'S NOTE: This recipe was tested in a 1,100-watt microwave.

HONEY-MUSTARD GREEN BEANS

CLARA COULSTON ❖ WASHINGTON COURT HOUSE, OHIO

I used this recipe as an occasion to get my kids involved in cooking. They had fun snapping ends off the green beans, and they delighted in whisking together the dressing ingredients. In addition, I was surprised how much they liked the beans with a hint of sweetness.

1/2 pound fresh green beans, trimmed
    1 teaspoon cider vinegar
    1 teaspoon olive oil
    1 teaspoon Dijon mustard
    1 teaspoon honey
1/8 teaspoon salt

Place beans in a small saucepan and cover with water. Bring to a boil. Cover and cook for 4-7 minutes or until crisp-tender.

Meanwhile, in a small bowl, combine the vinegar, oil, mustard, honey and salt. Drain beans; add to vinegar mixture and toss to coat. YIELD: 2 servings.

SAUSAGE RAISIN DRESSING

BRENDA LIZ PARKINSON
PRINCE GEORGE, BRITISH COLUMBIA

My mother was looking through a cookbook, and a clipping with this recipe fell to the floor. Mom, who's 80, told me the recipe came from her mother. We hope you relish this heirloom dish as much as we do.

    1 pound bulk pork sausage
3/4 cup *each* chopped celery, green pepper and onion
    6 cups cubed day-old bread (1/2-inch cubes), crusts removed
    1 can (8 ounces) sliced water chestnuts, drained and chopped
1/2 cup raisins
    1 teaspoon salt
1/8 teaspoon pepper
    2 eggs
1/2 cup chicken broth

In a large skillet, cook the sausage, celery, green pepper and onion over medium heat until meat is no longer pink; drain.

In a large bowl, combine the bread cubes, water chestnuts, raisins, salt and pepper. Add sausage mixture and toss to coat. Whisk the eggs and broth together; pour over bread mixture and toss to coat.

Transfer to a greased shallow 2-1/2-qt. baking dish. Cover and bake at 350° for 35 minutes. Uncover; bake 15-20 minutes longer or until golden brown. YIELD: 10 servings.

CREAMY FETTUCCINE WITH POPPY SEEDS

PAT STEVENS ❖ GRANBURY, TEXAS

The rich, creamy sauce coats the pasta well and makes a satisfying, pleasant side dish. I also serve this as an entree for the two of us. With a green salad and garlic bread, it makes a scrumptious homemade meal.

4 ounces uncooked fettuccine
1/4 cup butter, cubed
1 garlic clove, minced
2 tablespoons all-purpose flour
3/4 cup water
1/2 cup half-and-half cream
1/2 cup shredded Parmesan cheese
2 teaspoons dried parsley flakes
1/2 teaspoon poppy seeds
1/2 teaspoon pepper
1/4 teaspoon salt
4 fresh basil leaves, thinly sliced *or* 1/2 teaspoon dried basil

Cook fettuccine according to package directions. Meanwhile, melt butter in a small skillet over medium heat. Add garlic; cook and stir for 1 minute. Stir in flour until blended. Gradually whisk in water and cream. Cook and stir for 1-2 minutes or until thickened.

Stir in the Parmesan cheese, parsley, poppy seeds, pepper and salt until blended. Drain fettuccine; toss with cream sauce. Sprinkle with basil. YIELD: 2 servings.

PASTA POINTER

To cook pasta more evenly, prevent it from sticking together and avoid boil-overs, always cook pasta in a large kettle or Dutch oven. Unless you have a very large kettle, don't cook more than 2 pounds of pasta at a time.

BREADS, ROLLS & MORE

Fill your kitchen with the delectable aroma of fresh-from-the-oven muffins, sweet rolls, breads and more with the homespun recipes in this chapter.

🎀 STREUSEL PUMPKIN SWEET ROLLS

JULIE FEHR ❖ MARTENSVILLE, SASKATCHEWAN

My sons love anything that tastes like pumpkin, including these yummy rolls. I can't think of an easier way for me to get vitamin A into their diets!

    1 package (1/4 ounce) active dry yeast
1-1/4 cups warm 2% milk (110° to 115°)
    1 cup solid-pack pumpkin
    1/2 cup sugar
    1/2 cup butter, melted
    1 teaspoon salt
4-3/4 to 5-3/4 cups all-purpose flour

STREUSEL
1-1/2 cups all-purpose flour
    1 cup packed brown sugar
    1 teaspoon ground cinnamon
    1/2 teaspoon ground allspice
    3/4 cup cold butter, cubed

GLAZE
    1 cup confectioners' sugar
    1/2 teaspoon vanilla extract
    1 to 2 tablespoons 2% milk

In a large bowl, dissolve yeast in warm milk. Add the pumpkin, sugar, butter, salt and 4-3/4 cups flour. Beat until smooth. Stir in enough remaining flour to form a soft dough (the dough will be sticky).

Turn onto a floured surface; knead until smooth and elastic, about 6-8 minutes. Place in a greased bowl, turning once to grease top. Cover and let rise in a warm place until doubled, about 1 hour.

Punch the dough down; divide in half. Roll each portion into a 12-in. x 10-in. rectangle. Combine the flour, brown sugar, ground cinnamon and allspice; cut in the butter until crumbly. Set aside 1 cup.

Sprinkle remaining streusel over dough to within 1/2 in. of edges; press down lightly. Roll up jelly-roll style, starting with a long side; pinch seams to seal.

Cut each into 12 slices. Place cut side down in two greased 13-in. x 9-in. baking pans. Sprinkle with reserved streusel. Cover and let rise until doubled, about 30 minutes.

Bake at 375° for 20-25 minutes or until golden brown. Meanwhile, combine confectioners' sugar, vanilla and enough milk to achieve desired consistency; drizzle over rolls. Serve warm. YIELD: 2 dozen.

CINNAMON CRUMB MUFFINS

THERESA HOUZE ❖ SOUTHFIELD, MICHIGAN

When I was 13, these muffins won a blue ribbon at our own state fair. The coffee really enhances the cinnamon flavor, making these tender treats quite delicious.

    1 cup all-purpose flour
    1/3 cup sugar
    1 teaspoon baking powder
    1/4 teaspoon salt
    1/4 teaspoon ground cinnamon
    1 egg
    1/3 cup milk
    1/4 cup butter, melted
1-1/4 teaspoons instant espresso powder

CRUMB TOPPING
    4 teaspoons all-purpose flour
    2 teaspoons sugar
Pinch ground cinnamon
    2 teaspoons cold butter

In a small bowl, combine the first five ingredients. Whisk the egg, milk, butter and espresso powder until espresso powder is dissolved. Stir into the dry ingredients just until moistened. Fill greased or paper-lined muffin cups two-thirds full.

For topping, combine the flour, sugar and cinnamon. Cut in butter until mixture resembles coarse crumbs. Sprinkle about 1 teaspoon over each muffin.

Bake at 400° for 18-20 minutes or until a toothpick comes out clean. Cool for 5 minutes before removing to a wire rack. Serve warm. YIELD: 6 muffins.

CINNAMON MINCEMEAT BUNS

LINDA NEALLEY ❖ NEWBURGH, MAINE

My grandmother gave me this recipe a long time ago. Whenever I make these old-fashioned spiced rolls, I get rave reviews from family and friends.

    1 package (1/4 ounce) active dry yeast
    1 cup warm water (110° to 115°)
    3 tablespoons sugar
1-1/2 teaspoons salt
  1/4 cup canola oil
    1 egg
3-1/2 to 4 cups all-purpose flour

FILLING
    1 package (9 ounces) condensed mincemeat
  1/2 cup unsweetened apple cider *or* juice
  1/4 cup packed brown sugar
1-1/2 teaspoons ground cinnamon
    2 tablespoons butter

GLAZE
  3/4 cup confectioners' sugar
    1 tablespoon apple cider *or* juice
  1/2 teaspoon ground cinnamon

Dissolve the yeast in warm water. Beat in sugar, salt, oil, egg and 1 cup flour until smooth. Stir in enough remaining flour to form a soft dough. Turn onto a floured surface; knead until smooth and elastic, about 6-8 minutes. Place in a greased bowl, turning once to grease top. Cover and refrigerate 4 hours.

Crumble mincemeat into a small saucepan; add cider. Bring to a boil; cook and stir for 1 minute. Remove from the heat. Cool completely. Combine brown sugar and cinnamon; set aside.

Punch dough down. Turn onto a floured surface. Roll into a 16-in. x 12-in. rectangle. Spread filling to within 1/2 in. of edges; sprinkle with brown sugar mixture. Dot with butter.

Roll up jelly-roll style, starting with a long side; pinch seam to seal. Cut into 16 rolls. Place cut side up in two greased 9-in. round baking pans. Cover and let rise until doubled, about 1 hour.

Bake at 350° for 25-30 minutes or until golden brown. Combine the glaze ingredients and drizzle over warm rolls. YIELD: 16 rolls.

ONION CAKE

ANNELIESE DEISING ❖ PLYMOUTH, MICHIGAN

Refrigerated crescent dough creates a flaky crust for these savory squares. Moist and golden, each serving makes a comforting change from potatoes.

    3 bacon strips, diced
    4 medium onions, finely chopped
    3 tablespoons butter
  1/2 cup sour cream
    1 tablespoon all-purpose flour
  1/2 teaspoon salt
    3 eggs, beaten
    1 tube (8 ounces) refrigerated crescent rolls

In a large skillet, cook bacon until crisp; drain bacon and discard pan drippings. In the same skillet, cook onions in butter until tender. Cool.

In a large bowl, combine sour cream, flour and salt; add eggs. Stir in the bacon and onions; set aside.

Separate crescent roll dough into four rectangles. Pat dough onto the bottom and 1 in. up the sides of a greased 9-in. square baking pan, stretching as needed. Pinch edges together to seal. Pour onion mixture over dough.

Bake at 375° for 30 minutes or until the topping is set and crust is golden. Cool slightly before cutting into small squares. Serve warm. YIELD: 16 servings.

CARAMELIZED ONION FOCACCIA

DEIRDRE DEE COX ✢ MILWAUKEE, WISCONSIN

For a melt-in-your-mouth experience, top pizza crust with sweet cooked onions and your favorite cheese. The result is a focaccia-style snack that's fantastic!

- 3 large sweet onions, thinly sliced
- 2 tablespoons brown sugar
- 1 tablespoon marsala wine *or* apple juice
- 1/4 teaspoon salt
- 1/4 teaspoon pepper
- 2 tablespoons butter
- 1 tube (13.8 ounces) refrigerated pizza crust
- 1 tablespoon olive oil
- 1/4 cup shredded Parmesan cheese

In a large skillet, cook the onions, brown sugar, wine, salt and pepper in butter over medium heat for 15-20 minutes or until onions are golden brown, stirring frequently.

On a greased baking sheet, roll out pizza crust into a 13-in. x 10-in. rectangle. Brush with oil. Top with onions and cheese.

Bake at 400° for 15-18 minutes or until lightly browned. Serve warm. YIELD: 15 servings.

CRANBERRY CHEESE BREAD

SUZANNE GRUENBACHER ✢ COLWICH, KANSAS

Making this bread is really easy and the results are so tasty. It seems like an unlikely combination of cranberries and cheddar cheese but they are so delicious together.

- 2 cups all-purpose flour
- 1 cup sugar
- 2 teaspoons grated orange peel
- 1-1/2 teaspoons baking powder
- 1/2 teaspoon baking soda
- 1/2 teaspoon salt
- 2 tablespoons shortening
- 1 egg, lightly beaten
- 1-1/2 cups (6 ounces) shredded cheddar cheese
- 1/2 cup orange juice
- 1/4 cup water
- 1 cup fresh *or* frozen cranberries, thawed and halved
- 1/2 cup chopped walnuts

In a large bowl, combine the first six ingredients. Cut in shortening until crumbly. Combine the egg, cheese, orange juice and water. Make a well in the dry ingredients; stir in egg mixture just until moistened. Add the cranberries and the nuts.

Pour into a greased 9-in. x 5-in. loaf pan. Bake at 350° for 60-70 minutes or until a toothpick inserted near the center comes out clean. Cool for 10 minutes before removing from pan to a wire rack. Store in the refrigerator. YIELD: 1 loaf.

Yummy Quick Breads

A warm slice of delicious quick bread slathered in butter or topped with your favorite fruit spread is one of the most comforting snacks around.

In a large bowl, combine the first six ingredients. In another bowl, whisk the milk, butter and honey. Stir into dry ingredients just until moistened. Fold in the carrots, raisins, dates, almonds and pecans.

Transfer to three greased 8-in. x 4-in. loaf pans. Bake at 350° for 60-70 minutes or until a toothpick inserted near the center comes out clean. Cool for 10 minutes before removing from pans to wire racks. YIELD: 3 loaves (12 slices each).

ALMOND POPPY SEED BREAD

CAROLE DAVIS ✤ KEENE, NEW HAMPSHIRE

We hosted a beautiful wedding for our son and his bride, and served these lovely loaves to their guests. The recipe came from a dear friend.

2-1/4 cups sugar
    1 cup plus 2 tablespoons canola oil
    3 eggs
    3 tablespoons poppy seeds
1-1/2 teaspoons lemon juice
1-1/2 teaspoons almond extract
1-1/2 teaspoons vanilla extract
    3 cups all-purpose flour
1-1/2 teaspoons baking powder
    1 teaspoon salt
1-1/2 cups 2% milk

RAISIN WHOLE WHEAT QUICK BREAD

ELSIE SMITH ✤ INDEPENDENCE, MISSOURI

This delicious recipe has been a family favorite for many years. We especially enjoy it during the holidays. Once you bake this, you can't resist fixing it time and again.

    5 cups whole wheat flour
    1 cup wheat germ
    1 cup packed brown sugar
2-1/2 teaspoons baking powder
    1 teaspoon salt
1/4 teaspoon ground cinnamon
    3 cups 2% milk
1-1/2 cups butter, melted
1/4 cup honey
    3 cups grated carrots
    1 package (15 ounces) golden raisins
    1 cup chopped dates
1/2 cup chopped almonds
1/2 cup chopped pecans

GLAZE
- 3/4 cup confectioners' sugar
- 1/4 cup orange juice
- 1 teaspoon vanilla extract
- 1/2 teaspoon almond extract

In a large bowl, combine the sugar, oil, eggs, poppy seeds, lemon juice and extracts; beat until well blended. Combine the flour, baking powder and salt; add to sugar mixture alternately with milk, beating just until moistened.

Pour into two greased 8-in. x 4-in. loaf pans. Bake at 350° for 55-60 minutes or until a toothpick inserted near the center comes out clean.

Combine glaze ingredients until smooth; drizzle over warm loaves. Cool 10 minutes before removing from pans to wire racks. YIELD: 2 loaves (16 slices each).

BANANA NUT BREAD

SUSAN JONES ❖ LA GRANGE PARK, ILLINOIS

This quick bread is a tradition with us, so I always try to have ripe bananas on hand especially for this recipe. I'm sure your brood will love this nutty bread as much as mine. It's so good!

- 1/4 cup butter, softened
- 3/4 cup sugar
- 2 eggs
- 3/4 cup mashed ripe bananas (about 2 medium)
- 1/2 cup sour cream
- 2-1/4 cups all-purpose flour
- 1 teaspoon ground cinnamon
- 3/4 teaspoon baking soda
- 1/2 teaspoon salt
- 1/2 cup chopped walnuts

In a large bowl, cream the butter and sugar until light and fluffy. Add eggs, one at a time, beating well after each addition. Stir in bananas and sour cream. Combine the flour, cinnamon, baking soda and salt. Stir into banana mixture just until moistened. Fold in nuts.

Transfer to a greased 8-in. x 4-in. loaf pan. Bake at 350° for 1 hour or until a toothpick inserted near the center comes out clean. Cool for 10 minutes before removing from pan to a wire rack to cool completely. YIELD: 1 loaf (12 slices).

BAKING QUICK BREADS

For best results with quick breads, bake in a light aluminum pan rather than a darker nonstick pan. If you use a glass pan, lower your oven temperature by 25°.

CINNAMON ZUCCHINI BREAD

KATHIE MEYER ❖ ROUND ROCK, TEXAS

The only way Mom could get me to eat veggies was to bake this zucchini bread. When I grew up, I lightened her original recipe, so I can still eat it without guilt.

- 3/4 cup sugar
- 1/4 cup unsweetened applesauce
- 1/4 cup canola oil
- 2 egg whites
- 1 teaspoon vanilla extract
- 1-1/2 cups all-purpose flour
- 1-1/2 teaspoons ground cinnamon
- 1 teaspoon baking powder
- 1/2 teaspoon salt
- 1/2 teaspoon ground nutmeg
- 1/4 teaspoon baking soda
- 1-1/4 cups shredded peeled zucchini
- 1/2 cup raisins

In a small bowl, beat the sugar, applesauce, oil, egg whites and vanilla until well blended. Combine the flour, cinnamon, baking powder, salt, nutmeg and baking soda; gradually beat into sugar mixture. Fold in zucchini and raisins.

Transfer batter to an 8-in. x 4-in. loaf pan coated with cooking spray. Bake at 350° for 50-60 minutes or until a toothpick inserted near the center comes out clean. Cool for 10 minutes before removing from pan to a wire rack to cool completely. YIELD: 1 loaf (12 slices).

WHOLE WHEAT TOASTING BREAD

EVELYN DANBY ❖ SARINA, ONTARIO

This recipe for whole wheat bread is one of my favorites. Try it topped with butter and fruit spread!

      1 package (1/4 ounce) active dry yeast
  1/4 cup warm water (110° to 115°)
      1 cup warm milk (110° to 115°)
      1 tablespoon sugar
      2 tablespoons shortening
      1 egg
      1 teaspoon salt
3-1/2 to 4 cups whole wheat flour
      1 tablespoon butter, melted

In a large bowl, dissolve yeast in warm water. Add warm milk, sugar, shortening, egg, salt and 2 cups of flour; beat until smooth. Add enough remaining flour to form a soft dough.

Turn onto a floured surface; knead until smooth and elastic, about 6-8 minutes. Place in a greased bowl, turning once to grease top. Cover and let rise in a warm place until doubled, about 1-1/2 hours.

Punch dough down. Divide into thirds; roll each into a 12-in. rope. Braid ropes; place in a greased 8-in. x 4-in. loaf pan. Cover and let rise until doubled, about 45 minutes.

Bake at 375° for 25-30 minutes. Remove from pan and brush with melted butter. Cool on a wire rack. YIELD: 1 loaf.

PUMPKIN PATCH BISCUITS

LIZA TAYLOR ❖ SEATTLE, WASHINGTON

Often, I make a double batch of these moist, fluffy biscuits to meet the demand. My dad loves their pumpkiny goodness.

1-3/4 cups all-purpose flour
  1/4 cup packed brown sugar
2-1/2 teaspoons baking powder

  1/2 teaspoon salt
  1/4 teaspoon baking soda
  1/2 cup plus 1-1/2 teaspoons cold butter, *divided*
  3/4 cup canned pumpkin
  1/3 cup buttermilk

In a large bowl, combine the flour, brown sugar, baking powder, salt and baking soda. Cut in 1/2 cup butter until mixture resembles coarse crumbs. Combine pumpkin and buttermilk; stir into crumb mixture just until moistened.

Turn onto a lightly floured surface; knead 8-10 times. Pat or roll out to 1-in. thickness; cut with a floured 2-1/2-in. biscuit cutter. Place 1 in. apart on a greased baking sheet.

Bake at 425° for 18-22 minutes or until golden brown. Melt the remaining butter; brush over the biscuits. Serve warm. YIELD: 6 biscuits.

PIMIENTO-STUFFED OLIVE BREAD

VAL WILSON ❖ WABASHA, MINNESOTA

Salty olives pair well with this bread's cream cheese and chives. Even folks who normally avoid olives can't resist slices of this colorful bread.

      3 cups biscuit/baking mix
      2 tablespoons sugar
      1 egg
1-1/2 cups buttermilk
      1 cup (4 ounces) shredded Swiss cheese
      1 cup pimiento-stuffed olives
  3/4 cup chopped walnuts
      1 package (8 ounces) cream cheese, softened
      1 teaspoon minced chives

In a large bowl, combine biscuit mix and sugar. In another bowl, whisk egg and buttermilk. Stir into dry ingredients just until moistened. Fold in the Swiss cheese, olives and walnuts.

Transfer to a greased 9-in. x 5-in. loaf pan. Bake at 350° for 50-55 minutes or until a toothpick inserted near the center comes out clean. Cool for 10 minutes before removing from pan to a wire rack.

In a small bowl, combine cream cheese and chives. Serve with bread. Refrigerate leftovers. YIELD: 1 loaf (16 slices).

STORING NUTS IN THE FREEZER

So you don't run out of nuts at a crucial time, store them in freezer bags that are labeled. When you need them for a recipe, just pour out the amount you need.

ITALIAN TOMATO ROLLS

MARGARET PETERSON ❖ FOREST CITY, IOWA

No one believes me when I say it's pizza sauce that they're tasting in these tender, chewy rolls. The basil adds extra excitement. I like to serve these rolls with a hearty spaghetti and meatballs or a dinner-sized salad.

> 1 package (1/4 ounce) active dry yeast
> 1 teaspoon plus 2 tablespoons sugar, *divided*
> 1/4 cup warm water (110° to 115°)
> 1 cup pizza sauce
> 1/4 cup plus 2 tablespoons butter, melted, *divided*
> 1 egg
> 1 teaspoon salt
> 3/4 teaspoon dried basil
> 3 to 4 cups all-purpose flour

In a large bowl, dissolve yeast and 1 teaspoon sugar in warm water; let stand for 5 minutes. Add the pizza sauce, 1/4 cup butter, egg, salt, basil, 2 cups flour and the remaining sugar; beat until smooth. Stir in enough remaining flour to form a firm dough.

Turn onto a floured surface. Knead until smooth and elastic, about 6-8 minutes. Place in a greased bowl, turning once to grease top. Cover and let rise in a warm place until doubled, about 1-1/2 hours.

Punch the dough down. Turn onto a lightly floured surface; divide into 15 pieces. Shape each into a 2-in. ball. Place 2 in. apart on greased baking sheets. Cover and let rise until doubled, about 30 minutes.

Bake at 400° for 10-12 minutes or until golden brown. Remove from pans to wire racks. Brush with remaining butter. YIELD: 15 rolls.

🏵 COWBOY CORN BREAD

KAREN ANN BLAND ❖ GOVE, KANSAS

This corn bread is richer and sweeter than others I've tried, and especially luscious alongside ham and beans. I like to make an extra batch or two, cut into individual portions, wrap and freeze so I can use it at a later date.

> 2 cups biscuit/baking mix
> 1 cup yellow cornmeal
> 3/4 cup sugar
> 1/2 teaspoon baking soda
> 1/2 teaspoon salt
> 2 eggs
> 1 cup butter, melted
> 1 cup half-and-half cream

In a large bowl, combine the first five ingredients. In another bowl, combine the eggs, butter and cream; stir into the dry ingredients just until moistened. Spread into a greased 13-in. x 9-in. baking pan.

Bake corn bread at 350° for 25-30 minutes or until a toothpick inserted near the center comes out clean. Serve warm. YIELD: 12 servings.

★ CHOCOLATE PEPPERMINT SCONES

SHELLY PLATTEN ✤ AMHERST, WISCONSIN

Try my decadent scones as a breakfast or brunch treat or a snack served with coffee and mint tea. They're so festive for the special events or holidays, decked out in red and white peppermint candy.

```
  2 cups all-purpose flour
1/2 cup whole wheat pastry flour
1/2 cup baking cocoa
1/2 cup packed brown sugar
  2 teaspoons baking powder
  1 teaspoon baking soda
1/2 cup cold butter, cubed
3/4 cup (6 ounces) vanilla yogurt
1/2 cup buttermilk
  1 egg
  1 teaspoon peppermint extract
  1 cup 60% cacao bittersweet chocolate baking chips
  1 tablespoon coarse sugar
  2 ounces bittersweet chocolate, melted
1/4 cup crushed peppermint candies
```

In a large bowl, combine the first six ingredients. Cut in butter until mixture resembles coarse crumbs. In a small bowl, whisk the yogurt, buttermilk, egg and extract; add to crumb mixture just until moistened. Stir in chocolate chips.

Turn onto a floured surface; knead 10 times. Divide dough in half; transfer each portion to a greased baking sheet. Pat into a 6-in. circle. Cut into six wedges, but do not separate. Sprinkle with sugar.

Bake at 400° for 18-20 minutes or until puffed and tops are cracked. Remove to wire racks; cool slightly. Drizzle with melted chocolate and sprinkle with peppermint candies. Serve warm. YIELD: 1 dozen.

FRESH TOMATO FLATBREAD

MARLENE MOHR ✤ CINCINNATI, OHIO

Looking for an easy appetizer or side? All you need is a can of refrigerated crescent rolls, fresh tomatoes, a sprinkle of cheese, olive oil and savory seasonings.

```
  2 plum tomatoes
  1 tube (8 ounces) refrigerated crescent rolls
  1 small onion, thinly sliced
  2 tablespoons olive oil
  1 teaspoon Italian seasoning
  1 garlic clove, minced
1/4 teaspoon salt
1/8 teaspoon pepper
  1 tablespoon grated Parmesan cheese
```

Thinly slice the tomatoes; place on paper towels to drain. Unroll crescent dough; place on an ungreased baking sheet. Roll into a 14-in. x 10-in. rectangle; seal seams and perforations.

Arrange tomatoes and onion over crust. In a small bowl, combine the oil, Italian seasoning, garlic, salt and pepper; brush over top. Sprinkle with cheese.

Bake at 375° for 10-14 minutes or until lightly browned. Cut into squares. YIELD: 12 servings.

CRANBERRY ORANGE MUFFINS

SARA EICHENLAUB ❖ BURLINGTON, ONTARIO

These cranberry-studded muffins have a splash of orange flavor. They're so simple to fix, my husband and I enjoy one for breakfast almost every morning.

   2 cups whole wheat flour
1/3 cup sugar
   2 teaspoons baking powder
1/2 teaspoon baking soda
1/4 teaspoon salt
1-1/2 cups orange juice
1/4 cup canola oil
   1 egg
   1 cup fresh *or* frozen cranberries, halved

In a large bowl, combine the flour, sugar, baking powder, baking soda and salt. In another bowl, combine the orange juice, oil and egg; stir into the dry ingredients just until moistened. Fold in cranberries.

Coat muffin cups with cooking spray or use paper liners; fill three-fourths full with batter. Bake at 400° for 15-20 minutes or until a toothpick inserted near the center comes out clean. Cool for 5 minutes before removing from pans to wire racks. YIELD: 1 dozen.

MEASURING MUFFIN BATTER

Using a spoon to fill muffin cups with batter can get messy. Instead, use an ice cream scoop with a quick release or pour the batter from a measuring cup.

speed for 2 minutes. Add eggs and 1/2 cup flour; beat 2 minutes longer. Stir in enough remaining flour to form a soft dough (dough will be sticky).

Turn onto a floured surface; knead until smooth and elastic, about 6-8 minutes. Place in a greased bowl, turning once to grease the top. Cover and let rise in a warm place until doubled, about 1 hour.

Punch dough down; turn onto a floured surface. Roll into an 18-in. x 12-in. rectangle. Spread lemon curd to within 1/2 in. of edges. Roll up jelly-roll style, starting with a long side; pinch seams to seal. Cut into 12 slices.

Place rolls, cut side down, in a greased 13-in. x 9-in. baking dish. Cover and let rise until doubled, about 30 minutes. Brush with beaten egg and sprinkle with walnuts if desired.

Bake at 350° for 25-30 minutes or until golden brown. In a small bowl, combine the icing ingredients; drizzle over warm rolls. YIELD: 1 dozen.

BUTTERNUT SQUASH ROLLS

BERNICE MORRIS ❖ MARSHFIELD, MISSOURI

With their cheery yellow color and delicious aroma, these appealing buns will brighten your buffet table. I've found this recipe is a great way to use up extra winter squash from the garden.

  1 package (1/4 ounce) active dry yeast
  1 cup warm milk (110° to 115°)
1/4 cup warm water (110° to 115°)
  3 tablespoons butter, softened

TENDER LEMON ROLLS

SHIRLEY DUNCAN ❖ WILLIS, VIRGINIA

Light and tender, these golden rolls are filled with a lemon curd sauce and lightly glazed. Add a sprinkle of walnuts, and you'll have a sweet roll that's difficult to resist.

2-1/2 to 3 cups all-purpose flour
  1/3 cup sugar
    1 tablespoon active dry yeast
  1/2 teaspoon grated lemon peel
  1/4 teaspoon salt
  1/2 cup sour cream
  1/3 cup butter, cubed
  1/4 cup water
    2 eggs
  3/4 cup lemon curd
    1 egg, lightly beaten
  1/2 cup chopped walnuts, optional
ICING
  1/2 cup confectioners' sugar
    1 teaspoon water
    1 teaspoon lemon juice
  1/4 teaspoon grated lemon peel

In a large bowl, combine 1-1/2 cups flour, sugar, yeast, lemon peel and salt. In a small saucepan, heat the sour cream, butter and water to 120°-130°; add to dry ingredients. Beat on medium

2 teaspoons salt

1/2 cup sugar

1 cup mashed cooked butternut squash

5 to 5-1/2 cups all-purpose flour, *divided*

In a large bowl, dissolve yeast in milk and water. Add the butter, salt, sugar, squash and 3 cups flour; beat until smooth. Add enough remaining flour to form a soft dough.

Turn onto a floured surface; knead until smooth and elastic, about 6-8 minutes. Place in a greased bowl, turning once to grease top. Cover and let rise in a warm place until doubled, about 1 hour.

Punch dough down. Form into rolls; place in two greased 10-in. cast-iron skillets or 9-in. round baking pans. Cover and let rise until doubled, about 30 minutes.

Bake at 375° for 20-25 minutes or until golden brown. YIELD: 2 dozen.

CHEESY ROUND BREAD

RUTHE KROHNE ✤ FORT WAYNE, INDIANA

This bread, which looks similar to focaccia, has a light olive and garlic flavor. We love generous slices with soup.

1 package (16 ounces) hot roll mix

3/4 cup warm water (120° to 130°)

1 egg

1 tablespoon butter, softened

1-1/2 teaspoons garlic salt

1/2 teaspoon dried oregano

1/2 teaspoon paprika

3/4 cup shredded cheddar cheese

1/2 cup chopped ripe olives, well drained

1 egg white, lightly beaten

In a large bowl, combine the contents of the roll mix and yeast packets. Add warm water and mix well. Stir in the egg, butter and seasonings until blended.

Turn onto a floured surface. Knead in cheese and olives. Place in a greased bowl, turning once to grease top. Cover and let rise in a warm place until doubled, about 1 hour.

Punch dough down. Press into a 12-in. pizza pan. Cover and let rise in a warm place until doubled, 30 minutes.

ACTIVE DRY YEAST

Envelopes of yeast generally measure about 2-1/4 teaspoons. If your recipe calls for less, measure the amount called for in the recipe from an individual packet, then fold the packet closed and refrigerate the remaining yeast.

With a sharp knife, make three or four slashes across top of loaf. Brush with egg white. Bake at 325° for 40-45 minutes or until golden brown. Cool for 5 minutes before removing from pan to a wire rack. YIELD: 16 servings.

ENGLISH MUFFIN BREAD

ELSIE TRIPPETT ✤ JACKSON, MICHIGAN

Most of my cooking and baking is from scratch. I think it's worth the time and effort. Everyone enjoys homemade goodies like this delectable bread.

5 cups all-purpose flour, *divided*

2 packages (1/4 ounce *each*) active dry yeast

1 tablespoon sugar

2 teaspoons salt

1/4 teaspoon baking soda

2 cups warm milk (110° to 115°)

1/2 cup warm water (120° to 130°)

Cornmeal

In a large bowl, combine 2 cups flour, yeast, sugar, salt and baking soda. Add the warm milk and water; beat on low speed for 30 seconds, scraping the bowl occasionally. Beat on high for 3 minutes. Stir in the remaining flour (batter will be stiff). Do not knead.

Grease two 8-in. x 4-in. loaf pans. Sprinkle pans with cornmeal. Spoon batter into the pans and sprinkle cornmeal on top. Cover and let rise in a warm place until doubled, about 45 minutes.

Bake at 375° for 35 minutes or until golden brown. Remove from pans immediately to cool on wire racks. YIELD: 2 loaves.

BLUEBERRY YOGURT MUFFINS

CINDI BUDREAU ❖ NEENAH, WISCONSIN

With the addition of vanilla yogurt, these quick and easy muffins turn out moist and tender.

    1 cup all-purpose flour
    6 tablespoons sugar
    1/4 teaspoon salt
    1/4 teaspoon baking powder
    1/4 teaspoon baking soda
    1 egg
    1/2 cup vanilla yogurt
    3 tablespoons canola oil
    2 tablespoons 2% milk
    1/2 cup fresh *or* frozen blueberries

In a small bowl, combine flour, sugar, salt, baking powder and baking soda. In another bowl, combine the egg, yogurt, oil and milk. Stir into dry ingredients just until moistened. Fold in blueberries.

Fill greased or paper-lined muffin cups three-fourths full with muffin batter. Bake at 350° for 20-22 minutes or until a toothpick inserted near the centers of muffins comes out clean. Cool for 5 minutes before removing from pan to a wire rack. Serve warm. YIELD: 6 muffins.

EDITOR'S NOTE: If using frozen blueberries, use without thawing to avoid discoloring the batter.

LAZY DOUGHNUTS

ELOISE DEHOYOS ❖ TRACY, CALIFORNIA

These doughnuts have a great flavor without having to fry them. They come together quickly on those mornings that are particularly busy. I love the fact that I don't have to go to a doughnut shop to buy them!

    2 tablespoons plus 1-1/2 teaspoons shortening
    1/2 cup sugar
    2 eggs
    2 cups all-purpose flour
    2 teaspoons baking powder

1/2 teaspoon ground nutmeg

1/2 teaspoon salt

6 tablespoons milk

Butter, melted

Cinnamon-sugar

In a large bowl, cream shortening and sugar until light and fluffy. Add eggs, one at a time, beating well after each addition. Combine flour, baking powder, nutmeg and salt; gradually add to creamed mixture alternately with milk, beating well after each addition.

Fill greased muffin cups two-thirds full. Bake at 350° for 18 minutes or until a toothpick inserted near the centers comes out clean. Cool for 5 minutes before removing from pan to a wire rack. Dip doughnuts in melted butter, then roll in cinnamon-sugar. Serve warm. YIELD: about 10 servings.

RHUBARB-BUTTERMILK COFFEE CAKE

CINDY ASHLEY ❖ GREGORY, MICHIGAN

Take advantage of rhubarb's short season, and surprise your family with this yummy, scrumptious coffee cake. There's a nice balance of tart and sweet in each bite.

2 cups diced fresh *or* frozen rhubarb

1/4 cup plus 2/3 cup sugar, *divided*

1/2 cup butter, softened

2 eggs

1-1/2 teaspoons vanilla extract

1-1/2 cups all-purpose flour

1 teaspoon baking powder

1/2 teaspoon salt

1/8 teaspoon baking soda

3/4 cup buttermilk

2 tablespoons brown sugar

1/2 teaspoon ground cinnamon

In a small bowl, combine rhubarb and 1/4 cup sugar; set aside.

In a large bowl, cream butter and remaining sugar until light and fluffy. Add eggs, one at a time, beating well after each addition. Stir in vanilla. Combine the flour, baking powder, salt and baking soda; add to creamed mixture alternately with buttermilk, beating well after each addition. Fold in rhubarb.

Pour into a greased 9-in. square baking pan. Combine brown sugar and cinnamon; sprinkle over batter.

Bake at 350° for 25-30 minutes or until a toothpick inserted near the center comes out clean. Serve warm or at room temperature. YIELD: 9 servings.

EDITOR'S NOTE: If using frozen rhubarb, measure rhubarb while still frozen, then thaw completely. Drain in a colander, but do not press liquid out.

SUN-DRIED TOMATO CHEESE BISCUITS

LISA HUFF ❖ WILTON, CONNECTICUT

On busy weeknights, I whip up these biscuits, especially when we're eating Italian. By the time the pasta is done cooking, they're golden brown and ready to serve.

1-1/2 cups biscuit/baking mix

1/3 cup shredded part-skim mozzarella cheese

1/4 cup grated Parmesan cheese

1 teaspoon Italian seasoning

1/4 teaspoon onion powder

1/4 teaspoon garlic powder

1/2 cup buttermilk

3 tablespoons oil-packed sun-dried tomatoes, drained and finely chopped

1-1/2 teaspoons butter, melted

In a large bowl, combine the biscuit mix, cheeses, Italian seasoning, onion powder and garlic powder. Stir in buttermilk and tomatoes just until moistened.

Drop by 1/4 cupfuls 2 in. apart onto a greased baking sheet. Bake at 425° for 8-12 minutes or until golden brown. Brush with butter. Serve warm. YIELD: 6 biscuits.

COOKIES, BARS & CANDIES

There's no better way to satisfy your sweet tooth than with one of the scrumptious sweets featured in this chapter!

BUTTERSCOTCH SHORTBREAD

SANDRA MCKENZIE ✦ BRAHAM, MINNESOTA

After sampling these tender cookies in a specialty store, I knew I had to duplicate them. My version has lots of toffee bits and butterscotch chips. I give away dozens as home-baked gifts.

1 cup butter, softened
1/2 cup confectioners' sugar
1 teaspoon vanilla extract
1-3/4 cups all-purpose flour
1/2 cup cornstarch
1/4 teaspoon salt
1/2 cup butterscotch chips, finely chopped
1/2 cup milk chocolate English toffee bits

In a large bowl, cream butter and confectioners' sugar until light and fluffy. Beat in vanilla. Combine the flour, cornstarch and salt; gradually add to creamed mixture and mix well. Fold in butterscotch chips and toffee bits. Cover and refrigerate for 1 hour or until easy to handle.

On a lightly floured surface, roll out dough to 1/4-in. thickness. Cut with a floured 2-in. fluted round cookie cutter. Place 1 in. apart on ungreased baking sheets.

Bake at 350° for 10-12 minutes or until lightly browned. Remove to wire racks. YIELD: 4-1/2 dozen.

CRANBERRY ORANGE TRUFFLES

MOORE TERRYANN ✦ VINELAND, NEW JERSEY

My from-scratch truffles are a delicacy my family looks forward to every holiday. We love the combination of tart cranberries and rich chocolate—and the orange and almond put this recipe over the top.

12 ounces bittersweet chocolate, chopped
1/2 cup unsalted butter, cubed
4 egg yolks, beaten
1 cup dried cranberries, chopped
3 tablespoons thawed orange juice concentrate
1 teaspoon almond extract

COATING
12 ounces white candy coating, chopped
1/3 cup finely chopped almonds
1 ounce bittersweet chocolate, melted
1/4 cup dried cranberries

In a double boiler or metal bowl over simmering water, heat chocolate and butter until melted, stirring frequently. Whisk a small amount of mixture into egg yolks. Return all to the heat, whisking constantly. Cook and stir until mixture reaches at least 160° and coats the back of a metal spoon.

Remove from the heat; stir in the cranberries, orange juice concentrate and extract. Cool to room temperature, stirring occasionally. Refrigerate for 1 hour or until easy to handle. Shape into 1-in. balls.

In a microwave, melt candy coating. Dip truffles in coating; allow excess to drip off. Place on waxed paper-lined baking sheets; immediately sprinkle with almonds. Drizzle with bittersweet chocolate and garnish with dried cranberries. Refrigerate for 2 hours or until firm. Store in an airtight container in the refrigerator. YIELD: about 3 dozen.

In a large saucepan, bring sugar and corn syrup to a boil. Cook and stir until sugar is dissolved; stir in peanut butter.

Remove from the heat. Add cereal and mix well. Press into a greased 13-in. x 9-in. pan.

In a microwave-safe bowl, melt chips and shortening; stir until smooth. Spread over cereal mixture. Cover and refrigerate for at least 1 hour before cutting. YIELD: 2 dozen.

VINEGAR SUGAR COOKIES

JOSIE BOCHEK ❖ STURGEON BAY, WISCONSIN

Mom gave me this recipe when I was married. It's been in our family for generations. Young and old alike devour these scrumptious sugar cookies while I eat up the praise.

    1 cup butter, softened
3/4 cup sugar
    1 tablespoon white vinegar
1/2 teaspoon vanilla extract
    2 cups all-purpose flour
    1 teaspoon baking soda
Colored sugar

In a large bowl, cream butter and sugar until light and fluffy. Beat in vinegar and vanilla. Combine flour and baking soda; gradually add to creamed mixture and mix well.

APPLE OATMEAL COOKIES

NICKI WOODS ❖ SPRINGFIELD, MISSOURI

I brought these yummy cookies to work and they were gone in seconds. They're a great snack—and addictive, too!

    1 package (18-1/4 ounces) yellow cake mix
1-1/2 cups quick-cooking oats
1/2 cup packed brown sugar
    2 teaspoons ground cinnamon
    1 egg
3/4 cup unsweetened applesauce
    1 cup finely chopped peeled apple
1/2 cup raisins

In a large bowl, combine the cake mix, oats, brown sugar and cinnamon. In a small bowl, combine the egg, applesauce, apple and raisins. Stir into oats mixture and mix well.

Drop by heaping teaspoonfuls 2 in. apart onto baking sheets coated with cooking spray. Bake at 350° for 12-14 minutes or until golden brown. Let stand for 2 minutes before removing to wire racks to cool. YIELD: about 5 dozen.

CHOCOLATE SCOTCHEROOS

LOIS MAYS ❖ COVINGTON, PENNSYLVANIA

This recipe was given to me by one of my students at school. It has become one of my gang's favorites and is so simple to make.

    1 cup sugar
    1 cup light corn syrup
    1 cup creamy peanut butter
    6 cups crisp rice cereal
3/4 cup butterscotch chips
3/4 cup semisweet chocolate chips
3/4 teaspoon shortening

Roll into 1-in. balls. Place 2 in. apart on greased baking sheets. Flatten to 1/4-in. thickness; sprinkle with colored sugar.

Bake at 350° for 8-10 minutes or until edges are lightly browned. Cool for 1 minute before removing from pans to wire racks. Store in an airtight container. YIELD: 3-1/2 dozen.

CHEESECAKE DREAMS

BARBARA ALLSTRAND ❖ OCEANSIDE, CALIFORNIA

These bars are a "dream" because of their creamy filling and their easy preparation. Bet you can't eat just one!

1 cup all-purpose flour
1/3 cup packed brown sugar
1/2 cup chopped pecans
1/3 cup butter, melted

FILLING
1 package (8 ounces) cream cheese, softened
1/4 cup sugar
1 egg
2 tablespoons milk
1 tablespoon lemon juice
1 teaspoon vanilla extract

In a large bowl, combine the flour, brown sugar and pecans. Stir in butter until crumbly. Set aside 1/3 cup for topping. Press remaining mixture into a greased 8-in. square baking pan. Bake at 350° for 12-15 minutes or until lightly browned.

Meanwhile, in a large bowl, beat cream cheese and sugar until smooth. Beat in the egg, milk, lemon juice and vanilla. Pour over crust; sprinkle with reserved pecan mixture.

Bake for 20-25 minutes or until firm. Cool on a wire rack. Cut into 16 squares, then cut each square in half diagonally. Store in the refrigerator. YIELD: 32 bars.

COCONUT LEMON CRISPS

SEGARIE MOODLEY ❖ LONGWOOD, FLORIDA

We had these cookies at our wedding reception, where they brought smiles and compliments. They've become one of our anniversary dinner trademarks.

7 tablespoons butter, softened
1/4 cup sugar
1/2 teaspoon vanilla extract
1 cup all-purpose flour
1 egg white, beaten
1/2 cup flaked coconut

FILLING
1/3 cup sugar
4-1/2 teaspoons cornstarch
3/4 cup water
1 egg yolk, beaten
3 tablespoons butter, softened
2 tablespoons lemon juice

In a small bowl, cream the butter, sugar and vanilla until light and fluffy. Gradually add flour and mix well. On a lightly floured surface, roll out half of the dough to 1/8-in. thickness. Cut with a floured 2-in. round cookie cutter. Repeat with remaining dough, using a floured 2-in. doughnut cutter so the center is cut out of each cookie.

Place 1 in. apart on lightly greased baking sheets. Brush egg white over cookies with cutout centers; sprinkle with coconut. Bake at 350° for 8-10 minutes. Remove to wire racks to cool.

For filling, in a large saucepan, combine sugar and cornstarch; stir in water until smooth. Cook and stir over medium-high heat until thickened and bubbly. Reduce heat to low; cook and stir for 2 minutes longer. Remove from the heat. Stir a small amount of hot filling into egg yolk; return all to the pan, stirring constantly. Bring to a gentle boil; cook and stir for 2 minutes. Remove from the heat; gently stir in butter and lemon juice. Cool to room temperature without stirring.

Spread a teaspoonful of filling on the bottom of each solid cookie; place coconut topped cookie over lemon filling. Store in the refrigerator. YIELD: 1-1/2 dozen.

FREEZING COOKIES

To freeze cookies for up to 3 months, wrap the cookies in plastic wrap, stack in an airtight container, seal and freeze. When ready to use, simply thaw the wrapped cookies at room temperature and serve.

LEMON POPPY SEED COOKIES

CAROL OWEN ❖ SALINA, KANSAS

My family of lemon lovers has a weakness for these citrusy cookies. The poppy seeds add a pleasant nuttiness to the tangy treats.

1-1/4 cups sugar
1 cup butter-flavored shortening
2 eggs
1/4 cup light corn syrup
1 tablespoon grated lemon peel
1-1/2 teaspoons lemon extract
1 teaspoon vanilla extract
3 cups all-purpose flour
2 tablespoons poppy seeds
1 teaspoon ground ginger
3/4 teaspoon baking powder
1/2 teaspoon salt
1/2 teaspoon baking soda

In a large bowl, cream sugar and shortening until light and fluffy. Beat in the eggs, corn syrup, lemon peel and extracts. Combine the remaining ingredients; gradually add to creamed mixture and mix well.

Shape into three balls, then flatten into disks. Wrap in plastic wrap and refrigerate for 1 hour or until firm.

Roll each portion of the cookie dough between two sheets of waxed paper to 1/8-in. thickness. Cut with a floured 2-1/2-in. fluted round cookie cutter. Using a floured spatula, place the cookie dough pieces about 1 in. apart on greased baking sheets. Reroll scraps if desired.

Bake at 375° for 6-8 minutes or until edges are golden brown. Cool for 2 minutes before removing from pans to wire racks. YIELD: about 4-1/2 dozen.

HONEY-DATE PUMPKIN COOKIES

EUNICE STOEN ❖ DECORAH, IOWA

Just in time for harvest, here are some delicious drop cookies, plump with dates, pumpkins and nuts. The old-fashioned cream cheese frosting will remind you of Grandma's kitchen.

3/4 cup butter, softened
1-1/3 cups sugar
1/4 cup honey
1 egg
1 cup canned pumpkin
1 teaspoon milk
2-1/2 cups all-purpose flour
1 teaspoon baking powder
3/4 teaspoon salt
3/4 cup chopped dates
3/4 cup chopped pecans
2 tablespoons poppy seeds

FROSTING
1 package (3 ounces) cream cheese, softened
1/4 cup butter, softened
2 cups confectioners' sugar
2 tablespoons heavy whipping cream
1 teaspoon vanilla extract

In a large bowl, cream the butter and sugar until light and fluffy. Gradually beat in the honey and egg. Add the canned pumpkin and milk; mix well. Combine the flour, baking powder and salt; gradually add to the creamed mixture and mix well. Stir in the dates, pecans and poppy seeds.

Drop the batter by rounded tablespoonfuls 2 in. apart onto greased baking sheets. Bake at 350° for 12-15 minutes or until the edges are lightly browned. Remove cookies to wire racks to cool completely.

For the frosting, in a large bowl, beat the cream cheese, butter and confectioners' sugar together until light and fluffy. Beat in the heavy whipping cream and vanilla until smooth. Frost the cookies. Store in an airtight container in the refrigerator. YIELD: 5 dozen.

CHOCO-PEANUT BARS DELUXE

LAURA MCDOWELL ❖ LAKE VILLA, ILLINOIS

Satisfy your sweet tooth with the classic blend of peanut butter and chocolate. Together, the tender peanutty bar and crunchy chocolate topping are irresistible and will fly off a cookie tray in no time!

1/2 cup shortening
1/2 cup butter, softened
1-1/4 cups packed brown sugar
1 egg
1/3 cup chunky peanut butter
1 teaspoon vanilla extract
2-1/4 cups all-purpose flour
1/4 teaspoon salt

TOPPING
1-1/2 cups semisweet chocolate chips
3/4 cup chunky peanut butter
2-1/4 cups crisp rice cereal

In a large bowl, cream the shortening, butter and brown sugar until light and fluffy. Beat in the egg, peanut butter and vanilla. Combine flour and salt; gradually add to creamed mixture and mix well.

Spread into a greased 15-in. x 10-in. x 1-in. baking pan. Bake at 350° for 15-20 minutes or until golden brown. Cool for about 15 minutes.

For topping, melt the chocolate chips and peanut butter. Stir in the crisp rice cereal. Carefully spread over the top. Chill for 30 minutes or until firm. Cut into bars. Store in an airtight container. YIELD: 3 dozen.

EDITOR'S NOTE: Reduced-fat or generic brands of peanut butter are not recommended for this recipe.

TREASURE COOKIES

MICHELE PULFER ❖ OSSIAN, INDIANA

You'll want to bake a double batch of these cookies, because they'll disappear fast! Coconut and walnuts make them crunchy and chewy, and the milk chocolate chips turn them into comfort food.

1 can (14 ounces) sweetened condensed milk
1/2 cup butter, softened
1-1/2 cups graham cracker crumbs
1/2 cup all-purpose flour
2 teaspoons baking powder
1-1/3 cups flaked coconut
1 cup vanilla *or* white chips
1 cup milk chocolate chips
1 cup chopped walnuts

In a large bowl, beat milk and butter until blended. Combine the cracker crumbs, flour and baking powder; add to milk mixture and mix well. Stir in the coconut, chips and walnuts.

Drop by tablespoonfuls 2 in. apart onto ungreased baking sheets. Bake at 375° for 8-10 minutes or until lightly browned. Remove to wire racks. YIELD: 4 dozen.

1/3 cup shortening

1/2 cup sugar

1 egg

2 tablespoons molasses

1 cup all-purpose flour

1 teaspoon baking soda

1/2 teaspoon *each* ground cinnamon, cloves and ginger

1/8 teaspoon salt

Additional sugar

In a large bowl, cream the shortening and sugar until light and fluffy. Beat in the egg and molasses. Combine the flour, baking soda, cinnamon, cloves, ginger and salt; gradually add to the creamed mixture and mix well. Cover and refrigerate for at least 4 hours.

Shape tablespoonfuls of dough into balls. Roll in additional sugar. Place 2 in. apart on lightly greased baking sheets. Flatten slightly with a glass.

Bake at 350° for 8-10 minutes or until edges are lightly browned and tops are set and starting to crack. Cool for 2 minutes before removing to wire racks. YIELD: 2 dozen.

EDITOR'S NOTE: Cookie dough may be frozen. Freeze balls of dough on waxed paper-lined baking sheets until firm. Remove from the pan and place in resealable freezer bags for up to 3 months. To bake, place frozen balls of dough 2 in. apart on lightly greased baking or until edges are lightly browned and tops are set and starting to crack.

RASPBERRY DELIGHTS

GEORGIANA HAGMAN ❖ LOUISVILLE, KENTUCKY

These attractive bars have a rich, buttery crust holding the sweet jam topping. They're a big favorite on my Christmas cookie trays.

1 cup butter, softened

1 cup sugar

2 egg yolks

2 cups all-purpose flour

1 cup coarsely ground pecans

1 cup raspberry jam

In a large bowl, cream butter and sugar until light and fluffy. Beat in egg yolks. Gradually add the flour and mix well. Stir in the pecans.

Spread half into a lightly greased 13-in. x 9-in. baking pan. Top with the jam. Drop the remaining dough by teaspoonfuls over the jam topping.

Bake at 350° for 25-30 minutes or until top is golden brown. Cool on a wire rack. Cut into bars. YIELD: 3 dozen.

GINGERSNAPS

ELIZABETH FLATT ❖ KELSO, WASHINGTON

My friends and neighbors look for these old-time cookies on the goody trays that I give out every holiday. They're great for dunking in milk, and they bring back the spicy flavor of Christmases past.

CREAMY PASTEL MINTS

JAMIE GURNEY ❖ ODESSA, MISSOURI

My husband and I hosted a delicious dinner at my parents' house after our outdoor ceremony at a scenic spot. Our guests appreciated a tray of pretty, refreshing mints after the hearty meal. These mints are easy to make and have wonderful homemade flavor.

1 package (8 ounces) cream cheese, softened

1 teaspoon mint extract

6-2/3 cups confectioners' sugar

Red, green and yellow food coloring

Granulated sugar

In a small bowl, beat cream cheese and mint extract until smooth. Gradually beat in as much confectioners' sugar as possible; knead in remaining confectioners' sugar.

Divide the mixture into four portions. Tint one portion pink, one green and one yellow, leaving one portion white. For each color, shape into 1/2-in. balls. Dip one side of each ball into the granulated sugar. Press the sugared side of the balls into small candy molds; unmold the pastels and place on waxed paper. Let stand 1 hour or until dry before storing in airtight containers; refrigerate. May be stored for up to 1 week before serving. YIELD: about 12 -1/2 dozen.

EDITOR'S NOTE: Mints may also be made without molds by placing sugar side up on waxed paper. Flatten with a fork, forming a crisscross pattern.

DATE BARS

DOROTHY DELESKE ✦ SCOTTSDALE, ARIZONA

I used to be the cafeteria manager at a grade school, and these bars were always a big hit with the kids.

2-1/2 cups chopped dates
1/4 cup sugar
1-1/2 cups water
1/3 cup broken walnuts, optional
1-1/4 cups sifted all-purpose flour
1 teaspoon salt
1/2 teaspoon baking soda
1-1/2 cups quick-cooking oats
1 cup packed brown sugar
1/2 cup butter
1 tablespoon water

In a saucepan, combine dates, sugar and water. Cook, stirring frequently, until thick. Stir in nuts if desired.

Meanwhile, in a bowl, sift together flour, salt and baking soda. Add oats and brown sugar. Cut in butter until crumbly. Add water and mix lightly. Press half into a greased 13-in. x 9-in. baking pan. Spread date mixture on top. Cover with remaining oat mixture; pat lightly. Bake at 350° for 35-40 minutes or until lightly browned. YIELD: 3-4 dozen.

RICH CHOCOLATE BROWNIES

KAREN TRAPP ✦ NORTH WEYMOUTH, MASSACHUSETTS

I'm one of those people who needs chocolate on a regular basis. I looked high and low for a creamy brownie recipe that called for cocoa instead of chocolate squares and this is it. My family loves these brownies—they never last more than a day at our house.

1 cup sugar
2 eggs
1/2 teaspoon vanilla extract
1/2 cup butter, melted
1/2 cup all-purpose flour
1/3 cup baking cocoa
1/4 teaspoon baking powder
1/4 teaspoon salt
FROSTING
3 tablespoons baking cocoa
3 tablespoons butter, melted
2 tablespoons warm water
1 teaspoon instant coffee granules
1-1/2 cups confectioners' sugar

In a large bowl, beat the sugar, eggs and vanilla. Beat in butter. Combine the flour, cocoa, baking powder and salt; gradually add to batter and mix well.

Pour into a greased 8-in. square baking dish. Bake at 350° for 25-30 minutes or until a toothpick inserted near the center comes out clean. Cool on a wire rack.

For frosting, combine the cocoa and butter. Combine the water and coffee granules; add to cocoa mixture. Stir in sugar until smooth. Frost brownies. YIELD: 12 servings.

OATMEAL MOLASSES CRISPS

JORI SCHELLENBERGER ❖ EVERETT, WASHINGTON

In Amish and Mennonite homes, home cooking is guaranteed to be delicious, so when I found this recipe in an Amish cookbook, I knew I simply had to try it. It has become a true favorite of our family as well as the folks at our church fellowship.

2-1/2 cups butter, softened
5 cups sugar
4 eggs
1/3 cup dark molasses
3 teaspoons vanilla extract
4-1/3 cups all-purpose flour
4 teaspoons baking powder
3 teaspoons ground cinnamon
2 teaspoons salt
1 teaspoon baking soda
4-3/4 cups old-fashioned oats
2 cups finely chopped pecans

In a large bowl, cream butter and sugar until light and fluffy. Add eggs, one at a time, beating well after each addition. Beat in molasses and vanilla. Combine the flour, baking powder, cinnamon, salt and baking soda; gradually add to the creamed mixture and mix well. Transfer to a larger bowl if necessary. Stir in oats and pecans.

Drop by tablespoonfuls 2 in. apart onto greased baking sheets. Bake at 375° for 10-12 minutes or until edges are firm. Cool for 3 minutes before removing to wire racks. YIELD: 15 dozen.

CHOCOLATE TOPPED PEANUT BUTTER SPRITZ

DOLORES DEEGAN ❖ POTTSTOWN, PENNSYLVANIA

Peanut butter gives these scrumptious cookies a different flavor from other spritz. The chocolate drizzle makes them extra special.

1 cup butter, softened
1 cup peanut butter
1 cup sugar
1 cup packed brown sugar
2 eggs
2 cups all-purpose flour
1 teaspoon baking soda
1/2 teaspoon salt

CHOCOLATE TOPPING
1-1/2 cups semisweet chocolate chips
1 tablespoon shortening
Chopped peanuts

In a large bowl, cream the butter, peanut butter and sugars. Beat in eggs one at a time, beating well after each addition. Combine the flour, soda and salt; gradually add to creamed mixture. Chill for 15 minutes.

Using a cookie press fitted with bar disk, form dough into long strips on ungreased baking sheets. Cut each strip into 2-in. pieces (there is no need to separate the pieces). Bake at 350° for 6-8 minutes. (Watch carefully—cookies brown quickly.)

For topping, melt chocolate with shortening; stir until blended. Place in a heavy plastic bag; cut a small hole in the corner. Pipe a strip of chocolate down center of each cookie and sprinkle with chopped peanuts. YIELD: 16 dozen.

HEDGEHOG COOKIES

PAM GOODLET ❖ WASHINGTON ISLAND, WISCONSIN

Unlike the real woodland creatures, these chocolate-coated hedgehogs dwell on snack plates and cookie trays. The little guys are fun to make and eat. They make great treats anytime of the year!

1/3 cup butter, softened
1/4 cup confectioners' sugar
1/2 teaspoon vanilla extract
2/3 cup all-purpose flour
2/3 cup ground pecans
1/8 teaspoon salt
1/2 cup 60% cacao bittersweet chocolate baking chips
1/4 cup chocolate sprinkles

In a small bowl, cream the butter and confectioners' sugar until light and fluffy. Beat in the vanilla extract. Combine the flour, ground pecans and salt; gradually add to the creamed mixture and mix well. Shape 1 tablespoon of dough into a ball; pinch the dough to form a face. Repeat. Place 2 in. apart on a greased baking sheet.

Bake at 325° for 12-15 minutes or until lightly browned. Let stand for 5 minutes before removing to a wire rack to cool completely.

In a microwave, melt chocolate; stir until smooth. Holding a hedgehog cookie by the nose, spoon chocolate over the back (leave the face uncovered). Allow excess to drip off. Place on waxed paper; immediately coat the wet chocolate with sprinkles.

With a toothpick dipped in chocolate, make two eyes and a dot on the nose. Let stand until set. Store in an airtight container. YIELD: 16 cookies.

DIPPING COOKIES IN CHOCOLATE

When the chocolate is running low, it might be necessary to spoon it over the cookies. If the chocolate cools too much to coat the cookies properly, rewarm before finishing the dipping.

1 cup plus 2 tablespoons all-purpose flour, *divided*
1 cup quick-cooking oats
1-1/2 cups packed brown sugar, *divided*
1/2 cup cold butter, cubed
2 eggs
2 teaspoons vanilla extract
1-1/2 cups flaked coconut
1 cup chopped walnuts
1 teaspoon baking powder
1/4 teaspoon salt
1 cup (6 ounces) semisweet chocolate chips

In a large bowl, combine 1 cup flour, oats and 1/2 cup brown sugar; cut in butter until crumbly. Press into a greased 13-in. x 9-in. baking pan. Bake at 375° for 8-10 minutes or until golden brown. Cool on a wire rack.

In a large bowl, beat eggs, vanilla and remaining brown sugar. Combine the coconut, walnuts, baking powder, salt and remaining flour; gradually add to egg mixture and mix well. Stir in chocolate chips.

Spread evenly over crust. Bake for 18-20 minutes or until golden brown. Cut into bars while warm. Cool on a wire rack. YIELD: 4 dozen.

LEMON SHORTBREAD SQUARES

JANET SATER ✤ ARLINGTON, VIRGINIA

During the Christmas season, I keep homemade cookies available in my office to share with coworkers. These easy-to-prepare squares always get rave reviews.

1/2 cup plus 2 tablespoons butter, softened
1/2 cup confectioners' sugar
1/2 teaspoon lemon extract
1/2 teaspoon vanilla extract
1-1/4 cups all-purpose flour
1/4 teaspoon grated lemon peel, optional
1/2 cup chopped pecans

In a large bowl, cream butter and sugar until light and fluffy. Beat in extracts. Gradually add flour. Mix until dough forms a ball and pulls away from the side of the bowl. Stir in lemon peel if desired.

Press into an ungreased 9-in. square baking pan. Score with a sharp knife into 16 squares. Prick each square twice with a fork. Sprinkle with pecans; press firmly into dough.

Bake at 325° for 20-25 minutes or until lightly browned and pecans are toasted. Cool for 5 minutes. Cut along scored lines. Cool completely in pan on a wire rack. Store in an airtight container. YIELD: 16 squares.

DREAMY CHOCOLATE CHIP BARS

KATHARINE FLY ✤ FARWELL, TEXAS

This recipe is my children's favorite (and mine!). For even more sweet flavor, they always ask me to dust the bars with confectioners' sugar.

GINGER-CREAM BARS

CAROL NAGELKIRK ✤ HOLLAND, MICHIGAN

I rediscovered this old-time recipe recently and found it's a treat for everyone. Even 4-year-olds have asked for these frosted bars as nursery school treats.

1 cup sugar
1 cup butter, softened
2 cups all-purpose flour
1 teaspoon salt
2 teaspoons baking soda
1 tablespoon ground cinnamon
1 tablespoon ground cloves
1 tablespoon ground ginger
2 eggs
1/2 cup molasses
1 cup hot coffee

FROSTING
1/2 cup butter, softened
1 package (3 ounces) cream cheese, softened
2 cups confectioners' sugar
2 teaspoons vanilla extract
Chopped nuts, optional

In a medium bowl, cream sugar and butter. Sift together flour, salt, soda and spices; add to creamed mixture. Add eggs, one at a time, beating well after each addition, and molasses. Blend in coffee. Spread in a 15-in. x 10-in. x 1-in. baking pan.

Bake at 350° for 20-25 minutes. Cool. For frosting, cream butter and cream cheese; add sugar and vanilla. Spread over bars. Top with nuts if desired. YIELD: 5-6 dozen.

CHERRY COOKIES

JEAN DAVIS ❖ BRYSON CITY, NORTH CAROLINA

Studded with red cherries and nuts, these delicious cookies are worthy of setting out on a plate for Santa himself.

1 cup butter, softened
2 cups sugar
2 eggs
2 teaspoons vanilla extract
3 cups all-purpose flour
1 teaspoon baking soda
3/4 teaspoon salt
1 cup chopped pecans
1 cup chopped maraschino cherries

In a large bowl, cream butter and sugar until light and fluffy. Beat in eggs and vanilla. Combine the flour, baking soda and salt; gradually add to creamed mixture and mix well (dough will be thick). Stir in pecans and cherries.

Drop by rounded teaspoonfuls 2 in. apart onto ungreased baking sheets. Bake at 375° for 9-11 minutes or until set and lightly browned. YIELD: 6 dozen.

CHOCOLATE NUT BALLS

MURLIN MOORE ❖ CHAFFEE, MISSOURI

I make these simple no-bake treats for my family and have also taken them to church socials. They're so good that people often ask for the recipe.

2 cups graham cracker crumbs
2 cups chopped pecans
1 can (16 ounces) chocolate frosting
1 teaspoon vanilla extract
1-1/2 cups confectioners' sugar

In a large bowl, combine the first four ingredients. Shape into 1-in. balls; roll in sugar. Refrigerate for 1 hour before serving. YIELD: about 5 dozen.

CHOCOLATE ALMOND BRITTLE

PAT PARSONS ❖ BAKERSFIELD, CALIFORNIA

Here in Kern County, there are thousands of acres of almond orchards. I like to experiment with recipes to try to come up with something new. This candy is the result of altering, adding and a lot of taste-testing (somebody had to do it!). I think the recipe turned out rather well.

1 cup sugar
1/2 cup light corn syrup
1/8 teaspoon salt
1 cup coarsely chopped almonds
1 tablespoon butter
1 teaspoon vanilla extract
1-1/2 teaspoons baking soda
3/4 pound dark or milk chocolate candy coating

In a 1-1/2-qt. microwave-safe bowl, combine the sugar, corn syrup and salt. Microwave, uncovered, on high for 2-1/2 minutes. Stir in almonds; cook on high for 2-1/2 minutes. Add the butter and vanilla; cook on high for 1 minute.

Stir in baking soda. As soon as the mixture foams, quickly pour onto a greased metal baking sheet. Cool completely. Break into 2-in. pieces.

Melt chocolate coating in a microwave. Dip one side of brittle in chocolate and place on waxed paper to harden. Store in an airtight container. YIELD: about 1 pound.

EDITOR'S NOTE: This recipe was tested in a 1,100-watt microwave.

DAZZLING DESSERTS

This chapter is brimming with decadent sweets, including tender-crumb cakes, made-from-scratch pies, comforting cobblers and more!

BLUEBERRY BOUNTY CAKE

ALICE TESCH ❖ WATERTOWN, WISCONSIN

Everyone loves this golden cake bursting with blueberries and drizzled with fruity sauce. You'll have a hard time deciding whether to serve it for dessert, breakfast or brunch.

1-1/2 cups butter, softened
1-3/4 cups sugar
4 eggs
1 tablespoon grated lemon peel
2 teaspoons vanilla extract
3 cups cake flour
2-1/2 teaspoons baking powder
1/4 teaspoon salt
1 cup lemonade
1-1/2 cups fresh *or* frozen blueberries
BLUEBERRY SAUCE
2 teaspoons cornstarch
1/4 cup sugar
1/4 cup water
1 cup fresh *or* frozen blueberries, thawed

In a large bowl, cream butter and sugar until light and fluffy. Add eggs, one at a time, beating well after each addition. Beat in lemon peel and vanilla.

Combine the flour, baking powder and salt; add to creamed mixture alternately with lemonade, beating well after each addition. Fold in blueberries.

Pour into a greased and floured 10-in. fluted tube pan. Bake at 350° for 45-50 minutes or until a toothpick inserted near the center comes out clean. Cool for 20 minutes before removing from pan to a wire rack to cool completely.

In a small saucepan, combine cornstarch and sugar. Stir in water until smooth. Add blueberries; bring to a boil over medium heat, stirring constantly. Cook; stir 1 minute longer or until thickened. Serve warm with cake. YIELD: 12 servings (1 cup sauce).

EDITOR'S NOTE: If using frozen blueberries, use without thawing to avoid discoloring the batter.

SPICED PEACH PUFFS

AGNES WARD ❖ STRATFORD, ONTARIO

We always made cream puffs for special occasions when I was growing up in a family of seven. My favorite filling, then and now, is whipped cream and nutmeg-spiced peaches.

1 cup water
1/2 cup butter, cubed
1 teaspoon ground nutmeg
1/8 teaspoon salt
1 cup all-purpose flour
4 eggs
2 cups heavy whipping cream
1/2 cup confectioners' sugar
1 teaspoon vanilla extract
2 cups chopped peeled fresh *or* frozen peaches, thawed
Additional confectioners' sugar

In a large saucepan, bring the water, butter, nutmeg and salt to a boil. Add flour all at once and stir until a smooth ball forms. Remove from the heat; let stand for 5 minutes. Add eggs, one at a time, beating well after each addition. Continue beating until mixture is smooth and shiny.

Drop by tablespoonfuls 2 in. apart onto greased baking sheets. Bake at 400° for 25-30 minutes or until golden brown. Remove to a wire rack. Immediately split puffs open; remove tops and set aside. Discard soft dough from inside. Cool puffs.

For filling, in a large bowl, beat cream until it begins to thicken. Add confectioners' sugar and vanilla; beat until stiff peaks form.

Just before serving, fill puffs with whipped cream and peaches. Dust with confectioners' sugar. YIELD: 3 dozen.

In a large bowl, combine the flour, sugar, baking powder, salt and baking soda. In a bowl, whisk the egg yolks, oil, vanilla and poppy seeds with water. Add to dry ingredients; beat until well blended. In another large bowl, beat egg whites and cream of tartar until stiff peaks form. Fold into batter.

Pour into an ungreased 10-in. tube pan with a removable bottom. Cut through batter with a knife to remove air pockets. Bake at 325° for 50-55 minutes or until cake springs back when lightly touched. Immediately invert pan; cool completely, about 1 hour. Run a knife around side and center tube of pan. Remove cake to a serving plate.

In a small bowl, combine glaze ingredients. Pour over cake; garnish with flowers if desired. YIELD: 16 servings.

COUNTRY APPLE PRUNE CAKE

CLARA FOES ❖ VANCOUVER, WASHINGTON

I live in an area where prunes are the main crop. And since my state is also known for its apples, I feel this cake recipe really represents my region.

      2 cups sugar
  1-1/2 cups canola oil
      3 eggs
      2 cups shredded peeled apples
      3 cups all-purpose flour
      2 teaspoons baking soda
      1 teaspoon salt
      1 teaspoon ground cinnamon
  1/2 teaspoon ground cloves
      2 cups pitted dried plums, chopped
      1 package (12 ounces) dried pitted plums, chopped
      1 cup chopped nuts
  Confectioners' sugar

In a large bowl, beat sugar, oil and eggs for 2 minutes at medium speed; blend in apples. Combine dry ingredients; gradually beat into egg mixture. Stir in dried plums and nuts. Spoon into a greased and floured 10-in. tube pan.

Bake at 325° for 1 hour and 20 minutes or until a toothpick inserted near the center comes out clean. Cool in pan 15 minutes; invert onto wire rack to cool. Just before serving, dust cake with confectioners' sugar. YIELD: 12-14 servings.

POPPY SEED CHIFFON CAKE

MARILYN BECK ❖ MEDICINE HAT, ALBERTA

This attractive cake never seems to fail, and it's very moist. It's a great choice for any occasion, whether it's that special birthday celebration or an afternoon with friends.

  1/2 cup poppy seeds
      1 cup water
      8 eggs
      2 cups all-purpose flour
  1-1/2 cups sugar
      3 teaspoons baking powder
      1 teaspoon salt
  1/4 teaspoon baking soda
  1/2 cup canola oil
      2 teaspoons vanilla extract
  1/2 teaspoon cream of tartar
  GLAZE
      1 cup confectioners' sugar
  1/4 cup milk
      2 tablespoons butter, melted
  1/4 teaspoon vanilla extract
  Edible flowers, optional

In a small bowl, soak poppy seeds in water for 1 hour. Separate eggs; let stand at room temperature for 30 minutes.

MEASURING CHOPPED INGREDIENTS

If the word "chopped" appears before the ingredient, then chop it before measuring. If the word "chopped" comes after, then chop after measuring. For "1 cup nuts, chopped," measure 1 cup of nuts and then chop them.

MACADAMIA TOFFEE SNACK CAKE

MARIE ZAJDOWICZ ❖ RIVA, MARYLAND

Ever since I worked in a restaurant preparing desserts, I've been collecting recipes that make people happy. This mouthwatering cake is loaded with white chocolate chips, macadamia nuts and coconut.

      2 cups all-purpose flour
1-1/2 cups packed brown sugar
  1/2 cup cold butter
      1 teaspoon baking powder
  1/2 teaspoon salt
      1 egg
      1 cup milk
      1 teaspoon vanilla extract
      1 cup vanilla *or* white chips
  1/2 cup chopped macadamia nuts
  1/4 cup flaked coconut

In a large bowl, combine flour and brown sugar. Cut in butter until mixture resembles coarse crumbs. Set aside 1 cup for topping. Add baking powder and salt to remaining crumb mixture. In another bowl, whisk the egg, milk and vanilla. Stir into crumb mixture just until moistened.

Transfer to a greased 13-in. x 9-in. baking pan; sprinkle with reserved topping mixture, vanilla chips, nuts and coconut. Bake at 350° for 30-35 minutes or until golden brown and edges pull away from sides of pan. Cool completely on a wire rack before cutting. YIELD: 20 servings.

BLUEBERRY COBBLER

EVELYN DUNLAP ❖ NICOLLS, GEORGIA

As a child, I was reared on a small farm in southeast Georgia, and tobacco was our main crop. Now blueberries are the main crop in our small town, which has a blueberry festival each year. This recipe was the winner for 2008!

      6 cups fresh *or* frozen blueberries
1-1/2 cups sugar
  1/4 cup water
CRUST
  3/4 cup butter, softened
1-1/2 cups plus 2 tablespoons sugar, *divided*
      3 eggs
      1 teaspoon vanilla extract
1-1/2 cups all-purpose flour
      1 teaspoon baking powder
  1/2 teaspoon salt
  1/4 cup butter, melted
Vanilla ice cream, optional

Place blueberries in a greased 13-in. x 9-in. baking dish; set aside. In a small saucepan, bring sugar and water to a boil; cook and stir until sugar is dissolved. Pour over berries.

In a large bowl, cream butter and 1-1/2 cups sugar until light and fluffy. Add eggs, one at a time, beating well after each addition. Beat in vanilla. Combine the flour, baking powder and salt; add to creamed mixture. Spread over berry mixture. Drizzle with melted butter; sprinkle with remaining sugar.

Bake at 350° for 40-45 minutes or until golden brown. Serve warm with ice cream if desired. YIELD: 15 servings.

BANANA CUPCAKES

JANE DEARING ✦ NORTH LIBERTY, INDIANA

Go bananas when baking—especially when you have a bunch to quickly use up. Ripe bananas are the secret to these down-home cupcakes that look and taste the best!

1/2 cup shortening
1-1/2 cups sugar
2 eggs
1 cup mashed ripe bananas (about 2 medium)
1 teaspoon vanilla extract
2 cups all-purpose flour
3/4 teaspoon baking soda
1/2 teaspoon baking powder
1/2 teaspoon salt
1/2 cup buttermilk

LEMON BUTTER FROSTING
2 cups confectioners' sugar
1/3 cup butter, softened
3 tablespoons mashed ripe banana
1 tablespoon lemon juice

In a large bowl, cream shortening and sugar until light and fluffy. Add eggs, one at a time, beating well after each addition. Beat in bananas and vanilla. Combine the flour, baking soda, baking powder and salt; add to creamed mixture alternately with buttermilk, beating well after each addition.

Fill paper-lined muffin cups two-thirds full. Bake at 375° for 18-22 minutes or until a toothpick inserted near the center comes out clean. Cool for 10 minutes before removing from pan to a wire rack to cool completely.

In a small bowl, combine the frosting ingredients; beat until light and fluffy. Frost cupcakes. YIELD: 1-1/2 dozen.

CHERRY JUBILEE CAKE

DORIS HEATH ❖ FRANKLIN, NORTH CAROLINA

A luscious Bing cherry topping complements this light and tender cake. With a sprinkle of toasted almonds, the dessert is complete!

  2 egg whites
  2 tablespoons butter, melted
  3 tablespoons brown sugar
  2 cans (15 ounces *each*) pitted dark sweet cherries, drained
  3 tablespoons butter, softened
2/3 cup sugar
  1 cup cake flour
  1 teaspoon baking powder
1/4 teaspoon salt
1/3 cup milk
1/2 teaspoon almond extract
1/4 cup slivered almonds, toasted
Whipped cream

Let egg whites stand at room temperature for 30 minutes. Pour melted butter into a 9-in. round baking pan; sprinkle with brown sugar. Arrange cherries in a single layer over sugar.

In a large bowl, beat softened butter and sugar until crumbly, about 2 minutes. Combine the flour, baking powder and salt; add to the butter mixture alternately with milk. Stir in extract. In another bowl, beat egg whites until stiff peaks form; fold into batter. Spoon over cherries.

Bake at 350° for 30-35 minutes or until a toothpick inserted near the center comes out clean. Cool for 10 minutes before inverting onto a serving plate. Sprinkle with almonds. Serve warm with whipped cream. YIELD: 8 servings.

LEMON CHEESECAKE PIES

LORRAINE FOSS ❖ PUYALLUP, WASHINGTON

I've been making these scrumptious pies for at least 50 years. There's little cleanup, and kids and adults alike love the lemony, fluffy filling.

  1 can (12 ounces) evaporated milk
  2 packages (3 ounces *each*) lemon gelatin
  2 cups boiling water
  1 package (8 ounces) cream cheese, cubed
  1 tablespoon lemon juice
  1 cup sugar
  4 graham cracker crusts (9 inches)
TOPPING
  1 cup graham cracker crumbs
1/4 cup butter, melted
  2 tablespoons sugar

Pour milk into a large metal bowl; cover and refrigerate for at least 2 hours.

In a large bowl, dissolve gelatin in boiling water. Cool for 10 minutes. Add cream cheese and lemon juice; beat until blended. Set aside.

Beat chilled milk until soft peaks form. Gradually add sugar. Beat in gelatin mixture. Pour into crusts.

Combine topping ingredients; sprinkle over pies. Refrigerate for 4 hours or until set. YIELD: 4 pies (8 slices each).

BOSTON CREAM CUPCAKES

JEANNE HOLT ❖ MENDOTA HEIGHTS, MINNESOTA

Boston cream bismarcks have been my favorite bakery treat since I was a child, so I put together this easy-to-make cupcake version.

  3 tablespoons shortening
1/3 cup sugar
  1 egg
1/2 teaspoon vanilla extract
1/2 cup all-purpose flour
1/2 teaspoon baking powder
1/4 teaspoon salt
  3 tablespoons 2% milk
2/3 cup prepared vanilla pudding
1/2 cup semisweet chocolate chips
1/4 cup heavy whipping cream

In a small bowl, cream shortening and sugar until light and fluffy. Beat in egg. Beat in vanilla. Combine the flour, baking powder and salt; add to the creamed mixture alternately with milk, beating well after each addition.

Filled paper-lined muffin cups half full. Bake at 350° for 15-20 minutes or until a toothpick inserted near the center comes out clean. Cool for 10 minutes before removing from pan to a wire rack to cool completely.

Cut a small hole in the corner of a pastry or plastic bag; insert a small tip. Fill with pudding. Push the tip through the top to fill each cupcake.

Place chocolate chips in a small bowl. In a small saucepan, bring cream just to a boil. Pour over chocolate; whisk until

smooth. Cool, stirring occasionally, to room temperature or until ganache thickens slightly, about 10 minutes. Spoon over cupcakes. Let stand until set. Store in an airtight container in the refrigerator. YIELD: 1/2 dozen.

🏵 TRIPLE-BERRY CRUMB PIE

KATHERINE BARRETT ❖ BELLEVUE, WASHINGTON

Berries and hazelnuts are plentiful here in the Pacific Northwest, so ingredients for this treat are often at my fingertips. I like to freeze a couple of pies to enjoy in winter.

1-1/2 cups all-purpose flour
1-1/2 cups ground hazelnuts
  1 cup sugar, *divided*
3/4 cup cold butter, cubed
  2 cups fresh blackberries
  2 cups fresh blueberries
  2 cups fresh strawberries, sliced
  3 tablespoons cornstarch

In a large bowl, combine the flour, hazelnuts and 1/2 cup sugar; cut in butter until crumbly. Set aside 1-1/2 cups crumb mixture for topping. Press remaining mixture onto the bottom and up the sides of an ungreased 9-in. deep-dish pie plate.

Place the berries in a large bowl; sprinkle with cornstarch and remaining sugar. Stir until well blended. Spoon into crust. Sprinkle with reserved crumb mixture.

Bake at 375° for 55-60 minutes or until crust is golden brown and filling is bubbly (cover edges with foil during the last 15 minutes to prevent overbrowning if necessary). Cool on a wire rack. YIELD: 8 servings.

STRAWBERRY RHUBARB COBBLER

LILY JULOW ❖ GAINESVILLE, FLORIDA

Chock-full of berries and rhubarb, this pretty cobbler is the perfect finale for a dinner for two. Pecans in the topping and the delicious dessert sauce make it extra special.

 1 cup sliced fresh *or* frozen rhubarb
 1 cup sliced fresh strawberries
 1/4 cup sugar
 1 tablespoon quick-cooking tapioca
 1 teaspoon lemon juice
Dash salt

TOPPING
 1/3 cup all-purpose flour
 1/4 cup chopped pecans
 3 tablespoons sugar
 1/8 teaspoon baking powder
Dash salt
 2 tablespoons cold butter
 1 egg

SAUCE
 1/2 cup vanilla ice cream
2-1/4 teaspoons marsala wine

Combine the first six ingredients; divide between two greased 8-oz. ramekins or custard cups. Let stand for 15 minutes.

In a small bowl, combine the flour, pecans, sugar, baking powder and salt; cut in butter until the mixture resembles coarse crumbs. Stir in the egg. Drop by spoonfuls over the fruit mixture; spread evenly.

Bake at 375° for 25-30 minutes or until filling is bubbly and a toothpick inserted in topping comes out clean.

In a microwave-safe bowl, combine ice cream and wine. Cook, uncovered, at 50% power for 1-2 minutes or until heated through; stir until blended. Serve with warm cobbler. YIELD: 2 servings.

HONEY BAKED APPLES

RACHEL HAMILTON ❖ GREENVILLE, PENNSYLVANIA

My baked apple recipe is very old-fashioned but tried and true. It's definitely a comfort food.

 2 medium tart apples
 1/4 cup dried cranberries
 2/3 cup water
 1/4 cup packed brown sugar
 1 tablespoon honey
Vanilla ice cream

Core apples, leaving bottoms intact. Peel the top third of each apple; place in a greased 8-in. x 4-in. glass loaf pan. Fill each with cranberries.

In a small saucepan, combine the water, brown sugar and honey; cook and stir over medium heat until sugar is dissolved. Pour over apples.

Bake, uncovered, at 350° for 45-55 minutes or until tender, basting occasionally with pan juices. Serve with ice cream. YIELD: 2 servings.

VARIETIES OF TART APPLES

There are many varieties of tart baking apples to choose from, including: Granny Smith, Baldwin, Cortland, Ida Red, Jonathan, Lady Apple and McIntosh. Select apples that are firm, crisp and deeply colored.

DARK CHOCOLATE CREAM PIE

KEZIA SULLIVAN ✤ SACKETS HARBOR, NEW YORK

Caress every taste bud with this rich, creamy pie. Topped with a dollop of fluffy whipped cream, it will have chocolate fans standing in line.

1-1/4 cups sugar
1/4 cup cornstarch
1/4 teaspoon salt
3 cups milk
3 ounces unsweetened chocolate, chopped
4 egg yolks, lightly beaten
3 tablespoons butter
1-1/2 teaspoons vanilla extract
1 pastry shell (9 inches), baked

In a large saucepan, combine the sugar, cornstarch and salt. Stir in milk and chocolate. Cook and stir over medium-high heat until thickened and bubbly. Reduce heat; cook and stir 2 minutes longer. Remove from the heat.

Stir a small amount of hot filling into egg yolks; return all to the pan, stirring constantly. Bring to a gentle boil; cook and stir 2 minutes longer. Remove from the heat.

Gently stir in the butter and vanilla. Spoon into pastry shell. Cool on a wire rack. Cover and chill for at least 3 hours. YIELD: 8 servings.

DANISH RICE PUDDING (RISENGROD)

JYTTE KLARLUND ✤ LAWSON, MISSOURI

We use this traditional Danish dish as our first course on Christmas Eve, but many other times as well. It has a smooth, delicate flavor and is true comfort food.

2 cups milk
6 tablespoons medium grain rice
1/4 teaspoon salt

1 tablespoon sugar
1/4 teaspoon ground cinnamon
1 tablespoon butter

In a small heavy saucepan, bring the milk, rice and salt to a boil. Reduce heat; simmer, uncovered, for 35-40 minutes or until slightly thickened, stirring frequently.

Spoon pudding into individual dishes. Combine sugar and cinnamon; sprinkle over the tops. Dot with butter. Serve immediately. YIELD: 3 servings.

CINNAMON CHOCOLATE MOUSSE

CAMILLA SAULSBURY ✤ NACOGDOCHES, TEXAS

This eggless stovetop mousse is super silky. Its homemade chocolate sauce blends perfectly with cinnamon to create a sophisticated taste.

1 cup cold whole milk
2-1/4 teaspoons unflavored gelatin
1-3/4 cups semisweet chocolate chips, *divided*
3 cups heavy whipping cream, *divided*
1/2 cup sugar
1/2 to 3/4 teaspoon ground cinnamon
1/2 teaspoon vanilla extract
1/2 cup light corn syrup
Chocolate curls, optional

Pour milk into a small bowl; sprinkle gelatin over the top. Let stand for 5 minutes or until softened. Place 3/4 cup chocolate chips in a large bowl; set aside.

In a small saucepan, bring 2 cups cream and sugar to a boil; remove from the heat. Gradually pour over chips, whisking until smooth. Fold in the gelatin mixture. Stir in the cinnamon and vanilla. Pour into five dessert dishes. Cover and chill for at least 2 hours.

Place remaining chocolate chips in a small bowl. In a small heavy saucepan, bring the corn syrup and remaining cream to a boil; remove from the heat. Gradually pour over the chips, whisking until smooth. Cool to room temperature; carefully spoon over each dessert. Garnish with chocolate curls if desired. YIELD: 5 servings.

 BERRY & CREAM CHOCOLATE CUPS

AMY BLOM ✤ MARIETTA, GEORGIA

These cute chocolate cups are fun and easy to make ahead of time. They are yummy heaped with cool pastry cream filling, or you can spoon in ice cream or mousse. I like to serve them on Valentine's Day.

    1 package (12 ounces) dark chocolate chips
    2 ounces cream cheese, softened
  1/2 cup sour cream
  1/3 cup sugar
    2 tablespoons cornstarch
1-1/2 cups milk
    2 egg yolks, lightly beaten
1-1/2 teaspoons vanilla extract
1-1/2 cups thinly sliced fresh strawberries

In a microwave, melt chocolate chips; stir until smooth. Spread melted chocolate over the bottoms and up the sides of 12 foil muffin cup liners. Refrigerate for 25 minutes or until firm.

In a small bowl, beat cream cheese until fluffy; beat in sour cream until smooth. Set aside.

In a small saucepan, combine sugar and cornstarch. Stir in milk until smooth. Cook and stir over medium-high heat until thickened and bubbly. Reduce heat to low; cook and stir 2 minutes longer.

Remove from the heat. Stir a small amount of the hot mixture into the egg yolks; return all to the pan, stirring constantly. Bring to a gentle boil; cook and stir for 2 minutes. Remove from the heat; stir in the vanilla and reserved sour cream mixture. Cool to room temperature, stirring occasionally. Refrigerate until chilled.

Carefully remove liners from chocolate cups. Fill cups with pastry cream and berries. Chill until serving. YIELD: 1 dozen.

Old-Fashioned Flavor

"Best of Country Cooking" is known for its traditional recipes, and these classic desserts are comforting, rich and scrumptious.

⬤ GRANDMA'S CHRISTMAS CAKE

LINDA STEMEN ✦ MONROEVILLE, INDIANA

One bite of this old-fashioned spice cake will bring back memories. Chock-full of raisins and nuts, it tastes extra special drizzled with a rich, buttery sauce.

2 cups sugar
2 cups raisins
2 cups water
1 cup butter, cubed
3-1/2 cups all-purpose flour
1 teaspoon baking soda
1 teaspoon ground cinnamon
1/2 teaspoon *each* ground nutmeg and cloves
1 cup chopped pecans

BRANDY BUTTER SAUCE
1 cup heavy whipping cream
1 cup butter, cubed
1 cup sugar
4 egg yolks, lightly beaten
1/4 cup brandy

In a large saucepan, combine sugar, raisins, water and butter. Bring to a boil. Reduce heat to medium; cook, uncovered, for 5 minutes or until sugar is dissolved. Remove from heat; cool.

In a large bowl, combine flour, baking soda and ground spices. Add raisin mixture; beat until blended. Fold in pecans.

Pour into a greased and floured 10-in. fluted tube pan. Bake at 350° for 45-55 minutes or until cake springs back when lightly touched. Cool for 10 minutes before removing from pan to a wire rack to cool completely.

For sauce, in a large saucepan, bring cream to a boil; stir in butter and sugar until smooth. Reduce heat; stir a small amount of hot liquid into egg yolks. Return all to the pan, stirring constantly. Cook until sauce slightly thickens and reaches 160° (do not boil). Remove from the heat; stir in brandy. Serve warm with cake. YIELD: 12 servings.

MAPLE BREAD PUDDING

SUSAN PLANTE ✦ BENNINGTON, VERMONT

Simple to put together, this very comforting dessert has a pleasant maple flavor and aroma. My mouth is watering as I write this description!

2 eggs
1 cup milk
3/4 cup maple syrup
2 tablespoons butter, melted
4 slices egg bread *or* brioche, cut into cubes
Whipped cream

In a large bowl, whisk the eggs, milk, syrup and butter; stir in bread cubes.

Transfer to a well-greased 1-qt. pudding mold or ovenproof bowl; cover tightly. Place on a rack in a deep kettle; add 3 in. of hot water to pan. Bring to a gentle boil; cover and steam for 1 hour or until a knife inserted near the center comes out clean, adding water to pan as needed.

Let stand for 5 minutes before unmolding onto a serving plate; serve warm with whipped cream. Refrigerate leftovers. YIELD: 4 servings.

BLUEBERRY CUSTARD PIE

SONJA JENNER ✦ BARTLESVILLE, OKLAHOMA

This is one of my husband's favorite pies. We pick our own fresh blueberries, which makes the pie even better. One piece is never enough.

Pastry for single-crust pie (9 inches)
  1/2 cup sugar
    3 tablespoons cornstarch
  1/8 teaspoon ground cinnamon
    3 cups fresh or frozen blueberries
  1/4 cup orange juice

CUSTARD
  1/2 cup sugar
    2 tablespoons cornstarch
  1/8 teaspoon salt
1-1/4 cups whole milk
    3 egg yolks

MERINGUE
    3 egg whites
  1/4 teaspoon cream of tartar
    6 tablespoons sugar

Line a 9-in. pie plate with pastry; trim and flute edges. Line unpricked pastry with a double-thickness of heavy-duty foil. Bake at 450° for 8 minutes. Remove foil; bake 5 minutes longer. Cool on a wire rack.

In a large saucepan, combine the sugar, cornstarch and cinnamon. Stir in blueberries and orange juice. Bring to a boil; cook and stir for 2 minutes or until thickened. Remove from the heat. Cover and set aside.

For custard, in a small saucepan, combine sugar, cornstarch and salt. Stir in milk until smooth. Cook and stir over medium-

high heat until thickened and bubbly. Reduce heat; cook and stir 2 minutes longer. Remove from heat. Stir a small amount of hot filling into egg yolks; return all to pan, stirring constantly. Bring to a gentle boil; cook and stir 2 minutes longer. Remove from heat. Cool to room temperature without stirring; set aside.

In a large bowl, beat egg whites and cream of tarter on medium speed until soft peaks form. Gradually beat in the sugar, 1 tablespoon at a time, on high until stiff glossy peaks form and the sugar is dissolved.

Pour blueberry mixture into pie shell; top with custard. Spread meringue evenly over hot filling, sealing edges to crust. Bake at 350° for 12-15 minutes or until the meringue is golden brown. Cool on a wire rack for 1 hour. Refrigerate at least 3 hours before serving. Store leftovers in the refrigerator. YIELD: 8 servings.

PEAR UPSIDE-DOWN CAKE

TASTE OF HOME TEST KITCHEN

Using a packaged cake mix speeds up the preparation time of this tasty fall cake. Topped with pecans and golden pears, this moist cake is pretty to look at and luscious, too.

    3 tablespoons butter, melted
    2 medium pears, peeled and sliced
    3 tablespoons brown sugar
  1/2 cup chopped pecans
    1 package (9 ounces) yellow cake mix
  1/2 cup milk
    1 egg

Spread butter in an 8-in. square baking dish. Arrange pear slices in rows on top. Sprinkle with brown sugar and pecans.

Prepare cake batter according to package directions, using the milk and egg. Pour over pears.

Bake at 350° for 35-40 minutes or until a toothpick inserted near the center comes out clean. Cool on a wire rack for 5 minutes before inverting onto a serving plate. YIELD: 9 servings.

HOLIDAY WALNUT TORTE

EILEEN KORECKO ✤ HOT SPRINGS VILLAGE, ARKANSAS

This torte is one of my grandma's best-loved recipes—tender layers of nut-filled cake put together with apricot glaze and cream cheese frosting. It is just divine!

    3 eggs
1-1/2 cups sugar
    3 teaspoons vanilla extract
1-3/4 cups all-purpose flour
    1 cup ground walnuts
    2 teaspoons baking powder
    1/2 teaspoon salt
1-1/2 cups heavy whipping cream
GLAZE
    2/3 cup apricot preserves
    1 tablespoon sugar
FROSTING
    1/2 cup butter, softened
    1 package (3 ounces) cream cheese, softened
    2 cups confectioners' sugar
    1 teaspoon vanilla extract
3/4 cup ground walnuts, *divided*

In a large bowl, beat eggs, sugar and vanilla on high speed for 5 minutes or until thick and lemon-colored. Combine the flour, walnuts, baking powder and salt; beat into egg mixture. Beat cream until stiff peaks form; fold into batter.

Pour into two greased and floured 9-in. round baking pans. Bake at 350° for 25-30 minutes or until a toothpick inserted near the center comes out clean. Cool for 10 minutes before removing from pans to wire racks to cool completely.

In a small saucepan over medium heat, cook and stir preserves and sugar until sugar is dissolved. Set aside 1/2 cup. Brush remaining glaze over cake tops.

In a large bowl, beat butter and cream cheese until fluffy. Add confectioners' sugar and vanilla; beat until smooth. Spread 1/2 cup frosting over one cake; top with second cake and 3/4 cup frosting. Sprinkle 1/2 cup walnuts over the top.

Spread reserved glaze over sides of cake; press remaining walnuts onto sides. Pipe remaining frosting around top edge of cake. Store in the refrigerator. YIELD: 10-12 servings.

RHUBARB BERRY TART

MARY ANN LEE ❖ CLIFTON PARK, NEW YORK

I am a retired housewife who's always loved to bake. To make this dessert lighter, try using low-fat sour cream and a dollop of fat-free whipped topping.

1/2 cup sugar
4 teaspoons quick-cooking tapioca
3 cups sliced fresh *or* frozen rhubarb
2 cups sliced fresh strawberries
2 tablespoons orange liqueur *or* juice
1 teaspoon grated lemon peel

CRUST
1/2 cup butter, softened
1/2 cup sugar
1 egg
1/2 teaspoon almond extract
1-1/2 cups all-purpose flour
1-1/2 teaspoons baking powder

TOPPING
2 cups (16 ounces) sour cream
1/2 cup sugar
2 egg yolks
1 teaspoon vanilla extract

In a large bowl, combine sugar and tapioca. Add rhubarb and strawberries; toss to coat. Stir in liqueur and lemon peel. Let stand for 15 minutes.

Meanwhile, in a small bowl, cream butter and sugar until light and fluffy. Beat in the egg and almond extract. Combine flour and baking powder; gradually add to the creamed mixture and mix well.

Press dough onto the bottom of a greased 10-in. springform pan. Top with fruit mixture.

Combine the topping ingredients; spoon over fruit. Place pan on a baking sheet.

Bake at 350° for 55-60 minutes or until set. Cool on a wire rack for 10 minutes. Carefully run a knife around edge of pan to loosen. Cool cake completely. Store cake in the refrigerator. YIELD: 12 servings.

EDITOR'S NOTE: If using frozen rhubarb, measure rhubarb while still frozen, then thaw completely. Drain in a colander, but do not press liquid out.

STRAWBERRY CHEESECAKE MOUSSE

VIRGINIA ANTHONY ❖ JACKSONVILLE, FLORIDA

Indulge your sweet tooth with this refreshing berry dessert. I've been making it for years. It's like a no-bake cheesecake without the crust.

1/2 teaspoon unflavored gelatin
1/4 cup cold water
1 quart fresh strawberries, halved
2 tablespoons reduced-sugar strawberry preserves
1 package (8 ounces) reduced-fat cream cheese
1/2 cup sugar, *divided*
1/4 cup reduced-fat sour cream, *divided*
1/2 cup heavy whipping cream

Sprinkle gelatin over cold water; let stand for 1 minute. Microwave on high for 20 seconds. Stir and let stand for 1 minute or until gelatin is completely dissolved. Meanwhile, combine strawberries and preserves; set aside.

In a large bowl, beat the cream cheese, 1/4 cup sugar and 2 tablespoons sour cream until blended; set aside.

In another bowl, beat whipping cream and remaining sour cream until it begins to thicken. Add the gelatin mixture and remaining sugar; beat until stiff peaks form. Fold into cream cheese mixture.

In each of six dessert dishes, layer 1/2 cup strawberry mixture and 1/3 cup cream cheese mixture. Refrigerate until chilled. YIELD: 6 servings.

CARAMEL APPLE CREME BRULEE

CHERYL PERRY ✦ HERTFORD, NORTH CAROLINA

Here's the cream of the apple dessert crop. Fruit, caramel and cinnamon flavors enhance the rich, velvety custard. Served warm or chilled, it's a classic end to a meal.

- 3 medium tart apples, peeled and thinly sliced
- 6 tablespoons caramel ice cream topping
- 1/4 cup plus 2 tablespoons sugar, *divided*
- 1/4 cup plus 2 tablespoons packed brown sugar, *divided*
- 1/2 teaspoon ground cinnamon
- 2 cups heavy whipping cream
- 5 egg yolks, beaten
- 1 teaspoon vanilla extract

Place apples in a microwave-safe dish; cover with water. Cover and microwave on high for 3-4 minutes or until tender; drain well. Arrange apples in the bottoms of six 6-oz. ramekins or custard cups. Top with caramel topping; set aside.

In a small saucepan, combine 1/4 cup sugar, 1/4 cup brown sugar and cinnamon; stir in cream. Heat over medium heat until bubbles form around sides of pan. Remove from the heat; stir a small amount of hot mixture into the egg yolks. Return all to the pan, stirring constantly. Stir in vanilla.

Pour into prepared ramekins. Place ramekins in a baking pan; add 1 in. of boiling water to pan. Bake, uncovered, at 325° for 25-30 minutes or until centers are just set (mixture will jiggle). Remove ramekins from water bath; cool for 10 minutes. Cover and refrigerate overnight.

If using a creme brulee torch, combine the remaining sugars and sprinkle evenly over custards. Heat sugar with the torch until caramelized. Serve immediately.

If broiling the custards, place ramekins on a baking sheet; let stand at room temperature for 15 minutes. Combine remaining sugars; sprinkle over custards. Broil 8 in. from the heat for 4-7 minutes or until sugar is caramelized. Refrigerate for 1-2 hours or until firm. YIELD: 6 servings.

EDITOR'S NOTE: This recipe was tested in a 1,100-watt microwave.

STRAWBERRY PINEAPPLE PIE

IRENE CARON ✦ LOUDON, NEW HAMPSHIRE

Treat your loved ones to a spring fruit pie. This luscious change-of-pace dessert has a pretty pink filling and a fluffy whipped cream topping.

- 1 can (20 ounces) crushed pineapple, undrained
- 10 frozen unsweetened whole strawberries, thawed
- 3 tablespoons quick-cooking tapioca
- 2 egg yolks
- 3/4 cup plus 1 tablespoon sugar, *divided*
- 3/4 teaspoon lemon extract, *divided*
- 5 drops red food coloring, optional
- 1 pastry shell (9 inches), baked
- 1 cup heavy whipping cream

Place pineapple and strawberries in a food processor; cover and process until smooth. Transfer to a saucepan. Stir in the tapioca, egg yolks and 3/4 cup sugar; let stand for 5 minutes.

Cook and stir over medium heat until mixture comes to a full boil. Remove from the heat; stir in 1/2 teaspoon extract and food coloring if desired. Pour into pastry shell; refrigerate for 1 hour.

In a small bowl, beat cream until it begins to thicken. Add remaining sugar and extract; beat until stiff peaks form. Spread over top of pie. Refrigerate for at least 4 hours or until set. YIELD: 8 servings.

LEMON POUND CAKE

CORKEY ADDCOX ❖ MT. SHASTA, CALIFORNIA

I take this cake when asked to bring dessert for potluck lunches, and the ladies sometimes come to blows to see who gets to take home the leftovers.

1/3 cup sugar
1 egg
3 tablespoons canola oil
3 tablespoons orange juice
1/2 teaspoon lemon extract
2/3 cup all-purpose flour
3/4 teaspoon baking powder
1/8 teaspoon salt
1 teaspoon poppy seeds, optional
1/3 cup confectioners' sugar
2 tablespoons lemon juice

In a small bowl, combine the sugar, egg, oil, orange juice and extract. Combine the flour, baking powder and salt; add to egg mixture and mix well. Stir in poppy seeds if desired.

CITRUS-FLAVORED EXTRACTS

Keep lemon and orange extracts handy when you don't have fresh citrus peel. If your recipe calls for 1 teaspoon grated orange or lemon peel, substitute 1/2 teaspoon extract. Add the extract with the rest of the liquid ingredients.

Pour into a greased and floured 5-3/4-in. x 3-in. x 2-in. loaf pan. Bake at 350° for 30-35 minutes or until a toothpick inserted near the center comes out clean. Cool for 10 minutes before removing from pan to a wire rack to cool completely.

For glaze, in a small bowl, whisk confectioners' sugar and lemon juice until smooth; drizzle over cake. YIELD: 1 mini loaf (6 slices).

TOFFEE-CHOCOLATE PASTRY BUNDLE

TASTE OF HOME TEST KITCHEN

Chocolate chips and toffee bits ooze sweetness when you bite into this flaky puff pastry. For maximum enjoyment, eat it while slightly warm with vanilla ice cream.

1 sheet frozen puff pastry, thawed
1 cup milk chocolate English toffee bits
1 cup dark chocolate chips
1/2 cup coarsely chopped pecans
1 teaspoon confectioners' sugar
Vanilla ice cream, optional

Unfold puff pastry sheet on a lightly floured surface; roll into a 14-in. square. Combine the toffee bits, chocolate chips and pecans; place in center of pastry. Fold pastry over filling and pinch edges to seal.

Place seam side down on an ungreased baking sheet. Bake at 400° for 18-20 minutes or until golden. Cool on a wire rack for 10 minutes. Dust with confectioners' sugar. Serve warm with ice cream if desired. YIELD: 12 servings.

In a small saucepan, combine sugar and cornstarch; stir in water and 1-1/2 cups raspberries. Bring to a boil; cook and stir for 2 minutes or until thickened. Transfer to a bowl; refrigerate until chilled.

Spread topping over filling. Garnish with remaining berries. YIELD: 8 servings.

BERRY APPLE PIE

HEIDI JO KERANEN ❖ BRUNO, MINNESOTA

Our active family is full of big eaters, so I'm happy for our raspberry patch, our apple orchard and pie recipes like this one. You can substitute frozen berries for fresh.

    1 cup sugar
    3 tablespoons quick-cooking tapioca
    3 cups coarsely chopped peeled tart apples
    3 cups fresh *or* frozen raspberries
Pastry for double-crust pie (9 inches)
    2 tablespoons butter

In a large bowl, combine sugar and tapioca. Add apples and raspberries; toss to coat. Let stand for 15 minutes. Meanwhile, line a 9-in. pie plate with bottom crust; trim the pastry even with the edge.

Spoon filling into crust; dot with butter. Roll out remaining pastry to fit top of pie; place over filling. Trim, seal and flute edges. Cut slits in pastry.

Bake at 375° for 45-55 minutes or until crust is golden brown and apples are tender. Cool on a wire rack. YIELD: 8 servings.

RASPBERRY CREAM PIE

JULIE PRICE ❖ NASHVILLE, TENNESSEE

This recipe is delicious with either fresh-picked or frozen raspberries. That means you can make it year-round. One bite of raspberry pie will instantly turn winter to summer.

1-1/2 cups crushed vanilla wafers (about 45 wafers)
    1/3 cup chopped pecans
    1/4 cup butter, melted
FILLING
    1 package (8 ounces) cream cheese, softened
    2/3 cup confectioners' sugar
    2 tablespoons orange liqueur
    1 teaspoon vanilla extract
    1 cup heavy whipping cream, whipped
TOPPING
    1 cup sugar
    3 tablespoons cornstarch
    3 tablespoons water
2-1/2 cups fresh *or* frozen raspberries, *divided*

Combine the wafer crumbs, pecans and butter. Press onto the bottom and up the sides of a greased 9-in. pie plate.

In a large bowl, beat the cream cheese, confectioners' sugar, liqueur and vanilla until light and fluffy. Fold in whipped cream. Spread into crust. Chill until serving.

RASPBERRY CHOCOLATE CHEESECAKE

ROBINNE HURT ✦ CROSSFIELD, ALBERTA

This eye-catching cheesecake showcases red raspberries and heavenly dark chocolate. It's a treat in our house for special occasions.

2 cups chocolate wafer crumbs (about 38 wafers)
1/3 cup sugar
1/2 cup butter, melted

FILLING
1 envelope unflavored gelatin
3/4 cup cold water
2 cups heavy whipping cream
3 packages (two 8 ounces, one 3 ounces) cream cheese, softened
1/3 cup sugar
4 ounces semisweet chocolate, melted and cooled

1 cup fresh or frozen raspberries
Fresh raspberries and mint, optional

Combine the wafer crumbs, sugar and butter. Press onto the bottom and 1 in. up the sides of a greased 9-in. springform pan; set aside.

In a small saucepan, sprinkle gelatin over cold water; let stand for 1 minute. Heat over low heat, stirring until gelatin is completely dissolved; cool slightly.

In a small bowl, beat cream until stiff peaks form; set aside. In a large bowl, beat cream cheese and sugar; stir in cooled gelatin. Transfer half of the mixture to another bowl.

To one bowl, fold in the melted chocolate and half of the whipped cream. Pour over prepared crust. To the other bowl, carefully fold in the remaining whipped cream, then the raspberries. Pour over the chocolate layer. Cover and refrigerate for 6 hours or overnight.

Carefully run a knife around edge of pan to loosen. Remove sides of pan before slicing. Garnish with berries and mint if desired. Refrigerate leftovers. YIELD: 12 servings.

LEMON CHESS PIE

HANNAH LARUE RIDER ❖ EAST POINT, KENTUCKY

This creamy, lemony pie cuts beautifully and has a smooth texture. It's one of my favorites.

    1 sheet refrigerated pie pastry
    4 eggs
1-1/2 cups sugar
    1/2 cup lemon juice
    1/4 cup butter, melted
    1 tablespoon cornmeal
    2 teaspoons all-purpose flour
    1/8 teaspoon salt

Unroll pastry on a lightly floured surface. Transfer to a 9-in. pie plate. Trim pastry to 1/2 in. beyond edge of plate; flute edges.

In a large bowl, beat eggs for 3 minutes. Gradually add sugar; beat for 2 minutes or until the mixture becomes thick and lemon-colored. Beat in lemon juice, butter, cornmeal, flour and salt.

Pour into the pastry shell. Bake at 350° for 35-40 minutes or until a knife inserted near the center comes out clean; cool on a wire rack for 1 hour. Refrigerate for 3 hours before serving. YIELD: 6 servings.

APRICOT SHERBET

ORPHA CAMPBELL ❖ MIDLAND, TEXAS

Searching for a light and refreshing dessert that you can make ahead? Try this pretty sherbet that bursts with the invigorating flavor of apricot. It's the perfect summertime treat that doesn't require you to use the oven!

2-1/4 cups apricot nectar
1-1/2 cups milk
3/4 cup heavy whipping cream
1-1/2 cups sugar
3 tablespoons lemon juice

In a large bowl, combine all ingredients. Fill cylinder of ice cream freezer; freeze according to manufacturer's directions.

Transfer to a freezer container; freeze for 4 hours or until firm. YIELD: 1-1/2 quarts.

VANILLA ICE CREAM

DIANE SHAW ❖ GNADENHUTTEN, OHIO

My family had a two-hand crank ice-cream machine when I was young. We three kids took turns cranking until the ice cream began to harden, then Dad finished it. We tried many recipes, but Dad always liked this one the most.

2 cups sugar
1/4 cup all-purpose flour
1/2 teaspoon salt
6 cups half-and-half cream
4 eggs, lightly beaten
4 cups milk
3 teaspoons vanilla extract

In a large saucepan, combine the sugar, flour and salt. Gradually add cream; stir until smooth. Bring to a boil over medium heat; cook and stir for 2 minutes or until thickened. Remove from the heat; cool slightly.

Whisk a small amount of the hot mixture into the eggs. Return all to the pan, whisking constantly. Cook and stir over low heat until mixture reaches at least 160° and coats the back of a metal spoon. Remove from the heat. Cool quickly by placing pan in a bowl of ice water; stir for 2 minutes. Stir in milk and vanilla.

Press waxed paper onto surface of custard. Refrigerate for several hours or overnight.

Fill cylinder of ice cream freezer two-thirds full; freeze according to the manufacturer's directions. Refrigerate remaining mixture until ready to freeze. When ice cream is frozen, transfer to a freezer container; freeze for 2-4 hours before serving. YIELD: 3 quarts.

LIME PUDDING CAKES

ETHEL KOZMA ❖ WESTPORT, NEW YORK

This zesty, old-time dessert was always a real treat. My mother, Lois, baked it for us. Now I share it with my loved ones, too.

2 tablespoons butter, softened
1-1/2 cups sugar
1/3 cup all-purpose flour
1/4 teaspoon salt
1/2 cup lime *or* lemon juice
1 teaspoon grated lime *or* lemon peel
3 eggs, *separated*
1-1/4 cups 2% milk

In a small bowl, beat butter and sugar until crumbly. Add the flour, salt, lime juice and peel; mix well. Beat in egg yolks and milk until smooth. In another bowl, beat egg whites until stiff peaks form; gently fold into batter.

Pour into six ungreased 6-oz. custard cups. Place cups in a large baking pan; add 1 in. of boiling water to pan.

Bake, uncovered, at 325° for 40-45 minutes or until a knife inserted near the center comes out clean and top is golden. Serve warm or at room temperature. YIELD: 6 servings.

Cool & Creamy Finales

On a hot summer's day, these luscious desserts that use ice cream or frozen yogurt as the main ingredient will become instantly popular with your family!

FUDGE SUNDAE PIE

MARGARET RILEY ❖ TALLAHASSEE, FLORIDA

My son always asks for this guilt-free frozen yogurt pie for his birthday. Complete with peanut butter, fudge topping and nuts, it tastes ice cream parlor-good, but it's healthier.

1/4 cup plus 3 tablespoons light corn syrup, *divided*
3 tablespoons reduced-fat butter
2 tablespoons brown sugar
2-1/2 cups crisp rice cereal
1/4 cup reduced-fat creamy peanut butter
1/4 cup fat-free hot fudge ice cream topping, warmed
1/4 cup chopped unsalted peanuts
4 cups fat-free vanilla frozen yogurt, softened

In a large saucepan, combine 1/4 cup corn syrup, butter and brown sugar. Bring to a boil; cook and stir for 1 minute.

Remove from the heat; stir in cereal until blended. Press onto the bottom and up the sides of a greased 9-in. pie plate.

In a small bowl, combine the peanut butter, hot fudge topping and remaining corn syrup. Set aside 1/3 cup for topping. Spread remaining mixture over crust; sprinkle with half of the peanuts. Top with frozen yogurt and remaining peanuts. Cover and freeze for 6 hours or until firm.

Warm reserved peanut butter mixture; drizzle over pie. Let stand at room temperature for 5 minutes before cutting. YIELD: 8 servings.

EDITOR'S NOTE: This recipe was tested with Land O'Lakes light stick butter.

CARAMEL BANANA ICE CREAM PIE

APRIL TIMBOE ❖ SILOAM SPRINGS, ARKANSAS

With six ingredients and a prepared graham cracker crust, this pie is simple to make and luscious, too. Guests will enjoy the symphony of caramel, banana and toffee bits.

1/4 cup plus 1 tablespoon caramel ice cream topping, *divided*
1 graham cracker crust (9 inches)
1 cup cold 2% milk
2 packages (3.4 ounces *each*) instant banana cream pudding mix
1 quart vanilla ice cream, softened
1-3/4 cups whipped topping
1 English toffee candy bar (1.4 ounces), chopped

Spread 1/4 cup caramel topping into crust. In a large bowl, beat milk and pudding mix on low speed for 2 minutes. Add ice cream; mix well.

Spoon into prepared crust. Top with whipped topping. Drizzle with the remaining caramel topping; sprinkle with chopped candy bar.

Cover and freeze for 2 hours or until firm. Remove from the freezer 15 minutes before serving. YIELD: 8 servings.

MOCHA-FUDGE ICE CREAM DESSERT

CARRIE BURKE ✤ CONWAY, MASSACHUSETTS

This recipe looks and tastes like you spent lots of time and effort, but it's super easy. My kids like chocolate chip ice cream the best. In addition to its versatility, this recipe is a great make-ahead and you don't need to heat up the oven.

3-3/4 cups crushed cream-filled chocolate sandwich cookies
1/2 cup butter, melted
1 jar (16 ounces) hot fudge ice cream topping, warmed
1/2 gallon coffee ice cream, softened
1 carton (8 ounces) frozen whipped topping, thawed
Chocolate curls or sprinkles, optional

Combine cookie crumbs and butter; press onto bottom and 1 in. up sides of a 13-in. x 9-in. dish. Freeze for 1 hour or until firm.

Spread hot fudge topping evenly over the crust and freeze for 30 minutes.

Layer with ice cream and whipped topping. Cover and freeze for 8 hours or overnight. Garnish with chocolate curls or sprinkles if desired. YIELD: 15 servings.

HOW TO SOFTEN ICE CREAM

To soften, place ice cream in the refrigerator 20-30 minutes before using. Or let it stand at room temperature for 10-15 minutes. Hard ice cream can be softened in the microwave at 30% power for about 30 seconds.

MOCHA ICE CREAM CAKE ROLL

AGNES WARD ✤ STRATFORD, ONTARIO

Homemade chocolate cake rolled together with coffee ice cream makes a dessert everyone will enjoy. This is a real treasure to keep frozen for unexpected company.

3 eggs
1 cup sugar
1/3 cup water
1 teaspoon vanilla extract
1 cup cake flour
1/4 cup baking cocoa
1 teaspoon baking powder
1/4 teaspoon salt
4 teaspoons confectioners' sugar, *divided*
3 cups coffee ice cream, softened
White and semisweet chocolate curls, optional

Line a greased 15-in. x 10-in. x 1-in. baking pan with waxed paper; grease the paper and set aside.

In a large bowl, beat the eggs for 3 minutes. Gradually add sugar; beat for 2 minutes or until mixture becomes thick and lemon-colored. Beat in the water and vanilla. Combine the flour, cocoa, baking powder and salt; fold into the egg mixture (the batter will be thin).

Spread evenly into prepared pan. Bake at 375° for 10-13 minutes or until cake springs back when lightly touched. Cool for 5 minutes.

Invert cake onto a kitchen towel dusted with 2 teaspoons confectioners' sugar. Gently peel off waxed paper. Roll up cake in the towel jelly-roll style, starting with a short side. Cool completely on a wire rack.

Unroll cake; spread ice cream evenly over cake to within 1/2 in. of edges. Roll up again. Place seam side down on a serving platter. Freeze until firm. Just before serving, dust with remaining confectioners' sugar. Garnish with chocolate curls if desired. YIELD: 10 servings.

Place the apples and raspberries in a large bowl. Add sugar and 3 tablespoons all-purpose flour; toss gently to coat. Transfer to a greased 13-in. x 9-in. baking dish.

In a small bowl, combine the oats, brown sugar, whole wheat flour and remaining all-purpose flour. Cut in butter until crumbly; sprinkle over top (dish will be full).

Bake, uncovered, at 350° for 40-50 minutes or until the filling is bubbly and the topping is golden brown. Serve warm. YIELD: 12 servings.

CHOCOLATE CHERRY PIE

LISA VARNER ❖ CHARLESTON, SOUTH CAROLINA

You may want to make two of these easy ice cream pies to serve and the other to store in the freezer for company. The combination of chocolate and cherries is irresistible.

> 3/4 cup dried cherries
> 2 cups boiling water
> 3-1/2 cups chocolate ice cream, softened
> 3/4 cup miniature semisweet chocolate chips
> 1 chocolate crumb crust (9 inches)
> Hot fudge ice cream topping and maraschino cherries, optional

Place dried cherries in a small bowl; cover with boiling water. Let stand for 5 minutes; drain.

In a large bowl, combine the ice cream, chocolate chips and cherries. Spread into crust. Cover and freeze until firm.

Slice; drizzle each piece with fudge topping and garnish with a maraschino cherry if desired. YIELD: 8 servings.

🏵 APPLE RASPBERRY CRISP

GINGER PRICE ❖ ELVERSON, PENNSYLVANIA

This crisp is so delicious served with a scoop of vanilla ice cream. Guests are sure to love the crumble topping and sweet-tart filling.

> 10 cups thinly sliced peeled tart apples (about 10 medium)
> 4 cups fresh raspberries
> 1/3 cup sugar
> 3 tablespoons plus 3/4 cup all-purpose flour, *divided*
> 1-1/2 cups old-fashioned oats
> 1 cup packed brown sugar
> 3/4 cup whole wheat flour
> 3/4 cup cold butter

A BIT ABOUT OATS

Although quick-cooking and old-fashioned oats are processed differently, they can be used interchangeably in recipes. However, old-fashioned oats will give the recipe outcome a more chewy texture.

CHOCOLATE TREASURE BOXES

SAMUEL NICHOLS ❖ MESA, ARIZONA

This tasteful container is constructed with candy bars. Consider personalizing the box lid with a conversation heart or a special message written with white chocolate or frosting.

1 carton (7 ounces) milk chocolate for dipping
4 fresh strawberries
5 milk chocolate candy bars (1.55 ounces *each*)
1/2 cup vanilla *or* white chips, melted
1/2 cup cold milk
1/4 cup instant chocolate pudding mix
1-1/4 cups whipped topping

Melt dipping chocolate according to package directions; dip strawberries into chocolate and allow excess to drip off. Place on a waxed paper-lined baking sheet; set aside.

Cut candy bars in half widthwise. Drizzle with white chocolate; refrigerate until set. Dip the short sides of two candy bar halves into melted chocolate; place at right angles to each other on a waxed paper-lined baking sheet, forming two walls of a box. Dip the short sides of two more candy bar halves; attach at right angles to form a four-walled box. Repeat, forming a second box. Refrigerate boxes and strawberries until set, about 10 minutes.

Meanwhile, in a small bowl, whisk milk and pudding mix for 2 minutes. Let stand for 2 minutes or until soft-set; fold in whipped topping.

Place boxes on serving plates. Cut a small hole in the corner of a pastry or plastic bag; insert star pastry tip. Fill bag with pudding mixture; pipe into boxes.

Reheat dipping chocolate if necessary. Dip the long sides of the remaining candy bar halves into melted chocolate; adhere to a top edge of each box, forming a lid. Garnish with chocolate-covered strawberries. Refrigerate for 10 minutes or until set. YIELD: 2 boxes (2 servings each).

PEANUT BUTTER-FILLED BROWNIE CUPCAKES

CAROL GILLESPIE ❖ CHAMBERSBURG, PENNSYLVANIA

I have made this outstandingly delicious recipe for years. These rich cupcakes are sure to delight everyone you share them with.

    1 package fudge brownie mix (8-inch square pan size)
1/2 cup miniature semisweet chocolate chips
1/3 cup creamy peanut butter
    3 tablespoons cream cheese, softened
    1 egg
1/4 cup sugar
1/2 teaspoon confectioners' sugar

Prepare brownie batter according to package directions; stir in chocolate chips. For filling, in a small bowl, beat peanut butter, cream cheese, egg and sugar until smooth.

Fill paper-lined muffin cups one-third full with batter. Drop filling by teaspoonfuls into the center of each cupcake. Cover with remaining batter.

Bake at 350° for 15-20 minutes or until a toothpick inserted in brownie portion comes out clean. Cool for 10 minutes before removing from pan to a wire rack to cool completely. Dust with confectioners' sugar. Store in the refrigerator. YIELD: 1 dozen.

TINY BANANA CREAM PIES

JENNIFER LOEWEN ❖ ALTONA, BRITISH COLUMBIA

These petite pies take very little time to prepare and make an impressive, delectable dessert. Since my husband's work hours are erratic, we don't eat at the same time every day, so I often have these chilling in the refrigerator several hours in advance of mealtime.

    1 cup cold milk
1/3 cup instant vanilla pudding mix
    1 small banana, sliced
    4 individual graham cracker tart shells
1/2 cup whipped topping
    2 tablespoons flaked coconut, toasted
Additional banana slices, optional

In a small bowl, whisk milk and pudding mix for 2 minutes. Arrange the banana slices over the tart shell bottoms; top with the pudding.

Cover with whipped topping; sprinkle with coconut. Cover and refrigerate until serving. Garnish with additional banana slices if desired. YIELD: 4 servings.

CHOCOLATE SNACK CAKE

DEVOTA ANGELL ✦ ALLENSTOWN, NEW HAMPSHIRE

I have made this cake for over 50 years. Otherwise known as "crazy cake," this classic, tender and moist confection requires only a two-step procedure to make.

1/2 cup sugar
1/2 cup water
2 tablespoons plus 1 teaspoon canola oil
1-1/2 teaspoons white vinegar
1/2 teaspoon vanilla extract
3/4 cup all-purpose flour
4-1/2 teaspoons baking cocoa
1/2 teaspoon baking soda
1/4 teaspoon salt
Confectioners' sugar, optional

In a small bowl, beat the sugar, water, oil, vinegar and vanilla until well blended. Combine the flour, cocoa, baking soda and salt; gradually beat into sugar mixture until blended.

Pour into a greased 9-in. x 5-in. loaf pan. Bake at 350° for 20-25 minutes or until a toothpick inserted near the center comes out clean.

Cool for 10 minutes before removing from pan to a wire rack to cool completely. Dust with confectioners' sugar if desired. YIELD: 4 servings.

EDITOR'S NOTE: This recipe does not use eggs.

PEACHES & CREAM PIE

PATRICIA RITTER ✦ LEESBURG, FLORIDA

When fresh peaches are available, I make this pie all the time. My husband and I periodically sponsor a dessert party for our friends, and the peach cream pie remains as everyone's favorite.

1 sheet refrigerated pie pastry
1 egg
1/2 cup half-and-half cream
1/4 cup sugar
1 tablespoon all-purpose flour
1 tablespoon butter, melted
2 cups sliced peeled fresh or frozen peaches, thawed

Cut pastry sheet in half. Repackage and refrigerate one half for another use. On a lightly floured surface, roll out remaining half into an 8-in. circle. Transfer to a 7-in. pie plate; flute edges.

Line unpricked pastry shell with a double thickness of heavy-duty foil. Bake at 400° for 8 minutes. Remove foil; bake 5 minutes longer. Cool on a wire rack.

In a small bowl, combine the egg, cream, sugar, flour and butter. Arrange peach slices in crust; pour egg mixture over top. Bake for 10 minutes.

Reduce heat to 350°. Bake 35-45 minutes longer or until center is almost set. Cool on a wire rack. Store in the refrigerator. YIELD: 4 servings.

PEELING FRESH PEACHES

Place peaches in a large pot of boiling water for 10-20 seconds or until the skin splits. Remove with a slotted spoon and immediately place in an ice water bath to cool. Use a paring knife to peel the skin, which should easily peel off.

COOKING FOR TWO

For recipes that are small in quantity but big on taste,
turn to these yummy dishes that are the perfect size for a duo.

CREAMED SPINACH AND MUSHROOMS

MICHELLE FERRARIO ❖ IJAMSVILLE, MARYLAND

When my gang was snowed in one time, we had to make do with what we had on hand, so I was able to put this recipe together. I find that it is very versatile and takes only 10 minutes to make from start to finish.

1-1/2 cups sliced fresh mushrooms
   2 tablespoons olive oil
1/2 teaspoon butter
   1 package (6 ounces) fresh baby spinach
   3 ounces reduced-fat cream cheese, cubed
1/4 teaspoon salt
1/8 teaspoon pepper

ABOUT BABY SPINACH

Baby spinach is simply a variety of spinach with a small flat leaf that is tender in texture. Found in grocery stores in bulk or in several different size cellophane bags already cleaned, it can be eaten cooked or uncooked.

In a small skillet, saute mushrooms in oil and butter until tender. Add spinach; cover and cook for 1 minute or until wilted.

Stir in the cream cheese, salt and pepper. Serve immediately. YIELD: 2 servings.

ONION BRUNCH PIE

KERRY MASON ❖ KENDALLVILLE, INDIANA

I found this recipe in a cookbook in a chapter called, "Recipes for Busy Days." I love quiche but hate the hassle in making a crust. This recipe solves that problem for me. I continue to make this dish for brunches, and it's a favorite for our family Christmas breakfast.

1-1/2 cups thinly sliced onions
   2 tablespoons butter, *divided*
   3 eggs
1/2 cup 2% milk
1/4 teaspoon salt
1/8 teaspoon pepper
1/4 cup shredded cheddar cheese
1/2 cup crushed saltines (about 15 crackers)

In a large skillet over medium heat, cook onions in 1 tablespoon butter for 8-10 minutes or until golden brown, stirring frequently. Remove from the heat.

In a small bowl, beat the eggs, milk, salt and pepper. Stir in onions. Pour into a greased 7-in. pie plate. Sprinkle with cheese. Melt remaining butter; toss with cracker crumbs. Sprinkle over the cheese.

Bake at 350° for 30-35 minutes or until a knife inserted near the center comes out clean. Let stand for 5 minutes before cutting. YIELD: 2 servings.

ITALIAN CHICKEN SALAD SANDWICHES

GIOVANNA KRANENBERG ✤ MAHNOMEN, MINNESOTA

My whole family loves this recipe. The Italian pickled vegetables give it a distinctive taste. I also serve it on a bed of lettuce or as an appetizer on crackers.

2/3 cup shredded cooked chicken breast
3 tablespoons shredded carrot
3 tablespoons finely chopped celery
2 tablespoons mild giardiniera, chopped
2 teaspoons finely chopped onion
1 small garlic clove, minced
1/4 cup fat-free mayonnaise
Dash pepper
4 slices sourdough bread
2 lettuce leaves

In a small bowl, combine the first six ingredients. Add the mayonnaise and pepper; toss to coat. Spoon 1/2 cup salad onto two bread slices; top with the lettuce and remaining bread. YIELD: 2 servings.

BEEF STEW FOR TWO

ALLISON ECTOR ✤ ARDMORE, PENNSYLVANIA

Here's an easy stew that's ready in just an hour...even though it offers a simmered-all-day flavor. The tender beef and colorful vegetables are the perfect ingredients for a comforting meal.

1/4 cup all-purpose flour
1/2 teaspoon dried thyme, *divided*
3/4 pound beef cubed steaks, cubed
1 tablespoon canola oil
1 cup water
1 can (8 ounces) tomato sauce
1/2 cup beef broth
1 small potato, peeled and cubed
1/2 small onion, cut into wedges
1/2 cup sliced fresh carrots
1/3 cup chopped sweet red pepper
1 teaspoon onion soup mix
1 teaspoon Worcestershire sauce
1/2 teaspoon dried rosemary, crushed
1/4 teaspoon garlic powder
1/4 teaspoon pepper
1/2 cup frozen peas

In a large resealable plastic bag, combine flour and 1/4 teaspoon thyme. Add beef, a few pieces at a time, and shake to coat.

In a large skillet, brown meat in oil on all sides. Add the water, tomato sauce, broth, potato, onion, carrots, red pepper, soup mix, Worcestershire sauce, rosemary, garlic powder, pepper and remaining thyme.

Bring to a boil. Reduce heat; simmer, uncovered, for 45 minutes. Stir in peas. Return to a boil. Reduce heat; simmer 5-10 minutes longer. YIELD: 2 servings.

GRITS CASSEROLE

LEAH SELLERS ✤ FLORENCE, KANSAS

This recipe belonged to my husband's great aunt, and we think she clipped it from a newspaper. The unusual casserole quickly became a family favorite, often requested at reunions, birthday or holiday dinners. Even though the recipe was shared with many, nobody could quite duplicate Aunt Hazel's most popular dish.

2 cups water
1/2 teaspoon salt
1/2 cup quick-cooking grits
3/4 cup shredded cheddar cheese
2 tablespoons butter
2 tablespoons beaten egg
1/4 teaspoon garlic powder
Dash hot pepper sauce
2/3 cup corn chips, crushed

In a small saucepan, bring water and salt to a boil. Slowly stir in grits. Reduce heat; cook and stir for 4-5 minutes or until thickened.

Remove from the heat. Stir in the cheese, butter, egg substitute, garlic powder and pepper sauce.

Pour into a small greased baking dish. Sprinkle with corn chips. Bake, uncovered, at 325° for 20-25 minutes or until bubbly. YIELD: 2 servings.

PERSONAL VEGGIE PIZZAS

AMBER GERRITY ✤ WEST SENECA, NEW YORK

My mom and I like eating healthy—so this figure-friendly pizza is our favorite. The assorted veggies and the crisp, golden crust is so tasty, no one will miss the sauce.

    1 package (6-1/2 ounces) pizza crust mix
    2 tablespoons olive oil
    2 garlic cloves, minced
1/2 teaspoon dried oregano
1/4 teaspoon salt
1/4 teaspoon pepper
    2 tablespoons grated Parmesan cheese
    1 plum tomato, thinly sliced
1/4 cup crumbled tomato and basil feta cheese
    1 cup (4 ounces) shredded part-skim mozzarella cheese
1/4 cup chopped sweet onion
3/4 cup sliced fresh mushrooms
1/4 cup chopped fresh or frozen chopped broccoli
1/4 to 1/2 teaspoon crushed red pepper flakes

Prepare crust mix according to package directions. Divide dough in half; press each into a 7-in. circle on a greased baking sheet. Build up edges slightly.

In a small bowl, combine the oil, garlic, oregano, salt and pepper; spread over crusts. Sprinkle with Parmesan cheese. Top with tomato, feta, mozzarella, onion, mushrooms, broccoli and pepper flakes.

Bake at 450° for 12-15 minutes or until crust is golden brown and cheese is melted. YIELD: 2 servings.

MOUSSAKA

MARJORIE PALLA ✤ MORAGA, CALIFORNIA

A nice surprise in this moussaka recipe is the touch of cinnamon, just enough to give it a fresh taste. This dish would serve nicely as a meatless entree.

    1 small onion, chopped
    1 garlic clove, minced
    4 teaspoons canola oil, *divided*
    2 medium tomatoes, peeled and chopped
    1 tablespoon lemon juice
    1 teaspoon dried basil
1/4 teaspoon salt
1/8 teaspoon ground cinnamon
1/8 teaspoon pepper
    1 small eggplant, cut into 1/4-inch slices
1/3 cup shredded Swiss cheese

In a small skillet, saute onion and garlic in 1 teaspoon oil until tender. Stir in the tomatoes, lemon juice, basil, salt, cinnamon and pepper. Bring to a boil. Reduce heat; simmer, uncovered, for 15 minutes.

Meanwhile, brush eggplant slices with remaining oil. Broil 4 in. from the heat for 1-2 minutes on each side or until lightly browned. Spread 2 tablespoons sauce mixture into a greased 3-cup baking dish. Top with half of the eggplant slices. Spread with 1/2 cup sauce mixture. Repeat layers. Cover and bake at 350° for 20 minutes. Uncover; sprinkle with cheese. Bake 5-10 minutes longer or until cheese is melted. YIELD: 2 servings.

NEW YEAR'S EVE TENDERLOIN STEAKS

AGNES WARD ❖ STRATFORD, ONTARIO

I found this recipe in a cookbook I bought on a cruise. My friend and I tried it, and it is now one of our favorites.

2 beef tenderloin steaks (1 inch thick and 5 ounces *each*)
1/4 teaspoon pepper
1 tablespoon canola oil
3 shallots, finely chopped
2 tablespoons Cognac
1/4 teaspoon whole peppercorns, crushed
1/2 cup dry red wine *or* beef broth
1/4 cup beef broth
2 ounces fresh goat cheese, crumbled

Sprinkle steaks with pepper. In a large skillet, cook steaks in oil over medium heat for 4-6 minutes on each side or until meat reaches desired doneness (for medium-rare, a meat thermometer should read 145°; medium, 160°; well-done, 170°). Remove to a baking sheet and keep warm.

Reduce the heat to low and add the shallots, Cognac and peppercorns, stirring to loosen browned bits from pan. Stir in wine and broth. Bring to a boil over medium heat; cook until liquid is reduced to 1/2 cup.

Top steaks with cheese. Broil 6 in. from the heat for 2-3 minutes or until cheese is soft. Serve sauce mixture with steaks. YIELD: 2 servings.

PORTOBELLO-SPINACH SALAD

LISA WALLER ❖ ESCONDIDO, CALIFORNIA

This salad makes a great entree as well. The flavor of the onions and mushrooms is enhanced by the dressing.

4-1/2 teaspoons balsamic vinegar
2 tablespoons plus 1-1/2 teaspoons olive oil
1-1/2 teaspoons minced fresh basil *or* 1/2 teaspoon dried basil
1-1/2 teaspoons Dijon mustard
1 small garlic clove, minced
1/8 teaspoon salt
1/8 teaspoon pepper
SALAD
1 large portobello mushroom, sliced
1 small onion, thinly sliced
1 tablespoon olive oil
2 cups fresh baby spinach
1/2 cup cherry tomatoes, halved
2 tablespoons crumbled Gorgonzola cheese

In a small bowl, whisk the first seven ingredients; set aside.

In a large skillet, saute mushroom and onion in oil until tender. In a serving bowl, combine the spinach, mushroom mixture and tomatoes. Drizzle with dressing; toss to coat. Sprinkle with cheese. YIELD: 2 servings.

ROASTED GARLIC TWICE-BAKED POTATO

NANCY MUELLER ❖ MENOMONEE FALLS, WISCONSIN

The creamy texture flavored with the roasted garlic makes this potato side dish a winner. It's easy to prepare and a perfect choice to accompany a hearty meat entree.

1 large baking potato
1 teaspoon canola oil, *divided*
6 garlic cloves, unpeeled
2 tablespoons butter, softened
2 tablespoons 2% milk
2 tablespoons sour cream
1/4 teaspoon minced fresh rosemary *or* dash dried rosemary, crushed
1/8 teaspoon salt
1/8 teaspoon pepper

Scrub and pierce potato; rub with 1/2 teaspoon oil. Place garlic on a double thickness of heavy-duty foil. Drizzle with remaining oil. Wrap foil around garlic. Place potato and garlic on a baking sheet. Bake at 400° for 15 minutes. Remove garlic; bake potato 45 minutes longer or until tender.

When potato is cool enough to handle, cut potato in half lengthwise. Scoop out the pulp, leaving thin shells.

Squeeze softened garlic into a small bowl; add potato pulp and mash. Stir in remaining ingredients. Spoon into potato shells. Place on an ungreased baking sheet. Bake, uncovered, at 350° for 25-30 minutes or until heated through. YIELD: 2 servings.

CHOCOLATE LAVA CAKES

HEIDI WILCOX ❖ LAPEER, MICHIGAN

Since this dessert is served hot, it can be baking in the oven while you eat the main course. The recipe can easily be increased to serve more. It's a great choice for those who are chocolate lovers.

1/3 cup semisweet chocolate chips
1/4 cup butter, cubed
1/3 cup superfine sugar
1 egg
4-1/2 teaspoons all-purpose flour
1/4 cup white baking chips
Confectioners' sugar

Grease the bottom and sides of two 6-oz. ramekins or custard cups. Place ramekins on a baking sheet; set aside.

In a microwave, melt semisweet chocolate and butter; stir until smooth. Set aside to cool.

Combine sugar, egg and flour; stir in chocolate mixture. Fold in white baking chips. Spoon batter into prepared ramekins.

Bake at 400° for 15-18 minutes or until a thermometer reads 160° and cake sides are set. Remove ramekins to a wire rack to cool for 5 minutes. Invert onto serving plates; dust with confectioners' sugar. YIELD: 2 servings.

BAVARIAN BEEF PIE

CINDY SECOR ✦ GRAHAM, WASHINGTON

I found this recipe in an old church cookbook of my grandmother's when I was in 4-H. With its combination of ingredients and spices, it has a unique flavor that receives rave reviews when we fix it for family and friends.

    1 cup all-purpose flour
1/4 teaspoon salt
1/3 cup shortening
    2 egg yolks, *divided*
1/4 teaspoon white vinegar
    1 tablespoon plus 2 to 3 teaspoons cold water

FILLING
    1 beef top sirloin steak (3/4 pound), cut into 1/2-inch cubes
    2 teaspoons canola oil
    1 tablespoon butter
    1 small potato, peeled and cut into 1/2-inch cubes
    1 small onion, chopped

1/2 cup shredded peeled tart apple
    1 garlic clove, minced
    2 teaspoons all-purpose flour
1-1/2 teaspoons beef bouillon granules
    1 teaspoon minced fresh parsley
1/8 teaspoon celery seed
1/8 teaspoon dill weed
1/8 teaspoon dried thyme
1/8 teaspoon pepper
1/2 cup plus 2 teaspoons water, *divided*

In a small bowl, combine flour and salt; cut in the shortening until crumbly. Stir in 1 egg yolk and vinegar. Gradually add water, tossing with a fork until dough forms a ball. Divide dough in half so that one portion is slightly larger than the other. Cover and refrigerate for 30 minutes or until easy to handle.

Meanwhile, in a small skillet, brown beef in oil. Remove with a slotted spoon; set aside. In the same skillet, saute the potato, onion and apple in butter for 2-3 minutes or until onion is tender. Stir in garlic; cook 1 minute longer. Stir in flour until blended.

Add the bouillon, seasonings, beef and 1/2 cup water. Bring to a boil; cook and stir for 2 minutes or until thickened.

On a lightly floured surface, roll out larger portion of dough to fit a 7-in. pie plate. Transfer pastry to pie plate. Trim pastry even with edge. Fill with beef mixture. Roll out remaining pastry to fit top of pie. Place over filling. Trim, seal and flute edges. Cut slits in the pastry. Beat the remaining egg yolk and water; brush over pastry. Bake at 375° for 30-35 minutes or until golden brown. YIELD: 3 servings.

PUMPERNICKEL MUFFINS

NANCY MUELLER ❖ BLOOMINGTON, MINNESOTA

These dense muffins are a perfect accompaniment to a hearty entree. The rye flour gives the muffins some texture and the dried cherries add flavor.

- 3/4 cup rye flour
- 2/3 cup all-purpose flour
- 3 tablespoons sugar
- 1 teaspoon baking powder
- 1/2 teaspoon ground cinnamon
- 1/4 teaspoon baking soda
- 1/4 teaspoon salt
- 1 egg
- 2/3 cup buttermilk
- 1/4 cup canola oil
- 1 tablespoon molasses
- 1/2 ounce unsweetened chocolate, melted and cooled
- 1/4 cup dried cherries

In a large bowl, combine the flours, sugar, baking powder, cinnamon, baking soda and salt.

In another bowl, combine the egg, buttermilk, oil, molasses and chocolate. Stir into dry ingredients just until moistened. Fold in cherries.

Fill greased or paper-lined muffin cups three-fourths full. Bake at 400° for 15-20 minutes or until a toothpick comes out clean. Cool for 5 minutes before removing from pan to a wire rack. Serve warm. YIELD: 6 muffins.

SPINACH SALAD WITH HOT BACON DRESSING

WANDA COVER ❖ MEDIAPOLIS, IOWA

After having a salad like this at a restaurant years ago, I came up with this recipe. It is especially good when the spinach comes right from the garden to the table.

- 2 cups fresh baby spinach, torn
- 2 hard-cooked eggs, sliced
- 4 cherry tomatoes, halved
- 3 medium fresh mushrooms, sliced
- 1/4 cup salad croutons
- 6 pitted ripe olives, halved
- 3 slices red onion, halved

DRESSING
- 4 bacon strips, diced
- 1 tablespoon chopped onion
- 2 tablespoons sugar
- 2 tablespoons ketchup
- 1 tablespoon red wine vinegar
- 1 tablespoon Worcestershire sauce

Divide the spinach between two plates. Arrange the hard-cooked eggs, tomatoes, mushrooms, croutons, olives and red onion over the top.

In a small skillet, cook bacon over medium heat until crisp. Using a slotted spoon, remove to paper towels; drain, reserving 2 tablespoons drippings. Saute onion in drippings until tender.

Stir in the sugar, ketchup, vinegar and Worcestershire sauce. Bring to a boil. Reduce heat; simmer, uncovered for 1-2 minutes or until thickened. Sprinkle bacon over salads; drizzle with dressing. YIELD: 2 servings.

APPLE CREAM CHEESE KUCHEN

TRUDY WOLBERT ❖ MARYVILLE, MISSOURI

This is a very old recipe that my mother made often, when I was a child in Germany. It was our Sunday dessert. You can also use other fruit as a topping, such as plums, fresh peaches or apricots.

- 1-1/4 teaspoons active dry yeast
- 2 tablespoons warm water (110° to 115°)
- 1 egg
- 1/4 cup warm milk (110° to 115°)
- 2 tablespoons butter, softened
- 2 tablespoons sugar
- 1 teaspoon grated lemon peel
- 1/4 teaspoon salt
- 1-1/4 to 1-1/2 cups all-purpose flour

TOPPING
- 4 ounces cream cheese, softened
- 1 tablespoon sugar
- 1 large tart apple, peeled and sliced
- 2 teaspoons butter, melted

Confectioners' sugar

In a small bowl, dissolve yeast in warm water. Add the egg, milk, butter, sugar, lemon peel, salt and 3/4 cup flour. Beat until smooth. Stir in enough remaining flour to form a soft dough (dough will be sticky).

Turn onto a floured surface. With floured hands, knead until smooth and elastic, about 6-8 minutes. Press into a greased 8-in. square baking dish; build up edges slightly.

For topping, in a small bowl, combine cream cheese and sugar. Gently spread over dough. Arrange apple slices over top; brush with butter. Cover and let rise in a warm place until doubled, about 1 hour.

Bake at 350° for 30-40 minutes or until golden brown and apples are tender. Cool on a wire rack. Dust with confectioners' sugar. Refrigerate leftovers. YIELD: 6 servings.

Sweet Treats for Two

Sometimes you just want a little something to end your craving for sweets, and these recipes make modest servings. They're the perfect size for a pair.

APPLE DUMPLINGS WITH CARAMEL SAUCE

LOIS STACHE ✤ BRILLION, WISCONSIN

Of all my autumn recipes, apple dumplings are a hands-down favorite. I found this treat years ago in an Amish cookbook. A scrumptious, homemade caramel sauce tops them off.

2/3 cup all-purpose flour
  2 teaspoons sugar
1/2 teaspoon baking powder
1/8 teaspoon salt
1/4 cup cold butter, cubed
1/4 cup milk
  2 medium apples, peeled and cored
  4 teaspoons brown sugar
1/4 teaspoon ground cinnamon
  4 teaspoons butter

SAUCE
  2 teaspoons all-purpose flour
1/2 cup water
1/3 cup sugar
1/3 cup packed brown sugar
  3 tablespoons butter
Dash salt

In a small bowl, combine the flour, sugar, baking powder and salt; cut in cold butter until crumbly. Gradually add milk, tossing with a fork until dough forms a ball; divide dough in half. Cover and refrigerate for 1 hour or until easy to handle.

On a well-floured surface, roll each portion of dough into an 8-in. square. Cut apples in half horizontally; place an apple bottom on each square. Place brown sugar and cinnamon in the core of each bottom; dot each with 2 teaspoons butter. Replace apple tops.

Gently bring up corners of pastry to center; pinch edges to seal. Place in a greased 8-in. baking dish. Bake, uncovered, at 350° for 15 minutes.

Meanwhile, in a small saucepan, combine flour and water until smooth. Add the sugars, butter and salt. Bring to a boil; cook and stir until smooth and blended. Pour over dumplings.

Bake 35-40 minutes longer or until apples are tender and pastry is golden brown. Serve warm. YIELD: 2 servings.

RASPBERRY PARFAITS

JOELYN HANHAM ✤ CHESTER, NEW YORK

Looking for a carefree way to impress someone special? These rich and creamy raspberry parfaits are guaranteed to dazzle them.

  2 ounces cream cheese, softened
  2 tablespoons seedless raspberry jam
1/2 cup whipped topping, *divided*
1/2 cup fresh *or* frozen raspberries

In a small bowl, beat cream cheese and jam until smooth. Fold in 1/4 cup whipped topping.

Place 2 tablespoons raspberries in each of two small parfait glasses or dessert dishes; layer with cream cheese mixture and remaining berries. Top with remaining whipped topping. Refrigerate until serving. YIELD: 2 servings.

RAISIN-NUT BREAD PUDDING

LAVERNA M.JONES ✤ MOORHEAD, MINNESOTA

My husband and I are retired and our children are all grown, so this small-size dessert works perfectly for us. When my oldest son comes to eat, dinner wouldn't be complete if I didn't serve this bread pudding for dessert.

      1 cup soft bread cubes
      1 egg
  2/3 cup milk
      3 tablespoons brown sugar
      1 tablespoon butter, melted
  1/2 teaspoon ground cinnamon
  1/4 teaspoon ground nutmeg
Dash salt
  1/3 cup raisins
  1/4 cup chopped walnuts

WHAT IS BREAD PUDDING?

Bread puddings are made with cubes or slices of bread baked in a custard mixture. They can be enriched with fruits, nuts, chocolate and spices. Bread puddings are done when a knife inserted near the center comes out clean.

Whipped cream and ground cinnamon

Place bread cubes in a greased 20-oz. baking dish.

In a bowl, whisk egg and milk. Add brown sugar, butter, cinnamon, nutmeg and salt; mix well. Pour over bread; sprinkle with raisins and nuts.

Bake, uncovered, at 350° for 35-40 minutes or until a knife inserted near the center comes out clean.

Serve warm with whipped cream; sprinkle with cinnamon. YIELD: 2 servings.

LIME PARADISE

ADDISON GLAZNER ✤ DUMAS, TEXAS

I am 10 years old and love to watch my mom cook. I also enjoy watching cooking programs on TV. One hot day last summer, Mom let me experiment with something cool and refreshing. When I was done, I had a messy but very tasty drink that is full of lime flavor.

  1/4 cup fresh mint leaves
  1/4 cup lime juice
      2 tablespoons sugar
Ice cubes
      2 cups water

In two rocks glasses, muddle the mint, lime juice and sugar. Add ice; pour in water. YIELD: 2 servings.

TWICE-BAKED SWEET POTATOES

LINDA CALL ✤ FALUN, KANSAS

I like to make these twice-baked potatoes because they can be prepared ahead of time. With the addition of cream cheese, they are very rich and not overly sweet. It is so easy to increase the quantity to any number.

- 2 medium sweet potatoes
- 2 ounces cream cheese, softened
- 1 tablespoon brown sugar
- 1/4 teaspoon ground cinnamon
- 2 tablespoons chopped pecans

Scrub and pierce the sweet potatoes. Bake at 375° for 1-1/4 hours or until tender. When cool enough to handle, cut a thin slice off the top of each potato and discard. Scoop out the pulp, leaving thin shells.

In a small bowl, mash the sweet potato pulp with the cream cheese. Stir in the brown sugar and cinnamon. Spoon into the potato shells and then sprinkle with the chopped pecans. Place on a baking sheet.

Bake, uncovered, at 375° for 15-20 minutes or until heated through. YIELD: 2 servings.

BACON JALAPENO POPPERS

BERNICE KNUTSON ✤ DANBURY, IOWA

For a scrumptious appetizer for two, try this spicy recipe that is better than a restaurant's version. The bacon adds a smoky flavor to the traditional popper.

- 2 bacon strips, halved
- 4 teaspoons shredded Colby cheese
- 4 teaspoons cream cheese, softened
- 2 jalapeno peppers, halved lengthwise and seeded

In a small skillet, cook the bacon strips over medium heat until partially cooked but not crisp. Remove to paper towels to drain and keep warm.

Combine cheeses; spread into each pepper half. Wrap a piece of bacon around each pepper half. Place on a baking sheet.

Bake, uncovered, at 350° for 20-25 minutes or until bacon is crisp and filling is heated through. YIELD: 2 servings.

EDITOR'S NOTE: When cutting hot peppers, disposable gloves are recommended. Avoid touching your face.

SOUTHWESTERN SHEPHERD'S PIE

VERONICA GRECO ✤ TAMPA, FLORIDA

This wonderful dish is perfectly portioned for two. It can be served alone or with a side salad and corn bread. It has a delectable flavor with some spice!

- 2 medium potatoes, peeled and cubed
- 1/2 pound lean ground beef (90% lean)
- 1/2 cup canned diced tomatoes
- 1/3 cup medium salsa
- 2 tablespoons canned chopped green chilies
- 1/2 teaspoon salt, *divided*
- 1/2 teaspoon pepper, *divided*
- 1 cup (4 ounces) shredded cheddar cheese, *divided*
- 1 cup frozen corn
- 2 tablespoons butter

Place potatoes in a large saucepan and cover with water. Bring to a boil. Reduce heat; cover and simmer for 10-15 minutes or until tender.

Meanwhile, in a large skillet, cook beef over medium heat until no longer pink; drain. Stir in tomatoes, salsa, chilies and 1/4 teaspoon salt and pepper; heat through. Stir in 1/2 cup cheese. Transfer to a greased 4-cup baking dish; sprinkle with corn.

Drain potatoes and place in a large bowl. Mash potatoes with butter and remaining salt and pepper. Spread over top; sprinkle with remaining cheese.

Bake at 350° for 20-25 minutes or until pie is bubbly. YIELD: 2 servings.

PEPPER JACK MUFFINS

DEBORAH FORREST ✤ OCEAN SPRINGS, MISSISSIPPI

Here's a great change-of-pace recipe everyone is sure to enjoy. This savory muffin recipe is ideal with soup, chili or your favorite casserole. Use cheddar instead of pepper Jack for a milder muffin.

- 1 cup all-purpose flour
- 1 tablespoon sugar
- 1 teaspoon baking powder
- 1/4 teaspoon salt
- 1 egg
- 1/2 cup milk
- 2 tablespoons butter, melted
- 1/3 cup shredded pepper Jack cheese

In a small bowl, combine the flour, sugar, baking powder and salt. In another bowl, combine the egg, milk and butter. Stir into dry ingredients just until moistened. Fold in cheese.

Fill greased muffin cups three-fourths full. Bake at 400° for 15-20 minutes or until a toothpick comes out clean. Cool for 5 minutes before removing from pan to a wire rack. Serve warm. YIELD: 5 muffins.

CREAMY FLAN

AMANDA PETTIT ✤ LOGAN, OHIO

Flan has always been a hit with my family and friends so I downsized it to be just enough for two. It is such a delicious and creamy dessert!

    5 tablespoons sugar, *divided*
    1 cup milk
    1/3 cup egg substitute
1-1/2 teaspoons vanilla extract

In a small skillet over medium-low heat, cook 3 tablespoons sugar until melted, about 5 minutes. Do not stir. Reduce heat to low; cook for 5 minutes or until syrup is golden brown, stirring occasionally. Quickly pour into two ungreased 6-ounce custard cups or ramekins, tilting to coat bottom of dish. Let stand for about 10 minutes.

In a small saucepan, heat milk until bubbles form around sides of saucepan. Remove from the heat. In a small bowl, whisk egg substitute and remaining sugar. Stir half of the warm milk into egg mixture; return all to pan and mix well. Add vanilla. Slowly pour into prepared dishes.

Place dishes in a baking pan. Fill pan with boiling water to a depth of 3/4 in. Bake at 325° for 25-30 minutes or until center is just set (mixture will jiggle). Remove to a wire rack; cool for 1 hour. Refrigerate for at least 1 hour.

Run a knife around edge and invert each dish onto a small rimmed serving dish. Refrigerate leftovers. YIELD: 2 servings.

VENISON STEW

EDWARD MARTIN ❖ CORNING, OHIO

This flavorful stew works well with a variety of wild game. The meat turns out to be very tender, and the sauce is thick, with a nice pepper presence. We like the stew on the spicy side, so season to your taste.

  1/3 cup all-purpose flour
  1/4 teaspoon salt
  1/8 teaspoon pepper
  1/2 pound venison stew meat *or* boneless beef chuck roast, cut into 1-inch cubes
    2 tablespoons bacon drippings *or* canola oil
  1/3 cup chopped onion
    1 cup water
    1 small tomato, peeled and chopped
    1 teaspoon cider vinegar
    1 small garlic clove, minced
    1 bay leaf
    1 small carrot, sliced
    1 small potato, peeled and cubed
  1/4 cup chopped celery
  1/4 teaspoon lemon-pepper seasoning
  1/8 teaspoon cayenne pepper

In a large resealable plastic bag, combine the flour, salt and pepper. Add venison, a few pieces at a time, and shake to coat.

In a large heavy saucepan, brown meat in drippings on all sides. Add onion; cook and stir for 1 minute. Stir in the water, tomato, vinegar, garlic and bay leaf. Bring to a boil. Reduce heat; cover and simmer for 1 to 1-1/2 hours or until meat is tender.

Stir in the carrot, potato, celery, lemon-pepper seasoning and cayenne. Return to a boil. Reduce heat; cover and simmer 30-35 minutes longer or until vegetables are tender. Discard bay leaf. YIELD: 2 servings.

NAVAJO FRY BREAD

MILDRED STEPHENSON ❖ HARTSELLE, ALABAMA

While taking a trip to the Grand Canyon, my family drove through the Navajo reservation and stopped at a little cafe for dinner. I complimented the young Navajo waiter on the delicious bread he served to us and he gave me the recipe. It is very easy to make.

    1 cup all-purpose flour
    1 teaspoon baking powder
  1/8 teaspoon salt
  1/3 cup hot water
Oil for deep-fat frying

In a small bowl, combine the flour, baking powder and salt; stir in hot water to form a soft dough. Cover and let stand for about 30 minutes.

Divide dough in half. On a lightly floured surface, roll each portion into a 6-in. circle.

In an electric skillet, heat 1 in. of oil to 375°. Fry bread in hot oil for 2-3 minutes on each side or until golden brown; drain on paper towels. YIELD: 2 servings.

CRANBERRY-SESAME SPINACH SALAD

STEPHANIE SMOLEY ❖ ROCHESTER, MINNESOTA

This is a great salad for fall and is a refreshing side for a Thanksgiving feast. The dressing has a good balance of sweet and sour—the sesame and poppy seeds add crunch.

2 tablespoons slivered almonds
1 teaspoon butter
2-1/2 cups fresh baby spinach
2 tablespoons dried cranberries

DRESSING
2 tablespoons canola oil
1 tablespoon sugar
1 tablespoon cider vinegar
2 teaspoons sesame seeds, toasted
1/2 teaspoon dried minced onion
1/2 teaspoon poppy seeds
1/8 teaspoon salt
Dash paprika

In a small skillet, cook almonds and butter over low heat until almonds are lightly browned. In a serving bowl, combine the spinach and cranberries.

In a small bowl, whisk the dressing ingredients. Pour over salad; toss to coat. Sprinkle with almonds. YIELD: 2 servings.

BLUEBERRY CAKE WITH WOJAPI SAUCE

ANGELA "WINDDANCING" HATCHETT ❖ ALTOONA, ALABAMA

This is my grandmother's recipe, and the sauce is traditional Cherokee, which has been passed down for generations. It is very versatile and can be used on fry bread, pancakes, waffles and other desserts.

1/4 cup sugar
1/4 cup self-rising flour
1/4 cup milk
1/8 teaspoon vanilla extract
1 tablespoon butter, melted
1/4 cup fresh or frozen blueberries

WOJAPI SAUCE
2 tablespoons sugar
1-1/2 teaspoons cornstarch
1/4 cup water
1 cup fresh or frozen blueberries
Vanilla ice cream, optional

In a small bowl, combine sugar and flour; stir in milk and vanilla. Place butter in a greased 5-3/4-in. x 3-in. x 2-in. loaf pan. Pour batter into pan (do not stir). Sprinkle with blueberries.

Bake at 350° for 20-25 minutes or until a toothpick inserted near the center comes out clean. Cool for 10 minutes before inverting onto a serving plate.

In a small saucepan combine sugar and cornstarch. Stir in water until smooth; add blueberries. Cook and stir over medium heat until thickened and bubbly. Reduce heat; cook and stir 2 minutes longer. Serve warm over cake with ice cream if desired. YIELD: 2 servings.

SWISS MACARONI AND CHEESE

KATERI SCOTT ❖ AMSTERDAM, NEW YORK

Whenever we visited my husband's good friend, his wife made this dish. I was too shy to ask for the recipe, so I came up with this one. It is very creamy and rich, with a mild Swiss cheese flavor.

3/4 cup uncooked elbow macaroni
2 tablespoons chopped onion
2 tablespoons butter
1 tablespoon all-purpose flour
1 cup fat-free milk
1 cup (4 ounces) shredded Swiss cheese
1/4 teaspoon salt
1/8 teaspoon pepper

Cook macaroni according to package directions. Meanwhile, in a small saucepan, saute onion in butter until tender. Stir in flour until smooth; gradually add milk. Bring to a boil; cook and stir for 2 minutes or until thickened.

Add the cheese, salt and pepper. Drain macaroni. Add to cheese mixture; toss gently to coat. YIELD: 2 servings.

HONEY-GRILLED PORK TENDERLOIN

MILTON NICHOLAS ❖ BEAUMONT, TEXAS

I received this recipe from my daughter. We were having guests for dinner one night, and I thought this entree would be the perfect start in planning the menu.

    3 tablespoons reduced-sodium soy sauce
    2 garlic cloves, minced
    1/4 teaspoon ground ginger
    1 pork tenderloin (3/4 pound)
    4-1/2 teaspoons honey
    1 tablespoon brown sugar
    1 teaspoon sesame oil

In a large resealable plastic bag, combine the soy sauce, garlic and ginger; add the pork. Seal bag and turn to coat; refrigerate for at least 8 hours or overnight.

In a small saucepan, combine the honey, brown sugar and oil. Cook and stir over low heat until sugar is dissolved. Remove from the heat; set aside.

Drain and discard marinade. Moisten a paper towel with cooking oil; using long-handled tongs, lightly coat the grill rack. Prepare grill for indirect heat using a drip pan.

Place pork over drip pan and grill, covered, over indirect medium-hot heat for 20-25 minutes or until a meat thermometer reads 160°, basting frequently with honey mixture. Let stand for 5 minutes before slicing. YIELD: 2 servings.

SAUSAGE HASH

KARI CAVEN ❖ POST FALLS, IDAHO

I created this easy and quick recipe by using what I had in the refrigerator. Regular or spicy sausage can be used and red potatoes make it more colorful.

    1/2 pound bulk pork sausage
    2-1/2 cups cubed cooked potatoes

    1 cup thinly sliced sweet onion
    1 cup sliced fresh mushrooms
    2 tablespoons butter
    1/4 teaspoon salt
    1/4 teaspoon pepper

In a large heavy skillet over medium heat, cook the sausage until no longer pink; drain and set aside.

In the same skillet, cook the potatoes, onion and mushrooms in butter until potatoes are lightly browned. Stir in the sausage, salt and pepper; heat through. YIELD: 2 servings.

BLT SKILLET

EDRIE O'BRIEN ❖ DENVER, COLORADO

This weeknight meal is fast, and reminiscent of a BLT, with its chunks of bacon and tomato. The whole wheat linguine gives the skillet dish extra nutritional value and texture.

    4 ounces uncooked multigrain linguine
    4 bacon strips, cut into 1-1/2-inch pieces
    1 plum tomato, cut into 1-inch pieces
    1 garlic clove, minced
    1-1/2 teaspoons lemon juice
    1/4 teaspoon salt
    1/4 teaspoon pepper
    2 tablespoons grated Parmesan cheese
    1 tablespoon minced fresh parsley

Cook linguine according to package directions. Meanwhile, in a large skillet, cook bacon over medium heat until crisp. Remove to paper towels; drain, reserving 1 teaspoon drippings.

In the bacon drippings, saute the tomato and garlic for 1-2 minutes or until heated through. Stir in the bacon, lemon juice, salt and pepper.

Drain linguine; add to the skillet. Sprinkle with cheese and parsley; toss to coat. YIELD: 2 servings.

PORCUPINE MEATBALLS

VIOLET ALLWEIN ❖ LITITZ, PENNSYLVANIA

This was a favorite with my four boys as they grew up. The meatballs are tender, with a nice old-fashioned flavor.

1/4 cup uncooked instant rice
1/4 cup milk
  2 tablespoons chopped onion
1/4 teaspoon salt
1/4 teaspoon celery salt
1/8 teaspoon garlic salt
Dash pepper
1/2 pound ground beef
  1 tablespoon canola oil
  1 can (8 ounces) tomato sauce
1/2 cup water
1-1/2 teaspoons Worcestershire sauce

In a small bowl, combine the first seven ingredients. Crumble beef over mixture and mix well. Shape into four balls.

In a large skillet, brown meatballs in oil; drain. Stir in the tomato sauce, water and Worcestershire sauce. Bring to a boil. Reduce heat; cover and simmer for 30-35 minutes or until meatballs are no longer pink. YIELD: 2 servings.

BAKED ITALIAN TOMATOES

PHYLLIS SCHMALZ ❖ KANSAS CITY, KANSAS

I made this recipe into a family classic. We have a big garden each year, so most of the ingredients come right from the garden. There's nothing quite like a recipe made from fresh, traditionally Italian ingredients. Yum!

  2 large tomatoes
1/2 cup soft whole wheat bread crumbs
  2 tablespoons grated Parmesan cheese
  1 tablespoon olive oil
  1 garlic clove, minced
  1 teaspoon dried oregano
1/2 teaspoon dried basil
1/2 teaspoon dried thyme
1/4 teaspoon salt
1/4 teaspoon pepper

Halve and seed the tomatoes and invert onto paper towels to allow to drain.

In a small bowl, combine the remaining ingredients; spoon over tomato halves. Transfer to a greased 8-in. square baking dish. Bake, uncovered, at 350° for 25-30 minutes or until golden brown. YIELD: 2 servings.

MEALS IN MINUTES

A hot meal is easier to prepare than you think with these delectable recipes that each can be on the table in just 30 minutes...or less!

TURKEY WITH LIME BUTTER SAUCE

PATRICIA KILE ❖ ELIZABETHTOWN, PENNSYLVANIA

I also make this with leftover turkey from holiday meals. Just brown the meat lightly and it will give the sauce a wonderful flavor.

1/2 cup all-purpose flour
1/8 teaspoon salt
1/8 teaspoon Italian seasoning
1/8 teaspoon paprika
1/8 teaspoon pepper
 1 package (17.6 ounces) turkey breast cutlets
 2 tablespoons canola oil

LIME BUTTER SAUCE
 1 green onion, chopped
 2 garlic cloves, minced
1/4 cup reduced-sodium chicken broth
1/4 cup lime juice
1/2 cup butter, cubed
1/2 teaspoon minced chives
1/2 teaspoon minced fresh dill
1/2 teaspoon grated lime peel
Salt and pepper to taste

In a large resealable plastic bag, combine the first five ingredients. Add turkey, a few pieces at a time, and shake to coat. In a large skillet, cook turkey in oil in batches over medium heat for 1-2 minutes on each side or until meat is no longer pink. Remove and keep warm.

In the same skillet, cook the onion and garlic for about 1 minute. Add broth and lime juice stirring to loosen browned bits from pan. Bring to a boil. Reduce heat to low; stir in the remaining ingredients until butter is melted. Serve with turkey. YIELD: 4 servings.

SPICED ORANGE CHICKEN

ELIZABETH HACKETT ❖ TUCSON, ARIZONA

You'll want to add this jazzed-up chicken dish to your regular rotation of healthy poultry meals. The great orange and soy flavors meld perfectly with the herbs and spices.

 4 boneless skinless chicken breast halves (6 ounces *each*)
1/4 cup all-purpose flour
 1 teaspoon salt
1/4 teaspoon ground cinnamon
1/4 teaspoon ground cloves
1/4 teaspoon pepper
 1 tablespoon canola oil
 1 tablespoon butter
3/4 cup orange juice
 1 tablespoon brown sugar
 1 tablespoon soy sauce
 1 can (11 ounces) mandarin oranges, drained
Hot cooked rice

Flatten chicken to 1/2-in. thickness. In a large resealable plastic bag, combine the flour, salt, cinnamon, cloves and pepper. Add chicken, one piece at a time, and shake to coat.

In a large skillet over medium heat, cook chicken in oil and butter for 6-8 minutes on each side or until juices run clear.

In a small bowl, combine the orange juice, brown sugar and soy sauce. Remove chicken and keep warm. Add orange juice mixture to skillet; bring to a boil. Reduce heat; simmer, uncovered, for 5 minutes. Add oranges; heat through.

Serve the chicken with cooked rice and orange sauce. YIELD: 4 servings.

ALFREDO BACON MUSHROOM PIZZA

KAMI HORCH ✛ FRANKFORT, MAINE

My hearty party pizza is so convenient to make—but it looks and tastes gourmet. Creamy Alfredo sauce balances the creative combination of toppings.

    1 loaf (1 pound) frozen pizza dough, thawed
1/2 pound bacon strips
    1 cup roasted garlic Alfredo sauce
1-1/2 cups (6 ounces) shredded part-skim mozzarella cheese
1/4 cup grated Parmesan cheese
    2 large portobello mushrooms, stems removed
1/4 teaspoon pepper

Roll dough into a 15-in. circle; transfer to a greased 14-in. pizza pan and build up edges slightly. Bake at 425° for 6-8 minutes or until lightly browned. Meanwhile, in a large skillet, cook bacon just until done. Drain on paper towels; cut into 1-in. pieces.

Spread the Alfredo sauce over crust; sprinkle with cheeses. Cut mushrooms into 1/2-in. strips; place over cheese so they resemble spokes of a wheel. Sprinkle with bacon and pepper. Bake for 10-15 minutes or until heated through and cheese is melted. YIELD: 8 slices.

FROZEN SHREDDED CHEESE

To have shredded cheese on hand, buy a 5-pound bag and put small amounts in resealable freezer bags and freeze individually. When you need cheese, just thaw a bag.

STEAK WITH CHIPOTLE-LIME CHIMICHURRI

LAUREEN PITTMAN ✛ RIVERSIDE, CALIFORNIA

Steak gets a flavor kick from chimichurri. This piquant all-purpose herb sauce is so versatile, it goes with most any grilled meat, poultry or fish.

    2 cups chopped fresh parsley
1-1/2 cups chopped fresh cilantro
    1 small red onion, quartered
    5 garlic cloves, quartered
    2 chipotle peppers in adobo sauce
1/2 cup plus 1 tablespoon olive oil, *divided*
1/4 cup white wine vinegar
1/4 cup lime juice
    1 tablespoon dried oregano
    1 teaspoon grated lime peel
1-1/4 teaspoons salt, *divided*
3/4 teaspoon pepper, *divided*
    2 beef flat iron steaks *or* top sirloin steaks (1 pound *each*)

For chimichurri, place the parsley, cilantro, onion, garlic and chipotle peppers in a food processor; cover and pulse until minced. Add 1/2 cup oil, vinegar, lime juice, oregano, lime peel, 1/2 teaspoon salt and 1/4 teaspoon pepper; cover and process until blended. Cover and refrigerate until serving.

Drizzle steaks with remaining oil; sprinkle with remaining salt and pepper. Grill, covered, over medium heat for 8-10 minutes on each side or until meat reaches desired doneness (for medium-rare, a meat thermometer should read 145°; medium, 160°; well-done, 170°). Thinly slice across the grain; serve with chimichurri. YIELD: 8 servings.

SHRIMP WITH GINGER-CHILI SAUCE

CAROLE RESNICK ❖ CLEVELAND, OHIO

Sweet and peppery ginger complements spicy chili sauce in this cook-friendly shrimp stir-fry. It's ideal for nights when a quick, wholesome dinner is in order.

1-1/2 pounds uncooked large shrimp, peeled and deveined
   1 tablespoon cornstarch
1/4 cup orange juice
   2 tablespoons reduced-sodium soy sauce
   2 tablespoons honey
   1 tablespoon rice vinegar
1/4 to 1/2 teaspoon sriracha Asian hot chili sauce or 1/8 to 1/4 teaspoon hot pepper sauce
   2 garlic cloves, minced
   2 teaspoons minced fresh gingerroot
   2 tablespoons canola oil
   4 green onions, finely chopped, *divided*
   3 cups hot cooked rice

Pat shrimp dry with paper towels. In a large bowl, combine shrimp and cornstarch. In a small bowl, combine the orange juice, soy sauce, honey, vinegar and chili sauce; set aside.

In a wok or large skillet, stir-fry garlic and ginger in oil for 30 seconds. Add shrimp; stir-fry for 3 minutes. Stir half of the onions into the orange juice mixture; add to the pan.

Bring to a boil; cook and stir for 2 minutes or until sauce is thickened and shrimp turn pink. Sprinkle with remaining onions. Serve with rice. YIELD: 6 servings.

SCALLOPS WITH ANGEL HAIR

NANCY MUELLER ❖ MENOMONEE FALLS, WISCONSIN

Scallops taste extravagant, but they're actually low in fat. This recipe pairs them with superfine pasta, lightly coated with a lively white wine, garlic, onion and lemon sauce.

   8 ounces uncooked angel hair pasta
3/4 pound bay scallops
   2 teaspoons olive oil, *divided*
   1 small onion, chopped
   2 garlic cloves, minced
   1 cup vegetable broth
1/4 cup dry white wine *or* additional vegetable broth
   2 tablespoons lemon juice
1/4 teaspoon salt
1/8 teaspoon pepper
   2 teaspoons cornstarch
   2 teaspoons water
1/4 cup minced fresh parsley
Shredded Parmesan cheese and thinly sliced green onions, optional

Cook pasta according to package directions. Meanwhile, in a large nonstick skillet coated with cooking spray, cook scallops in 1 teaspoon oil over medium heat until firm and opaque; remove and keep warm.

In the same skillet, saute onion in remaining oil until tender. Add garlic; cook 1 minute longer. Stir in the broth, wine, lemon juice, salt and pepper. Bring to a boil. Combine cornstarch and water until smooth. Gradually stir into the pan. Bring to a boil; cook and stir for 2 minutes or until thickened. Stir in parsley and reserved scallops; heat through.

Drain pasta; serve with scallops. Sprinkle with cheese and green onions if desired. YIELD: 4 servings.

HOISIN CHICKEN SALAD

MICHELLE KRZMARZICK ✢ REDONDO BEACH, CALIFORNIA

Asian flavors enhance my convenient rotisserie chicken salad. It earns compliments every time I make it. Toasted sesame seeds add a nutty surprise.

- 8 cups torn romaine
- 3 cups shredded rotisserie chicken
- 2 medium tomatoes, chopped
- 2 green onions, thinly sliced
- 1/3 cup canola oil
- 1/4 cup lemon juice
- 1/4 cup hoisin sauce
- 1/4 teaspoon ground ginger
- 1/4 teaspoon garlic salt
- 1/8 teaspoon pepper
- 1/4 cup sesame seeds, toasted

In a large bowl, combine the romaine, rotisserie chicken, tomatoes and onions.

In a small bowl, whisk the oil, lemon juice, hoisin sauce, ginger, garlic salt and pepper. Drizzle over the salad and toss to coat. Sprinkle with toasted sesame seeds. Serve immediately. YIELD: 5 servings.

SAGE-DUSTED CHICKEN

VERONICA CALLAGHAN ✢ GLASTONBURY, CONNECTICUT

I use this "express" recipe for family meals and last-minute dinner parties. It's always met with rave reviews. I think the golden-brown chicken looks particularly scrumptious when served over cooked spinach.

- 4 boneless skinless chicken breast halves (6 ounces *each*)
- 3 teaspoons rubbed sage
- 1 teaspoon salt
- 1/2 teaspoon pepper
- 2 tablespoons butter
- 2 teaspoons olive oil
- 1/4 cup heavy whipping cream

Flatten chicken breast halves to 1/2-in. thickness; sprinkle with sage, salt and pepper.

In a large skillet over medium heat, cook chicken in butter and oil for 5-6 minutes on each side or until juices run clear. Remove and keep warm.

Add cream to the skillet, stirring to loosen browned bits. Cook and stir until sauce is thickened, about 4 minutes. Serve with chicken. YIELD: 4 servings.

WALDORF TURKEY SALAD

MITZI SENTIFF ✢ ANNAPOLIS, MARYLAND

Crisp apples, celery and walnuts teamed with lean poultry turn any meal into a picnic. The combination of tastes and textures makes this salad a cool classic that is as healthy as it is refreshing.

- 1 cup (8 ounces) plain yogurt
- 2 tablespoons honey
- 1/8 to 1/4 teaspoon ground ginger
- 1/4 teaspoon salt
- 2 cups cubed cooked turkey breast
- 1 cup cubed apple
- 1 cup seedless red grapes, halved
- 1/2 cup thinly sliced celery

1/2 cup raisins

4 lettuce leaves

2 tablespoons chopped walnuts

Whisk yogurt, honey, ginger and salt. In a large bowl, combine turkey, apple, grapes, celery and raisins; stir in yogurt mixture. Serve on lettuce; sprinkle with walnuts. YIELD: 4 servings.

MAHI MAHI WITH NECTARINE SALSA

MICHELLE AUGUSTINE ❖ CINCINNATI, OHIO

A ripe nectarine inspired me to put together a fruity salsa to serve with fish fillets. I received six thumbs-up from our three children for this easy, nutritious main dish.

1 medium nectarine, peeled and chopped

1/4 cup chopped onion

2 tablespoons chopped cucumber

1 tablespoon minced fresh cilantro

2 teaspoons chopped seeded jalapeno pepper

2 teaspoons lime juice

1/4 teaspoon salt

1/4 teaspoon pepper

1/4 teaspoon Louisiana-style hot sauce

FISH FILLETS

2 mahi mahi fillets (6 ounces *each*)

1 tablespoon olive oil

Dash salt

For salsa, in a small bowl, combine the first nine ingredients. Cover and refrigerate until serving.

Drizzle fillets with oil; sprinkle with salt. Moisten a paper towel with cooking oil; using long-handled tongs, lightly coat the grill rack. Grill fillets, covered, over medium heat or broil 4 in. from the heat for 3-5 minutes on each side or until fish just turns opaque. Serve with salsa. YIELD: 2 servings.

EDITOR'S NOTE: When cutting hot peppers, disposable gloves are recommended. Avoid touching your face.

COOKING FISH

When fish is overcooked, it tends to lose its flavor and become tough. As a general rule, fish should be cooked 10 minutes for every inch of thickness. When fish turns opaque and is flaky, it is cooked completely.

BEEF & SPINACH LO MEIN

DENISE PATTERSON ✤ BAINBRIDGE, OHIO

I discovered this dish at an international luncheon and brought the recipe home. It's quick, easy and always a hit with anyone who enjoys a stir-fry.

1/4 cup hoisin sauce
2 tablespoons soy sauce
1 tablespoon water
2 teaspoons sesame oil
2 garlic cloves, minced
1/4 teaspoon crushed red pepper flakes
1 pound beef top round steak, thinly sliced
6 ounces uncooked spaghetti
4 teaspoons canola oil, *divided*
1 can (8 ounces) sliced water chestnuts, drained
1/4 cup sliced green onions
1 package (10 ounces) fresh spinach, coarsely chopped
1 red chili pepper, seeded and thinly sliced

In a small bowl, combine the hoisin sauce, soy sauce, water, sesame oil, garlic and pepper flakes. Pour 1/4 cup into a large resealable plastic bag; add beef. Seal bag and turn to coat; refrigerate for 10 minutes. Set remaining marinade aside.

Cook spaghetti according to package directions. Meanwhile, in a large skillet or wok, stir-fry beef in 3 teaspoons canola oil in batches for 1-2 minutes or until no longer pink. Remove with a slotted spoon and keep warm.

Drain spaghetti and set aside. In the skillet or wok, stir-fry water chestnuts and onions in remaining oil until onions are tender. Stir in the spinach, spaghetti and reserved marinade. Cook and stir for 2-3 minutes or until spinach is wilted.

Return beef to the pan; heat through. Garnish with chili pepper. YIELD: 5 servings.

EDITOR'S NOTE: When cutting hot peppers, disposable gloves are recommended. Avoid touching your face.

TURKEY SAUSAGE WITH PASTA

MARY TALLMAN ✤ ARBOR VITAE, WISCONSIN

Love Italian food? You'll be craving what's good for you when this turkey dish is on the menu. It balances meat, pasta and the best of the garden's bounty.

1 pound Italian turkey sausage links, casings removed
1 large onion, chopped
1 large green pepper, chopped
1-1/4 cups sliced fresh mushrooms
2 garlic cloves, minced
2 cans (14-1/2 ounces *each*) diced tomatoes, undrained
1 teaspoon Italian seasoning
1 teaspoon chili powder
6 cups uncooked spiral pasta
1/2 cup shredded part-skim mozzarella cheese

Crumble sausage into a large nonstick skillet. Add onion, green pepper and mushrooms. Cook over medium heat until meat is no longer pink. Add garlic; cook 1 minute longer. Drain.

Stir in the tomatoes, Italian seasoning and chili powder. Bring to a boil. Reduce heat; simmer, uncovered, for 10 minutes.

Meanwhile, cook pasta according to package directions; drain. Serve sausage mixture over pasta; sprinkle with cheese. YIELD: 6 servings.

PISTACHIO-CRUSTED SALMON CAKES

MARY LOU TIMPSON ✤ COLORADO CITY, ARIZONA

It takes only half an hour to give salmon patties glamour. These time-saving fish cakes get a rich, buttery crunch from ground pistachio nuts.

1-1/4 pounds salmon fillets
1 egg
1/2 cup soft bread crumbs

1 tablespoon Dijon mustard

1 teaspoon grated lime peel

1/4 teaspoon salt

1/4 teaspoon pepper

1 cup coarsely ground pistachios

2 tablespoons canola oil

Lime wedges

In a large nonstick skillet, bring 4 cups water to a boil. Reduce heat; add fillets and poach, uncovered, for 8-10 minutes or until fish flakes easily with a fork. Remove from pan and cool slightly.

In a large bowl, combine the egg, bread crumbs, mustard, lime peel, salt and pepper. Shred salmon with two forks; fold into bread crumb mixture. Shape into eight patties. Coat both sides with pistachios.

In a large skillet over medium heat, cook patties in oil in batches for 1-2 minutes on each side or until golden brown. Serve with lime wedges. YIELD: 4 servings.

WORTH EVERY PENNE

JANET REIMER ✤ ARMSTRONG, BRITISH COLUMBIA

My husband is usually a meat and potatoes guy, but after I made this simple sauteed chicken and penne salad for him, he added it to his list of most-requested dinners.

1/4 cup balsamic vinegar

1/4 cup prepared pesto

2 tablespoons olive oil, *divided*

1 teaspoon honey

1/2 teaspoon salt

1/2 teaspoon pepper

2 cups uncooked penne pasta

3 cups sliced fresh mushrooms

1 large red onion, chopped

1 small sweet red pepper, julienned

1 small green pepper, julienned

3 cups fresh baby spinach

3 cups cubed cooked chicken breast

12 cherry tomatoes, halved

1/2 cup crumbled feta cheese *or* 1/4 cup grated Parmesan cheese

In a small bowl, combine the vinegar, pesto, 1 tablespoon oil, honey, salt and pepper; set aside. Cook pasta according to package directions.

Meanwhile, in a Dutch oven, saute the mushrooms, onion and peppers in remaining oil until tender. Stir in the spinach, chicken and tomatoes; cook until spinach is wilted.

Drain pasta; place in a large serving bowl. Add the chicken mixture, tomatoes and pesto mixture; toss to coat. Sprinkle with cheese. YIELD: 5 servings.

OUR FAVORITE PORK CHOPS

LINDA FOREMAN ✤ LOCUST GROVE, OKLAHOMA

My husband raves about these tender sweet-and-sour chops that top my list of best speedy dinners. They're on our menu regularly.

4 bone-in pork loin chops

2 tablespoons all-purpose flour

2 tablespoons olive oil

1 cup picante sauce

1 medium tart apple, peeled and chopped

2 tablespoons brown sugar

Coat pork chops with flour. In a large skillet over medium-high heat, brown chops in oil on both sides. Combine the picante sauce, apple and brown sugar; add to the pan. Reduce heat; cover and cook for 15-20 minutes or until a meat thermometer reads 160°. YIELD: 4 servings.

MEMORABLE MEALS

These all-time favorite-family meals bring you simple, satisfying dishes that have graced dinner tables all over the country.

BRACIOLE

COOKIE CURCI-WRIGHT ❖ SAN JOSE, CALIFORNIA

In our family, Braciole was served as a special treat for birthdays and holidays. It was Grandma's specialty, and the preparation was time-consuming. When the meat and sauce were fully cooked, Grandma called us into the kitchen to watch her lift the big roll from the sauce to the cutting board to slice it. The pinwheels of meat, laid side by side on the platter, topped with Grandma's delicious sauce, made a colorful picture.

        1 beef flank steak (1-1/2 pounds)
        4 tablespoons olive oil, *divided*
    1/2 cup soft bread crumbs
    1/2 cup minced fresh parsley
    1/2 cup grated Parmesan cheese
        2 garlic cloves, minced
        1 teaspoon dried oregano
    1/2 teaspoon salt, *divided*
    1/2 teaspoon pepper, *divided*
        1 medium onion, chopped
        2 cans (15 ounces *each*) tomato sauce
    1/2 cup water
        1 teaspoon Italian seasoning
    1/2 teaspoon sugar
    Hot cooked spaghetti, optional

Flatten steak to 1/2-in. thickness. Rub with 1 tablespoon oil. Combine the bread crumbs, parsley, cheese, garlic, oregano, 1/4 teaspoon salt and 1/4 teaspoon pepper. Spoon over beef to within 1 in. of edges; press down. Roll up jelly-roll style, starting with a long side; tie with kitchen string.

In a Dutch oven, brown meat in remaining oil on all sides. Add onion and cook until tender. Stir in the tomato sauce, water, Italian seasoning, sugar and remaining salt and pepper. Bring to a boil. Reduce heat; cover and simmer for 70-80 minutes or until meat is tender.

Remove the meat from the sauce and discard the string. Cut into thin slices; serve with sauce and spaghetti if desired. YIELD: 6 servings.

TUSCAN BREAD SALAD

MARY ANN DELL ❖ PHOENIXVILLE, PENNSYLVANIA

I have made this salad many times over the years, and it always receives many compliments. The addition of capers and Greek olives offers a unique flavor, and the bread cubes add a nice, crunchy texture. This salad is very easy to prepare and is one of our gang's favorites.

        4 cups cubed Italian bread
        1 small cucumber, seeded and cubed
    3/4 cup thinly sliced red onion
    1/4 cup sliced Greek olives
        2 tablespoons capers, drained
    3/4 cup balsamic vinaigrette, *divided*
        5 cups torn romaine

Place the bread cubes on an ungreased baking sheet. Bake at 350° for 15-20 minutes or until dried and toasted, stirring every 5 minutes. Cool to room temperature.

In a large bowl, combine the cucumber, onion, olives, capers and toasted bread. Drizzle with 1/2 cup vinaigrette; toss to coat. Let stand for 5-10 minutes.

Add romaine and remaining vinaigrette; toss to coat. YIELD: 6 servings.

GRANDMA'S RED VELVET CAKE

KATHRYN DAVISON ❖ CHARLOTTE, NORTH CAROLINA

No one thinks it's Christmas in our family without Red Velvet Cake. I baked the first one for Christmas in 1963 when I found the recipe in the newspaper, and my mother kept the tradition going into the '80s. This one is different from the other Red Velvet Cakes I've tasted over the years, since this one has a mild chocolate taste and the icing, although rich, is as light as snow.

1/2 cup butter, softened
1-1/2 cups sugar
2 eggs
2 bottles (1 ounce *each*) red food coloring
1 tablespoon white vinegar
1 teaspoon vanilla extract
2-1/4 cups cake flour
2 tablespoons baking cocoa
1 teaspoon baking soda
1 teaspoon salt
1 cup buttermilk

FROSTING
1 tablespoon cornstarch
1/2 cup water
2 cups butter, softened
2 teaspoons vanilla extract
3-1/2 cups confectioners' sugar

In a large bowl, cream butter and sugar until light and fluffy. Add eggs, one at a time, beating well after each addition. Beat in the food coloring, vinegar and vanilla. Combine the flour, cocoa, baking soda and salt; add to creamed mixture alternately with buttermilk, beating well after each addition.

Pour into two greased and floured 9-in. round baking pans. Bake at 350° for 20-25 minutes or until a toothpick inserted near the center comes out clean. Cool for 10 minutes before removing from pans to wire racks to cool completely.

For frosting, in a small saucepan, combine cornstarch and water until smooth. Cook and stir over medium heat for 2-3 minutes or until thickened and opaque. Cool to room temperature.

In a large bowl, beat butter and vanilla until light and fluffy. Beat in cornstarch mixture. Gradually add confectioners' sugar; beat until frosting is light and fluffy. Spread frosting between layers and over top and sides of cake. YIELD: 14 servings.

ITALIAN-STYLE LIMA BEANS

MARLENE MOHR ❖ CINCINNATI, OHIO

This Italian-style side dish will delight lima-bean lovers. Not only is it a beautiful addition to the menu, the lima beans have a bite, yet are tender and perfect with the delicate flavor of the cherry tomatoes.

3 garlic cloves, minced
1 tablespoon olive oil
2 cups cherry tomatoes, halved
2 cups frozen lima beans, thawed
2 teaspoons balsamic vinegar
1/2 teaspoon brown sugar
2 teaspoons grated lemon peel
1/2 teaspoon dried oregano
1/4 teaspoon salt
1/4 teaspoon crushed red pepper flakes
1 tablespoon minced fresh parsley, optional

In a large skillet, cook garlic in oil for 1 minute. Add tomatoes and lima beans; cook for 3-5 minutes or until tomatoes soften and beans are tender.

Stir in the vinegar, brown sugar, lemon peel, oregano, salt and pepper flakes; cook 1 minute longer. Sprinkle with parsley if desired. YIELD: 6 servings.

RASPBERRY CHOCOLATE RUGALACH

G.P. BUSAROW ❖ WHITEHALL, MONTANA

Since we celebrate both Hanukkah and Christmas, these traditional sweets are always on the menu every holiday season. The rugalach can be covered and refrigerated overnight or frozen for up to two months.

1/2 cup butter, softened
4 ounces cream cheese, softened
1 cup all-purpose flour
1/4 teaspoon salt

FILLING
1/4 cup dried currants
2 tablespoons sugar
1/2 teaspoon ground cinnamon
1/4 cup seedless raspberry jam
2/3 cup finely chopped pecans
1/4 cup miniature semisweet chocolate chips

In a large bowl, beat butter and cream cheese until smooth. Combine flour and salt; gradually add to creamed mixture and mix well.

Divide dough in half; form into two balls. Flatten to 5-in. circles; wrap in plastic wrap. Refrigerate for 8 hours or overnight.

Place currants in a small bowl. Cover with boiling water; let stand for 5 minutes. Drain well and set aside. Combine sugar and cinnamon; set aside.

On a lightly floured surface or pastry mat, roll one portion of dough into an 11-in. circle. Brush with half of the jam. Sprinkle with half of the cinnamon-sugar, pecans, chocolate chips and currants; press down gently.

Cut into 16 wedges. Roll up wedges from the wide end and place point side down 2 in. apart on a parchment paper-lined baking sheet. Curve the ends to form a crescent. Cover and refrigerate for 30 minutes before baking. Repeat with remaining dough and filling.

Bake at 350° for 18-22 minutes or until golden brown. Remove to wire racks to cool. YIELD: 32 cookies.

TZIMMES

CHERI BRAGG ❖ VIOLA, DELAWARE

I found this recipe a long time ago. It has become our classic side dish for every Hanukkah and Passover feast and is a favorite of young and old alike. It also complements chicken and turkey well.

3 pounds sweet potatoes (about 4 large), peeled and cut into chunks
2 pounds medium carrots, cut into 1/2-inch chunks
1 package (12 ounces) pitted dried plums, halved
1 cup orange juice
1 cup water
1/4 cup honey
1/4 cup packed brown sugar
2 teaspoons ground cinnamon
1/4 cup butter, cubed

In a greased 13-in. x 9-in. baking dish, combine the sweet potatoes, carrots and plums. Combine the orange juice, water, honey, brown sugar and cinnamon; pour over vegetables.

Cover and bake at 350° for 1 hour. Uncover; dot with butter. Bake 45-60 minutes longer, carefully stirring every 15 minutes, or until the vegetables are tender and sauce is thickened. YIELD: 12 servings.

VEGETABLE SLAW

VICKI STEH ❖ WAUSAU, WISCONSIN

This pretty combination of fresh veggies is low in fat, and to enhance the flavors, it can be made at least an hour before serving. For extra color, half-cup portions of squash and red and green pepper can be added.

1 small head cabbage (1-1/2 pounds), shredded
1 cup shredded carrots
1/2 cup fresh broccoli florets
1/2 cup fresh cauliflowerets
1/2 cup chopped celery
1/2 cup cherry tomatoes, halved
1/2 cup chopped peeled cucumber

DRESSING
6 tablespoons olive oil
3 tablespoons cider vinegar
4-1/2 teaspoons Dijon mustard
1-1/4 teaspoons garlic powder
3/4 teaspoon salt
1/4 teaspoon pepper
1 cup minced fresh parsley

In a large bowl, combine the first seven ingredients.

In a small bowl, whisk the oil, vinegar, mustard, garlic powder, salt and pepper. Pour over vegetables and toss to coat. Stir in parsley. Cover and refrigerate for at least 1 hour before serving. YIELD: 12 servings.

OLD-FASHIONED BEEF BRISKET

GERRY THORPE ❖ EAST FALMOUTH, MASSACHUSETTS

Tender slices of beef smothered in onions in a sweet tomato sauce give this entree an old-fashioned feel. It is simple to prepare and delicious comfort food.

1 fresh beef brisket (4 pounds)
2 tablespoons canola oil
2 large sweet onions, sliced
2 cups ketchup
2 cups water
1/2 cup dry red wine *or* beef broth

In a Dutch oven, brown meat in oil on all sides; drain. Top with onions. Combine the ketchup, water and wine; pour over meat and onions.

Cover and bake at 350° for 3 to 3-1/2 hours or until the meat is tender. Let stand for 5 minutes. Thinly slice the brisket across the grain. Thicken the sauce if desired; serve with beef. YIELD: 12 servings.

EDITOR'S NOTE: This is a fresh beef brisket, not corned beef.

USING LEFTOVER BRISKET

A great way to use leftover brisket is to layer the meat, sauteed onion and green pepper on a toasted sandwich roll, top it with Swiss cheese and then to broil it until the cheese is melted.

CURRY-GLAZED PORK CHOPS

PAT LANE ✣ PULLMAN, WASHINGTON

My sister-in-law gave me this recipe several years ago, and it has been a family favorite since. It is always a big hit at potlucks, and I have given the recipe to many friends. I am happy to share it with anyone who asks for it.

    8 boneless pork loin chops (6 ounces *each*)
    2 tablespoons canola oil
    1 large onion, chopped
    2 tablespoons all-purpose flour
    2 tablespoons brown sugar
1/2 teaspoon curry powder
1/2 teaspoon ground cinnamon
1/4 teaspoon salt
    1 cup water
1/3 cup apricots with mixed fruit baby food
1/4 cup flaked coconut
    2 tablespoons ketchup
    1 teaspoon beef bouillon granules
1/4 cup flaked coconut, toasted
Hot cooked rice

In a large skillet, brown chops in oil in batches; transfer to a greased 13-in. x 9-in. baking dish.

In the same skillet, saute onion until tender; stir in the flour, brown sugar, curry powder, cinnamon and salt until blended. Gradually add the water; stir in the baby food, coconut, ketchup and bouillon. Bring to a boil; cook and stir for 1-2 minutes or until thickened.

Spoon half of the sauce mixture over pork. Bake, uncovered, at 400° for 20 minutes. Top with remaining sauce; bake 10-15 minutes longer or until a meat thermometer reads 160°. Sprinkle with toasted coconut. Serve with rice. YIELD: 8 servings.

SHRIMP EGG ROLLS

DOROTHY WITKOWSKI ✣ TINLEY PARK, ILLINOIS

These very flavorful egg rolls are a special treat and one of our favorite hot hors d'oeuvres. They can be partially fried for re-heating later or cooked until golden brown.

    2 celery ribs, finely chopped
    2 tablespoons butter
1-1/2 pounds uncooked medium shrimp, peeled, deveined and chopped
    4 green onions, chopped
1/2 cup chopped water chestnuts
    2 tablespoons creamy peanut butter
    1 teaspoon salt
    1 teaspoon sugar
Dash pepper
Dash cayenne pepper
    9 egg roll wrappers
Oil for deep-fat frying
SWEET 'N' SOUR SAUCE
    1 can (12 ounces) apricot cake and pastry filling
1/2 cup sugar
1/2 cup white vinegar
1/4 cup water
1/4 teaspoon salt

In a large skillet, saute celery in butter until tender. Add shrimp and onions; cook until shrimp turns pink. Stir in the water chestnuts, peanut butter, salt, sugar, pepper and cayenne; heat through.

Place 2 heaping tablespoonfuls of shrimp mixture in the center of one egg roll wrapper. (Keep remaining wrappers covered with a damp paper towel until ready to use.) Fold bottom corner over filling. Fold sides toward center over filling. Moisten remaining corner with water; roll up tightly to seal. Repeat.

In an electric skillet or deep fryer, heat oil to 375°. Fry egg rolls, a few at a time, for 1-2 minutes on each side or until golden brown. Drain on paper towels. Combine sauce ingredients; serve with egg rolls. YIELD: 9 egg rolls (2 cups sauce).

KOREAN SPINACH SALAD

AUDREY MISNER ❖ PRICE, UTAH

This delicious salad is a flavorful twist on the classic spinach salad. The sweet and sour dressing has just the right balance, and there's a wonderful crunch from the beans and water chestnuts.

    1/2 cup canola oil
    1/3 cup sugar
    1/3 cup finely chopped onion
      3 tablespoons ketchup
      2 tablespoons white vinegar
Dash pepper

SALAD
    1/2 pound fresh spinach, torn
      1 cup canned bean sprouts
      1 can (8 ounces) sliced water chestnuts, drained
      4 bacon strips, cooked and crumbled
      1 hard-cooked egg, chopped

Place the first six ingredients in a jar with a tight fitting lid; shake well. Chill until serving.

In a large salad bowl, combine the spinach, sprouts and water chestnuts. Just before serving, shake the dressing and pour over salad; toss to coat. Sprinkle with the cooked bacon and egg. YIELD: 8 servings.

OLD-FASHIONED ORANGE LAYER CAKE

TASTE OF HOME TEST KITCHEN

This is a very traditional cake that is tender and moist and has a delicate orange flavor.

      1 cup butter, softened
      2 cups sugar
      5 eggs
    1/2 cup orange juice
      1 tablespoon grated orange peel
2-1/2 cups self-rising flour
      1 cup whole milk

GLAZE
    1/4 cup butter, softened
3-3/4 cups confectioners' sugar
    1/3 cup orange juice
      1 tablespoon grated orange peel

In a large bowl, cream butter and sugar until light and fluffy. Add eggs, one at a time, beating well after each addition. Beat in orange juice and peel. Add flour to the creamed mixture alternately with milk, beating well after each addition.

Pour into two greased and floured 9-in. round baking pans. Bake at 350° for 25-30 minutes or until a toothpick inserted near the center comes out clean. Cool for 10 minutes before removing from pans to wire racks to cool completely.

In a large bowl, beat butter until light and fluffy. Add the confectioners' sugar, orange juice and peel; beat until smooth. Spread glaze between layers and over the top and sides of cake. YIELD: 12 servings.

EDITOR'S NOTE: As a substitute for each cup of self-rising flour, place 1-1/2 teaspoons baking powder and 1/2 teaspoon salt in a measuring cup. Add all-purpose flour to measure 1 cup.

SWEET POTATO WEDGES WITH CHILI MAYO

RAYMONDE BOURGEOIS ❖ SWASTIKA, ONTARIO

We enjoy eating sweet potatoes regularly, and this is a delicious way to serve them. It is a great combination of flavors. The spicy seasoning of the mayo sauce pairs well with the taste of sweet potatoes.

　6 small sweet potatoes, peeled
　2 tablespoons olive oil
　2 to 3 tablespoons Cajun seasoning
　1 cup mayonnaise
　4 teaspoons lemon juice
　2 teaspoons chili powder *or* chili garlic sauce
　2 teaspoons Dijon mustard

Cut each sweet potato lengthwise into eight wedges; place in two greased 15-in. x 10-in. x 1-in. baking pans. Drizzle with oil. Sprinkle with Cajun seasoning; toss to coat.

　Bake at 400° for 30-35 minutes or until tender, turning once. Meanwhile, in a small bowl, combine the remaining ingredients; serve with potatoes. YIELD: 8 servings.

CRISPY CAJUN PANFISH

GAYLE COOK ❖ MINOT, NORTH DAKOTA

My mother was happiest with a fishing rod in her hands, and her method of frying her catch was always a hit.

　2 cups all-purpose flour
　2 teaspoons salt
　2 teaspoons Cajun seasoning

1-1/2 teaspoons pepper

1/8 teaspoon ground cinnamon

2 pounds bass *or* perch fillets

2 eggs

1/4 cup water

2 cups mashed potato flakes

6 tablespoons canola oil

In a large resealable plastic bag, combine the first five ingredients. Add fish, one piece at a time; shake to coat. Whisk eggs and water in a shallow dish. Place potato flakes in another shallow dish. Dip each fillet in eggs, then coat with potato flakes. Dip fish again in eggs and potato flakes.

In a large skillet, heat 3 tablespoons oil over medium-high heat. Cook the fish in batches for 3-4 minutes on each side or until fish flakes easily with a fork, adding oil as needed. YIELD: 8 servings.

PECAN PIE

R.K. HUGUNIN ❖ PHELAN, CALIFORNIA

This recipe came from a magazine published in the '70s. Since then, I have made hundreds of pecan pies. In addition to my family, I bake for senior groups and my husband's business acquaintances.

1 sheet refrigerated pie pastry

1/2 cup butter, softened

1 cup sugar

3 eggs

3/4 cup light corn syrup

1 teaspoon vanilla extract

1 cup pecan halves

Unroll pastry into a 9-in. pie plate; flute edges. In a large bowl, cream butter and sugar until light and fluffy. Beat in the eggs, corn syrup and vanilla. Pour into pastry shell; arrange pecans over top.

Bake at 375° for 50-55 minutes or until set. Cover the edges with foil during the last 15 minutes to prevent overbrowning if necessary. Cool on a wire rack. Refrigerate any leftovers. YIELD: 8 servings.

HEARTY BEAN SALAD

JEWELL DAWSON ❖ CULVER, OREGON

I discovered this salad years ago, when I was a teenager in a 4-H club. After I was married, I used the recipe as a base and added different beans and water chestnuts for more crunch. Getting the right balance between the sweet and the sour in the dressing is most important.

1 can (16 ounces) kidney beans, rinsed and drained

1 can (15-1/4 ounces) whole kernel corn, drained

1 can (14-1/2 ounces) cut wax beans, drained

1 can (14-1/2 ounces) cut green beans, drained

1 can (8 ounces) sliced water chestnuts, drained

1 small sweet red pepper, chopped

DRESSING

2/3 cup sugar

1/2 cup cider vinegar

1 small onion, finely chopped

1 teaspoon salt

1/4 teaspoon pepper

In a large bowl, combine the first six ingredients. In a small bowl, whisk the dressing ingredients; pour over the bean mixture and toss to coat.

Cover and refrigerate for at least 1 hour. Stir before serving. Serve with a slotted spoon. YIELD: 10 servings.

MERINGUE-TOPPED PEACH BREAD PUDDING

ROSALIND POPE ✦ GREENSBORO, NORTH CAROLINA

My English mother loved to make bread pudding, and when we were living in South Africa many years ago, I found a recipe that added the meringue topping. I adapted the idea and came up with my peach version. My mum declared it better than her original!

    1/2 cup packed brown sugar
      1 tablespoon cornstarch
    1/4 teaspoon ground cinnamon
    1/2 cup water
      4 cups sliced peeled peaches
      1 tablespoon lemon juice
      1 tablespoon butter
      4 eggs, *separated*
    1/8 teaspoon salt
    2/3 cup sugar, *divided*
      2 cups milk
      5 slices French bread (1 inch thick)

In a large saucepan, combine the brown sugar, cornstarch and cinnamon. Stir in water until smooth; add peaches. Cook and stir over medium heat until mixture comes to a boil. Cook and stir 1-2 minutes longer or until thickened. Remove from the heat; stir in lemon juice and butter. Set aside.

In a large bowl, beat egg yolks on high speed for 3 minutes or until light and fluffy. Gradually add salt and 1/3 cup sugar, beating until thick and lemon-colored. Stir in milk.

Dip bread into egg mixture; soak for 1 minute. Place slices into a greased 11-in. x 7-in. baking dish. Spoon peach mixture evenly over bread layer. Pour remaining egg mixture over peaches. Bake at 350° for 25-30 minutes or until center is set.

Meanwhile, in a small bowl, beat the egg whites on medium speed until soft peaks form. Gradually beat in remaining sugar,

1 tablespoon at a time, on high until stiff peaks form. Spread over the hot pudding, sealing the edges to pan. Bake 10-15 minutes longer or until the meringue is golden brown. Serve warm. YIELD: 8 servings.

MINTED MANDARIN SALAD

PAMELA SCHOTT ✦ CANTON, OHIO

I got the recipe for this salad several years ago and adjusted a few things. It has become very popular at potluck gatherings. Not only is it attractive, but the blend of flavors is distinctive.

    1/4 cup plus 2-1/2 teaspoons sugar, *divided*
    1/2 cup sliced almonds
      4 cups torn mixed salad greens
    1/2 cup halved and thinly sliced cucumber
      1 celery rib, sliced
      3 green onions, thinly sliced
    1/4 cup canola oil
      3 tablespoons balsamic vinegar
  1-1/2 teaspoons minced fresh parsley
  1-1/2 teaspoons minced fresh mint
    1/4 teaspoon lemon juice
    1/8 teaspoon salt
    1/8 teaspoon pepper
    1/8 teaspoon hot pepper sauce
      1 can (11 ounces) mandarin oranges, drained

In a small heavy skillet, melt 1/4 cup sugar over low heat. Add almonds and stir to coat. Spread onto a greased sheet of foil; break apart if necessary.

In a large bowl, combine the salad greens, cucumber, celery and onions.

For dressing, in a small bowl, whisk the oil, vinegar, parsley, mint, lemon juice, salt, pepper, pepper sauce and remaining sugar. Drizzle the desired amount over salad; toss to coat. Top with oranges and almonds. Refrigerate leftover dressing. YIELD: 8 servings.

BRAISED SHORT RIBS

SUSAN KINSELLA ❖ EAST FALMOUTH, MASSACHUSETTS
This recipe can be finished in a slow cooker, which makes it very helpful during those very busy days.

 4 pounds bone-in beef short ribs
 1 teaspoon pepper, *divided*
1/2 teaspoon salt
 3 tablespoons canola oil
 3 celery ribs, chopped
 2 large carrots, chopped
 1 large yellow onion, chopped
 1 medium sweet red pepper, chopped
 1 garlic clove, minced
 1 cup dry red wine *or* reduced-sodium beef broth
 4 cups reduced-sodium beef broth
 1 fresh rosemary sprig
 1 fresh oregano sprig
 1 bay leaf

Sprinkle ribs with 1/2 teaspoon pepper and salt. In an ovenproof Dutch oven, brown ribs in oil in batches. Remove and set aside.

In the drippings, saute the celery, carrots, onion, red pepper and garlic until tender. Add wine, stirring to loosen browned bits from pan. Bring to a boil; cook until liquid is reduced by half.

Return ribs to the pan. Add broth and remaining pepper; bring to a boil. Place rosemary, oregano and bay leaf on a double thickness of cheesecloth; bring up corners of cloth and tie with kitchen string to form a bag. Add to Dutch oven.

Cover and bake at 325° for 1-1/2 to 2 hours or until the meat is tender.

Remove ribs and keep warm. Discard spice bag. Skim fat from pan juices; thicken if desired. YIELD: 8 servings.

MASHED POTATO BAKE

JOAN ANTONEN ❖ ARLINGTON, SOUTH DAKOTA
I received this recipe from a friend, but over the years, I have added and subtracted ingredients until it was just right for my family. It's a great make-ahead dish with a delicious taste.

 4 medium potatoes, peeled and quartered
 1 package (8 ounces) cream cheese, softened
1/4 cup milk
 2 tablespoons butter
 1 egg
 1 jar (2 ounces) pimientos, drained
 2 garlic cloves, minced
 1 tablespoon grated onion

Place potatoes in a large saucepan and cover with water. Bring to a boil. Reduce heat; cover and cook for 15-20 minutes or until tender. Drain.

Place potatoes in a large bowl. Add the cream cheese, milk and butter; beat until smooth. Stir in the egg, pimientos, garlic and onion. Spoon into a greased 2-1/2-qt. baking dish.

Bake, uncovered, at 350° for 45-50 minutes or until heated through. YIELD: 8 servings.

SWEET & SOUR STUFFED CABBAGE

LAUREN KARGEN ❖ BUFFALO, NEW YORK

Everyone loves the taste of these cabbage rolls, and when I make them, I make a lot of extra filling to prepare meatballs. I adapted this recipe from one I found for sweet and sour stuffed green peppers.

      1/2 cup raisins
        1 cup boiling water
        1 medium head cabbage
        3 medium onions
        1 egg
        1 cup cooked instant rice
        1 cup shredded carrots
        1 teaspoon salt
        1 teaspoon pepper
  1-1/4 pounds lean ground beef
        1 can (15 ounces) tomato sauce
      1/2 cup packed brown sugar
      1/2 cup lemon juice

Place raisins in a small bowl; cover with boiling water. Let stand for 5 minutes; drain and set aside.

Fill a Dutch oven three-quarters full of water; bring to a boil. Add cabbage; cook for 2-3 minutes or just until leaves fall off head. Set aside 12 large leaves for rolls; chop remaining cabbage and set aside. Cut out the thick vein from the bottom of each reserved leaf, making a V-shaped cut.

Slice two onions and set aside; chop the remaining onion. In a large bowl, combine the chopped onions, egg, rice, carrots, salt, pepper and reserved raisins. Crumble the beef over the raisin mixture and mix well.

Place 1/4 cup meat mixture on each cabbage leaf; overlap cut ends of leaf. Fold in sides. Beginning from the cut end, roll up completely to enclose filling.

Place sliced onions and reserved chopped cabbage in a 13-in. x 9-in. baking dish. Arrange cabbage rolls, seam side down, on top. Combine the tomato sauce, brown sugar and lemon juice; pour over rolls.

Cover and bake at 350° for 1 hour or until the cabbage is tender and a meat thermometer reads 160°. Uncover; bake 5-10 minutes longer or until sauce reaches desired consistency. YIELD: 6 servings.

GRANDMA'S POLISH COOKIES

SHERINE ELISE GILMOUR ❖ BROOKLYN, NEW YORK

This traditional kruschiki recipe has been handed down through my mother's side from my great-grandmother. As a child, it was my job to loop the end of each cookie through its hole.

      4 cups all-purpose flour
      1 teaspoon salt
      1 cup cold butter
      4 egg yolks
      1 cup evaporated milk
      2 teaspoons vanilla extract
  Oil for deep-fat frying
  Confectioners' sugar

In a large bowl, combine flour and salt. Cut in butter until mixture resembles coarse crumbs. In another bowl, beat egg yolks until foamy; add milk and vanilla. Stir into crumb mixture until dough is stiff enough to knead.

Turn onto a lightly floured surface; knead 8-10 times. Divide dough into four pieces. Roll each portion into a 1/4-in.-thick rectangle; cut into 4-in. x 1-1/2-in. strips. Cut a 2-in. lengthwise slit down the middle of each strip; pull one of the ends through the slit like a bow.

In an electric skillet or deep-fat fryer, heat oil to 375°. Fry dough strips, a few at a time, until golden brown on both sides. Drain on paper towels. Dust with confectioners' sugar. YIELD: 40 cookies.

PICKLED EGGS WITH BEETS

MARY BANKER ❖ FORT WORTH, TEXAS

Ever since I can remember, my mother served pickled eggs at Easter. It was a tradition that my family expected. I made them for my granddaughter the last time she visited, and they were all gone before she left.

      2 cans (15 ounces *each*) whole beets
    12 hard-cooked eggs, peeled
      1 cup sugar
      1 cup water
      1 cup cider vinegar

Drain beets, reserving 1 cup juice (discard remaining juice or save for another use). Place beets and eggs in a 2-qt. glass jar.

In a small saucepan, bring the sugar, water, vinegar and reserved beet juice to a boil. Pour over beets and eggs; cool.

Cover tightly and refrigerate for at least 24 hours before serving. YIELD: 12 servings.

LAZY PIEROGI

JO KELLER ✦ LORAIN, OHIO

These tender little dumplings, with a mild cheese flavor, are delicious and a great side dish for any meat dish. Their homemade flavor is wonderful.

    2 cups (16 ounces) small curd cream-style cottage cheese
    2 eggs
1-1/4 cups all-purpose flour
    1 teaspoon salt
    3 tablespoons butter, melted, *divided*
    1 small onion, chopped
Sour cream

In a large bowl, combine cottage cheese and eggs. Stir in the flour, salt and 1 tablespoon butter.

In a Dutch oven, bring 3 qts. of water to a boil. Reduce heat. Drop batter by tablespoonfuls into simmering water, stirring gently to prevent sticking; cook pierogi in batches for 4-6 minutes or until slightly firm. Remove with a slotted spoon to paper towels to drain; cool slightly.

In a large skillet, saute the onion and pierogi in remaining butter until lightly browned. Serve with the sour cream. YIELD: 10 servings.

PEELING HARD-COOKED EGGS

Very fresh eggs can be difficult to peel. The American Egg Board recommends refrigerating eggs for a week to 10 days before cooking them. After cooking, crackle the shells all over before peeling by tapping on the kitchen counter.

GENERAL RECIPE INDEX

Bistro French Onion Chicken, 70
Braised Short Ribs, 171
Broccoli Mac & Cheese Bake, 44
Cherry-Glazed Pork Tenderloin, 69
Chicken Continental, 58
Chicken Fajita Pizza, 50
Chicken in White Wine Sauce, 44
Chorizo-Stuffed Turkey Breast with Mexican Grits, 47
Cordon Bleu Lasagna, 62
Crusted Baked Chicken, 63
Curry-Apple Turkey Loaf, 45
Curry-Glazed Pork Chops, 166
Grits Casserole, 138
Hearty Eggplant Parmesan, 70
Herbed Turkey Tetrazzini, 62
Hereford Casserole, 44
Holiday Glazed Ham, 45
Honey-Brined Turkey Breast, 54
Italian Tomato Pie, 61
Just-Like-Thanksgiving Turkey Meat Loaf, 43
Maple Chicken 'n' Ribs, 51
Moussaka, 139
Old-Fashioned Beef Brisket, 165
Onion Brunch Pie, 137
Pepper & Jack Smothered Cheeseburgers, 64
Personal Veggie Pizzas, 139
Poblanos Stuffed with Chipotle Turkey Chili, 46
Pork Chops with Sauerkraut, 55
Pork Tenderloin with Spiced Plum Sauce, 59
Reuben Casserole, 49
Roasted Citrus & Herb Turkey, 60
Rosemary-Garlic Roast Beef, 64
Sausage Ranch Breakfast Casserole, 68
Sole Thermidor, 67
Southwestern Shepherd's Pie, 144
Spinach, Mushroom & Three-Cheese Pizza, 70
Sweet & Sour Stuffed Cabbage, 172
Sweet & Spicy Chicken Drummies, 56
Turkey and Dressing Casserole, 55
Veggie-Tuna Noodle Casserole, 48

PASTA & NOODLES

Asparagus Pasta Salad, 21
Beef & Spinach Lo Mein, 158
BLT Skillet, 148
Broccoli Mac & Cheese Bake, 44
Cheesy Pasta Salad, 30
Herbed Turkey Tetrazzini, 62
Hot Bacon Macaroni Salad, 30
Layered Tortellini Salad, 31
Scallops with Angel Hair, 155

Swiss Macaroni and Cheese, 147
Tomato-Basil Salmon Steaks, 49
Turkey Sausage with Pasta, 158
Vegetable Pasta with Sun-Dried Tomato Sauce, 54
Veggie Bow Tie Salad, 30
Worth Every Penne, 159

PEACHES

Meringue-Topped Peach Bread Pudding, 170
Peaches & Cream Pie, 135
Spiced Peach Puffs, 111

PEANUT BUTTER

Choco-Peanut Bars Deluxe, 102
Chocolate Scotcheroos, 100
Chocolate Topped Peanut Butter Spritz, 106
Fudge Sundae Pie, 130
Peanut Butter-Filled Brownie Cupcakes, 134
Shrimp Egg Rolls, 166
Singapore Satay Sandwiches, 23

PEARS & DRIED PEARS

Gorgonzola Pear Salad, 32
Pear Tea Sandwiches, 19
Pear Upside-Down Cake, 121
Portobello Burgers with Pear-Walnut Mayonnaise, 58

PIES & TARTS
(also see Oven Entrees for savory pies)

Berry Apple Pie, 126
Blueberry Custard Pie, 121
Caramel Banana Ice Cream Pie, 130
Chocolate Cherry Pie, 132
Dark Chocolate Cream Pie, 118
Lemon Cheesecake Pies, 115
Lemon Chess Pie, 128
Peaches & Cream Pie, 135
Pecan Pie, 169
Raspberry Cream Pie, 126
Rhubarb Berry Tart, 123
Strawberry Pineapple Pie, 124
Tiny Banana Cream Pies, 134
Triple-Berry Crumb Pie, 116

PINEAPPLE

Holiday Glazed Ham, 45
Singapore Satay Sandwiches, 23
Strawberry Pineapple Pie, 124

PLUMS & DRIED PLUMS

Country Apple Prune Cake, 112
Pork Tenderloin with Spiced Plum Sauce, 59
Tzimmes, 164

PORK
(also see Ham & Bacon; Sausage)

Applesauce-Sauerkraut Spareribs, 63
Asian Barbecued Pork Loin, 51
Barbecued Meatballs, 5
Cherry-Glazed Pork Tenderloin, 69
Country-Style Pork Ribs, 63
Curry-Glazed Pork Chops, 166
Holiday Glazed Ham, 45
Honey-Grilled Pork Tenderloin, 148
Maple Chicken 'n' Ribs, 51
Our Favorite Pork Chops, 159
Pork Chops with Sauerkraut, 55
Pork Tenderloin with Spiced Plum Sauce, 59
Sausage Hash, 148
Sausage Sloppy Joes, 34
Sweet Onion & Cherry Pork Chops, 48

POTATOES
(also see Sweet Potatoes)

Country Potato Salad, 41
Favorite Fish Chowder, 36
Golden Potato Surprise, 77
Irish Herbed Potatoes, 77
Low Country Boil, 67
Mashed Potato Bake, 171
Moist Potato Pancakes, 76
Roasted Garlic Potato Soup, 38
Roasted Garlic Twice-Baked Potato, 140
Rosemary-Garlic Roast Beef, 64
Sausage Hash, 148
Southwestern Shepherd's Pie, 144
Swiss-Onion Potato Bake, 76

PUMPKIN

Honey-Date Pumpkin Cookies, 102
Pumpkin Patch Biscuits, 90
Streusel Pumpkin Sweet Rolls, 85

RASPBERRIES

Apple Raspberry Crisp, 132
Berry Apple Pie, 126
Festive Cranberry Fruit Salad, 28
Raspberry Chocolate Cheesecake, 127
Raspberry Chocolate Rugalach, 164
Raspberry Cream Pie, 126
Raspberry Delights, 104
Raspberry Parfaits, 150

RHUBARB

Rhubarb Berry Tart, 123
Rhubarb-Buttermilk Coffee Cake, 97
Strawberry Rhubarb Cobbler, 117

ALPHABETICAL RECIPE INDEX